Consumer Behaviour

Consumer Behaviour:
Irish Patterns and Perspectives

Margaret Linehan

Gill & Macmillan

Gill & Macmillan Ltd
Hume Avenue
Park West
Dublin 12
with associated companies throughout the world
www.gillmacmillan.ie

© Margaret Linehan 2008

978 07171 44563

Index compiled by Cover to Cover
Print origination in Ireland by Carole Lynch

The paper used in this book is made from the wood pulp of managed forests.
For every tree felled, at least one is planted, thereby renewing natural resources.

A CIP catalogue record for this book is available from the British Library.

Contents

Preface

Consumer Behaviour: Irish Patterns and Perspectives covers a wide range of topics within the rapidly changing field of consumer behaviour. Part of the challenge of writing this textbook was that the field of consumer behaviour is so dynamic and its researchers, particularly in the United States, so prolific. With this in mind, this book on the subject of consumer behaviour is written from a uniquely Irish perspective.

The book aims to achieve an appropriate balance of applying consumer behaviour principles and theories to Irish products and services. Each of the ten chapters contains two case studies and mini vignettes in order to highlight the relevance of consumer behaviour to our everyday lives. Each chapter begins with a number of key objectives which, along with the review questions at the end of each chapter, should help the student to focus in a clear and concise way on the ten different but related topics addressed in this textbook.

Consumer behaviour involves satisfying needs. This book seeks to meet the needs of consumers — students and lecturers of consumer behaviour — by providing a text that is succinct, and yet comprehensively explores key aspects of the discipline of consumer behaviour.

During the past decade, changes in Irish consumer behaviour patterns have been influenced by many factors, most noticeably the country's increased wealth, 24-hour shopping, more leisure time, online purchasing, and the influx of many thousands of foreign nationals. Additionally, as consumers in Ireland, we are typically exposed to over 2,000 advertisements by lunchtime each day and that figure is steadily rising.

Young children are also targeted by marketers of goods and services, with a gender divide evident at a very young age. On a recent shopping trip to a large toy store with my five-year-old nephew, Cormac, I jokingly suggested we could walk through the aisle containing dolls. He immediately refused, retorting, 'All dolls and all things in pink should be put in the rubbish bin!' Throughout this book, these newer patterns evident in Irish consumer behaviour along with the more traditional perspectives are explored.

Acknowledgments

I would first like to acknowledge my colleague, Dr Angela Wright, who came up with the idea for this book. Angela identified a gap in the Irish market for such a text for both students and lecturers. Angela, thank you as always for another of your good ideas.

Thanks to Marion O'Brien and Emma Farrell at Gill & Macmillan for your encouragement, enthusiasm, and professional support throughout the writing of this textbook.

Finally, very special thanks to my husband, Dr John Mullins, for your usual attention to detail in proofreading and editing the text and ensuring that all your favourite commas, dashes, hyphens, etc., were inserted correctly! More importantly, thank you for always being there for me and for your support and encouragement for all my work and projects.

1

Introduction to Consumer Behaviour

> **CHAPTER OBJECTIVES**
> After reading this chapter you should be able to:
> * Understand what is meant by consumer behaviour.
> * Trace the development of the marketing concept and consumer behaviour.
> * Explain market segmentation, targeting and positioning.
> * Discuss consumer value, satisfaction and retention.

WHAT IS CONSUMER BEHAVIOUR?

Consumer behaviour is a relatively young field of study. The first textbooks on consumer behaviour were written in the 1960s. In its early stages of development, the discipline was often referred to as *buyer behaviour*, reflecting an emphasis on the interaction between consumers and producers at the time of purchase. Most marketers now recognise that consumer behaviour is an *ongoing* process, not merely what happens at the moment a consumer hands over money or a credit or debit card and in turn receives a good or service.

Consumer behaviour is the study of the processes involved when individuals or groups select, purchase, use or dispose of products, services, ideas or experiences to satisfy needs and desires. A consumer is at one end of an *exchange process* in which resources are transferred between two parties. The exchange process is a fundamental element of consumer behaviour. Exchanges occur between consumers and organisations. Exchanges also occur between organisations, for example in industrial buying situations. Although exchange remains an important part of consumer behaviour, the expanded view emphasises the entire consumption process, which includes the issues that influence the consumer before, during and after a purchase. This sequence can occur over a matter of hours, days, weeks, months, or even years.

The term *consumer behaviour* describes two different kinds of consuming entities: the personal consumer and the organisational consumer. The *personal consumer* buys goods and services for his or her own use, for the use of the household, or as a gift for a friend. In each of these contexts, the products are bought for final use by individuals, who are referred to as *end users* or ultimate consumers. The second category of consumer — the organisational consumer — includes profit and not-for-profit businesses, government agencies (state, national, local) and institutions (e.g. schools, hospitals, universities), all of which must buy products, services and equipment in order to run their organisations (see Chapter 10). Despite the importance of both categories of consumer — individuals and organisations — this book will focus on the individual consumer, who purchases for his or her own personal use or for household use.

Consumer behaviour has changed dramatically in the past decade. Digital technologies allow much greater customisation of products, services and promotional messages than older marketing tools. They enable marketers to adapt the elements of the marketing mix to consumers' needs more quickly and efficiently, and to build and maintain relationships with consumers on a much greater scale. Today, consumers can order online many customised products ranging from clothing to computers. These customised products emphasise that as individual consumers we are all unique. Despite our differences, however, one factor we have in common is that we *are* all consumers. We regularly use or consume food, clothing, shelter, transportation, education, holidays, essential and luxury services and even ideas. As consumers, we play a vital role in the local, national and international economy. As consumers, the purchase decisions we make affect the demand for raw materials, transportation, the employment of workers and the deployment of resources, the success of some industries and the failure of others. In order to succeed in any business and especially in today's dynamic and rapidly evolving marketplace, marketers need to have as much information as possible about consumers. Marketers need to know what consumers want, what they think, how they work, when and where they shop and how they spend their leisure time. They also need to understand the personal and group influences that affect consumer decisions (see Chapter 10).

Consumer behaviour means more than just how a person buys products such as computers, mobile phones and cars. It also includes consumers' use of services, activities and ideas. Going to the dentist, taking a holiday, celebrating birthdays, donating to charity and saying no to drugs are all examples of consumer behaviour.

Consumer behaviour, therefore, is a broad field that studies the exchange process through which individuals and groups acquire, consume and dispose of goods, services, ideas and experiences. Very simply, understanding consumer behaviour is good business. A basic marketing concept holds that organisations exist to satisfy consumers' needs. These needs can only be satisfied to the extent that marketers understand the people or organisations that will use the products and services they are trying to sell, and that they do so better than their competitors.

Defining Consumer Behaviour

Consumer behaviour is defined as the study of the buying units and the exchange processes involved in acquiring, consuming and disposing of goods, services, experiences and ideas (Mowen 1995). The term 'buying units' is used in preference to 'consumers' because purchases may be made by either individuals or groups. This definition also suggests that the exchange process has three phases, beginning with the acquisition phase, moving to the consumption phase, before ending with the disposition of the product or service. An *exchange* involves 'a transfer of something tangible or intangible, actual or symbolic, between two or more social actors' (Bagozzi 1975). Exchange is the core concept of consumer behaviour. For an exchange to take place, several conditions must be satisfied. There must be at least two parties and each must have something of value to the other. Each party must also want to deal with the other party; each must be free to accept or reject the other's offer. Finally, each party must be able to communicate and deliver. These conditions simply make exchange *possible*. Whether exchange actually *takes place* depends on the parties coming to an agreement.

Much of the research on consumer behaviour has concentrated on the *acquisition phase*, in which marketers analyse the factors that influence the product and service choices of consumers. After consumers acquire a product or service, they typically use it in some manner. *Consumption* has important implications for marketers: for example, dissatisfied consumers may communicate negative experiences to others, causing negative results.

Finally, consumer behaviour examines *disposition*. This means finding out how consumers dispose of a product when they no longer have use for it. Disposition behaviour can have important implications for marketers. Many consumers, for example, who are concerned about the environment will pay extra for products that are biodegradable, are made from recycled materials, or do not pollute when disposed of.

A consumer, therefore, is generally thought of as a person who identifies a need or desire, makes a purchase and then disposes of the product during the three stages in the consumption process. The *purchaser* and *user* of a product might not be the same person, for example when parents are purchasing for children. In other cases, another person may act as an *influencer*, providing recommendations for or against certain products without actually buying or using them.

THE MEANING OF CONSUMPTION

In the exchange process, organisations receive monetary and other resources from consumers. In return, consumers receive products, services and other resources of value. For marketers to create a successful exchange, they must have an understanding of the factors that influence the needs and wants of consumers. One of the fundamental premises of the modern field of consumer behaviour is that people often buy products not for what they *do*, but for what they *mean*. This principle does not imply that a product's basic function is unimportant, but rather that the roles products play in the lives of consumers go well beyond the tasks they perform. The deeper meanings of a product may help it to stand out from other, similar goods and services — all things being equal, the purchaser will choose the brand that has an image consistent with their underlying needs.

When investigating the *consumption phase*, researchers analyse how consumers actually use a product or service and the experiences that the consumer obtains from such use. The investigation of the consumption process is particularly important for service industries. In some industries, such as restaurants, amusement parks and concerts, the consumption experience is the reason for the purchase.

IRISH CONSUMER BEHAVIOUR: CHRISTMAS 2007

Irish households spent an average of €1,431 for Christmas (2007), compared with €411 in the Netherlands; €420 in Germany; €556 in France; €592 in Switzerland; €624 in Belgium; and €951 in Spain. This was an increase of 6.9 per cent on 2006. Deloitte's annual consumer survey of Christmas spending saw Ireland retaining its top spot in Europe's spending league. Britain was placed second behind Ireland with an average household spend of €1,007.

Of the Irish figure, an estimated household total of €720 was spent on gifts; €431 on food; and €280 on socialising. Forty-nine per cent of respondents said that they buy the most expensive gift for their partner. When it came to children, 23 per cent said that their daughter or son would get the most expensive gift. These figures reflect a shift in the demographic structure of the Irish population. As the population continues to grow older, Christmas will continue to become more of an 'adult' event.

Books, gift vouchers and music are the most desired gifts by adults in Ireland, according to this survey. The survey also showed that 58 per cent of women surveyed would like to receive jewellery, but only 40 per cent of men purchase jewellery for women. Only 52 per cent of those surveyed believed they knew what their children wanted. The top three children's gifts for Christmas 2007 were action figures and play sets, Bratz and computer games. Teenagers' lists included music/CDs, cash and MP3 players.

With regard to food purchases, supermarkets still remain the most popular source, with traditional food shops, such as the butcher and baker, and discount food shops in the top three favourite stores. Looking at non-food products, 75 per cent of respondents buy these products in traditional department stores. Interestingly, 66 per cent also buy non-food products in supermarket chains, which is further evidence of the rise of supermarkets in Ireland.

Ethical questions continue to have an impact on consumer spending patterns, with 65 per cent of Europeans admitting that they are willing to pay more for an ethical product. Ethical concerns did not appear to be so high among Irish consumers.

Fifty-two per cent of respondents outlined their intention to buy on the Internet. In fact, the Irish are the second highest users of the Internet, just behind the Germans. Thirty-six per cent of respondents said that they buy products and services over the Internet, and 25 per cent use the Internet to research and compare prices. The reasons behind such Internet usage included greater product choice (36 per cent) and avoiding crowded stores (34 per cent). CDs, DVDs, books and tickets are currently the top items purchased on the Internet. Respondents said there are a number of factors that would deter them from using the Internet: for example, 44 per cent of respondents prefer to see or handle products. Only 11 per cent, however, stated they were concerned with fraud and online security.

Source: adapted from www.finfacts.com/irelandbusinessnews

DEVELOPMENT OF THE MARKETING CONCEPT AND CONSUMER BEHAVIOUR

The basic idea of an exchange process has its roots in very ancient history, when people began to produce crops or goods surplus to their own requirements. They then began to *barter* them for other things they wanted. In the late nineteenth and early twentieth centuries, goods were sufficiently scarce and competition sufficiently underdeveloped that producers could easily sell whatever they produced. This was known as *the production era*, from which the idea of *production orientation* was adopted.

The business leader who gave consumers the affordable car and the business approach known as the *production concept* was Henry Ford. Before the early 1900s, only wealthy consumers could afford cars because cars were assembled individually and it took some considerable time and expense to produce each car. Henry Ford quickly found out that he could not meet the overwhelming consumer demands for his affordable Model T car, so he introduced the assembly line. This new production method enabled Ford to produce good-quality cars more quickly and much less expensively.

The production concept assumes that consumers are mostly interested in product availability at low prices. Its implicit marketing objectives are cheap, efficient production and intensive distribution. This orientation makes sense when consumers are more interested in obtaining the product than in specific features and they will buy what is available rather than wait for what they really want. Marketers use this orientation today when the main objective is to expand their market.

The *product concept* assumes that consumers will buy the product that offers them the highest quality, the best performance and the most features. A product *orientation* leads a company to strive constantly to improve the quality of its product and to add new features that are technically feasible, without finding out first whether or not consumers really want these features. A product orientation often leads marketers to focus on the product rather than on the consumer needs it presumes to satisfy.

A natural evolution from both the production concept and the product concept is the *selling concept*, in which a marketer's primary focus is selling the product that it has produced. This became known as the *sales era*, which lasted into the 1950s. The assumption of the selling concept is that consumers are unlikely to buy the product unless they are aggressively persuaded to do so, mostly through the 'hard sell' approach. This leads to a heavy emphasis on personal selling and other sales-stimulating devices because products are 'sold, not bought'; thus an organisation focuses more strongly on the needs of the seller than those of the buyer. The problem with this approach is that it fails to consider consumer satisfaction. Today, the selling concept, for example, is used by marketers of timeshare properties.

The discipline of consumer behaviour evolved from a marketing strategy in the early 1960s, when some marketers began to realise that it would be easier for them to sell more if they produced only those goods that they had already determined consumers would buy. Instead of trying to persuade consumers to buy what the organisation had already produced, marketing-oriented organisations found that it was easier to produce products they had first confirmed, through market research, that consumers wanted. Consumer needs and wants became the organisation's primary focus. This consumer-oriented marketing philosophy became known as the *marketing concept*. The key assumption underlying the marketing concept is that, to be successful, a company must determine the needs and wants of specific target markets and deliver desired satisfaction better than its competitors. The marketing concept is based on the premise that a company should make what it can sell, instead of trying to sell what it has made. This meant that consumers took a central role in an organisation. According to Drucker (1986), 'marketing is the whole business seen from the point of view of its final result, that is, the customer's point of view'.

The widespread adoption of the marketing concept, therefore, provided the impetus for the study of consumer behaviour. To identify satisfied and unsatisfied consumer needs, companies had to engage in extensive market research. In doing so, they began to discover that consumers were highly complex individuals, subject to a variety of psychological and social needs quite apart from their survival needs. They also discovered that the needs and priorities of different consumer segments differed greatly and, in order to design new products and marketing strategies that would fulfil consumer needs, they had to study consumers and their consumption behaviour in depth.

The *societal marketing concept* holds that an organisation should determine the needs, wants and interests of target markets. It should then deliver the desired satisfaction more effectively and efficiently than competitors in a way that maintains or improves the consumer's *and the society's* well-being. The societal marketing concept questions whether the pure marketing concept is adequate in an age of environmental problems, resource shortages, rapid population growth and neglected social services. According to the societal marketing concept, the pure marketing concept overlooks possible conflicts between short-run consumer *wants* and long-run consumer *welfare*.

EXAMPLE: IRELAND'S LEADING COFFEE ENTREPRENEURS AND CONNECT ETHIOPIA

Brody Sweeney of O'Briens Sandwich Bars came up with an innovative idea of twinning a rich western country with a poor third-world country. This idea led him to set up a charity called Connect Ethiopia, which twins the business community in Ireland with the business community in Ethiopia. The first project involved bringing coffee retailers to the coffee-growing region in Ethiopia. As a result of these trips to Ethiopia, major coffee companies like O'Briens Sandwich Bars, La Croissanterie Group and Java Republic are now importing Fair Trade Ethiopian coffee into Ireland. According to Java Republic CEO David McKiernan, who

An Irish business initiative for trade & partnership

was part of the original group, 'this is a practical example of ethical trading in action. I was blown away on the trip to see the lives of the farmers and how our purchases could make a huge difference to them.' Brody Sweeney explained, 'the idea is to get the business community to drive it forward and to focus, so rather than Ireland trying to save the world and not making much of an impact, we could take a bite-size piece of the world and work on that.' As well as coffee, Connect Ethiopia is developing projects in other areas such as insurance, micro-finance, website design, textiles, tourism, property and medical supplies.

Source: adapted from www.irishentrepreneur.com and www.connectethiopia.com

MARKET SEGMENTATION, TARGETING AND POSITIONING

Market Segmentation

This is the process of dividing a market into subsets of consumers with common needs or characteristics and selecting one or more segments to target with a distinct marketing mix. Before the widespread acceptance of market segmentation, the prevailing way of doing business with consumers was through *mass marketing* — that is, offering the same product and marketing mix to all consumers.

If all consumers were alike — if they all had the same needs, wants and desires and the same background, education and experience — mass marketing would be a logical strategy. Its primary advantage is that it costs less. Only one advertising campaign is needed, only one marketing strategy is developed and usually only one standardised product is offered.

There are major drawbacks, however, in an undifferentiated marketing approach. When trying to sell the same product to every prospective consumer with a single advertising campaign, the marketer must portray its product as a means for satisfying a common or generic need and, therefore, can end up appealing to no one. Galtee rashers, for example, first appeared in Irish shops forty years ago. Galtee, however, no longer rely on their traditional Irish rasher but have expanded far beyond the rasher sector to include a full breakfast range, a sliced cooked meats range and snacking products. The last four decades have seen the rasher market expand and Galtee have introduced the 'Sinless' range for consumers who are increasingly conscious of health, obesity and dieting issues but do not want to compromise on taste. Galtee's Sinless rasher medallions have 70 per cent less fat, 20 per cent less salt and are naturally low in carbohydrates. Galtee is positioned as the number one rasher brand in Ireland (www.galtee.ie).

The strategy of segmentation allows companies to avoid head-on competition in the marketplace by differentiating their product not only on the basis of price but also through styling, packaging, promotional appeal, method of distribution and superior service. The first step in developing a segmentation strategy is for marketers to select the most appropriate base(s) on which to segment the market. The most popular bases for market segmentation include:

- *Age* — Consumers of different age groups have different needs and wants. Although people who belong to the same age group differ in many ways, they tend to share a set of values and common cultural experiences that they carry throughout life.
- *Gender* — Many products are targeted either at men or at women. Differentiating by gender starts at a very early age, for example, segmenting and targeting consumers in markets such as children's toys.
- *Social class and income* — Social class means people who are approximately equal in terms of their incomes and social standing. Segmentation by social class and income is of interest to marketers because it determines which groups have the greatest buying power and market potential.
- *Race and ethnicity* — As Irish society becomes increasingly multicultural, new opportunities develop to deliver specialised products to racial and ethnic groups and to introduce other groups to these offerings.
- *Lifestyle* — Lifestyle segmentation involves intangible variables such as the beliefs, attitudes and opinions of the potential consumer. Marketers can sell the product on benefits that can be seen to enhance that lifestyle on a more emotional level rather than on functional features.
- *Family structure* — A consumer's family/marital status has a big effect on their spending priorities. Young singles, families with young children and older couples all have different consumption requirements.
- *Geography* — Geographical segmentation divides the market into different units such as nations, regions, counties, cities, or neighbourhoods. A company may decide to operate in one or a few geographical areas or to operate in all areas but pay attention to geographical differences in needs and wants.

Once a company has identified its most promising market segments, it must decide whether to target one segment or several segments. The idea behind market segmentation is that each targeted segment receives a specially designed marketing mix, that is, a specially tailored product, price distribution network and a promotional campaign.

EXAMPLE: BISC& TARGETS IRISH MUMS AND CHILDREN

The Irish biscuit market is valued at approximately €177 million in annual retail sales and is relatively static, with growth occurring as consumers purchase more expensive products rather than more packs of biscuits. When the biscuit market is examined in more detail, most households have a very defined role for biscuits, with particular sub-categories of biscuits associated with certain situations. As a result of its market research, Masterfoods has chosen to launch the BISC& (pronounced bisc and) brand in the 'everyday treats' bay of the biscuit aisle and to promote it accordingly. This is a new departure for Masterfoods as, prior to the launch of BISC&, it only competed in the chocolate biscuit sub-segment with Twix and Twix Top. BISC& now brings the packaging advantages associated with the chocolate biscuit sub-segment to the everyday treats sub-segment and thereby broadens the usage occasions of this sector. In addition to its packaging, which ensures versatility of use, BISC& is expected to boost sales of this sub-segment because the range will appeal to adults and children alike. Currently the products in the everyday treats sector would appeal to adults only or children only.

Through market research with various groups of people, Masterfoods has identified the key purchaser of BISC& to be the modern mother with young children aged between five and twelve. In most cases, the purchaser is also the key decision maker. The research also found that each visit to a supermarket resulted in substantial quantities of biscuits and chocolate biscuits being purchased for all of the family. Indeed, Ireland has the highest consumption per person of biscuits in the world! The main reason for repeat purchase of biscuits was found to be that children enjoyed the product. Thus, while the mother was found to be the key purchaser, the children also had an important role in influencing the decision to purchase. As such, the central aim of the company was to introduce the BISC& brand as a new biscuit product that appeals to the key purchasers and consumers while leveraging the strength of existing established brands.

Source: adapted from www.business2000.ie/masterfoods

Market Targeting

Marketing segmentation reveals the market-segment opportunities an organisation can avail of. An organisation has to decide how many segments to cover and how to identify and target the best ones. There are broadly three market-coverage strategies available: *undifferentiated, differentiated* and *concentrated marketing.*

Undifferentiated Marketing

The undifferentiated approach assumes that the market is one great homogeneous unit, with no significant differences between individuals within that market. It focuses on what is *common* in needs of consumers rather than on what is *different.* It designs a product and marketing campaign that appeals to the majority of consumers. It relies on mass distribution and mass advertising. An advantage of this approach is that it involves relatively low costs: using just one marketing mix does not require the depth of research, fine tuning and updating that a concentrated or differentiated strategy would entail. Most marketers, however, would have doubts about this strategy. It is difficult to develop a product or brand that will satisfy all consumers.

Differentiated Marketing

Marketers using a *differentiated marketing* strategy decide to target several market segments and therefore design separate offers for each. This approach allows an organisation to tailor its offerings to suit the individual segments, thus maintaining satisfaction. It hopes that a stronger position in several segments will strengthen consumers' overall identification of the organisation with the product category. It also spreads risk across the market, so that if one segment declines, the organisation still has revenue from others.

To be implemented properly, this approach requires a detailed overview of the market and how it is developing, perhaps leading to the early detection of new opportunities or emerging segments. Overall, a differentiated strategy dilutes the organisation's effort through the thin spreading of resources. The organisation must, therefore, be careful not to over-reach itself in the number of segments it attempts to cover. Nevertheless, it can help an organisation to survive in highly competitive markets.

Concentrated Marketing

The concentrated approach is the most focused approach of the three and involves specialising in serving one specific segment. This can lead to very detailed knowledge of the target segment's needs and wants, with the added benefit that the organisation is seen as a specialist, giving it an advantage over its more mass-market competitors. Concentration is attractive because costs are kept down as there is only one marketing mix to manage.

Being a niche specialist, however, may make it more difficult for an organisation to diversify into other segments, whether through lack of experience and knowledge, or through problems of acceptance arising from being identified with the original niche. Additionally, if that segment fails, there is no fallback position.

Market Positioning

Once a company has decided which segments of the market it will enter, it must then decide what 'positions' it wants to occupy in those segments. A product's *position* is the way the product is *defined by consumers* on important attributes — the place the product occupies in consumers' minds relative to competing products. In the Irish daily newspaper industry, for example, the *Irish Times* and the *Irish Daily Mirror* would be positioned differently.

Consumers are overloaded with information about products and services. They cannot re-evaluate products every time they make a buying decision. To simplify buying decisions, companies organise products into categories — they 'position' products, services and companies in the minds of consumers. A product's position, therefore, is the complex set of *perceptions, impressions* and *feelings* that consumers hold for the product in comparison with competing products (Kotler & Armstrong 2007).

There are various positioning strategies that marketers can follow. They can position products on specific *product attributes*, for example supermarket chains Lidl and Aldi advertise their low prices, while Brown Thomas is positioned as a high-quality department store. In order to reinforce this positioning in its target market, Brown Thomas makes sure that its product range, its staff expertise, its displays and overall store ambience are of equally high quality.

Products can also be positioned on the needs they fill or the *benefits* they offer. For example, Irish-manufactured Glenisk organic yogurt is low in fat, contains two probiotic cultures for healthy digestion, is gluten-free, has no genetically modified ingredients and has eco-friendly packaging.

Alternatively, products can be positioned according to *usage occasions*. Each year coming up to Christmas over-the-counter medicine sales increase as Christmas parties, increased alcohol consumption and the cold weather wear down the population's resistance to bugs, flu and colds. Research has shown that the seasonal peak starts as early as October, with the majority of sales coming through the winter months. The grocery cold and flu remedy market is worth almost €7 million. The Irish-manufactured product Hedex remains a strong performer with Irish consumers for the relief of headaches and has particularly high levels of awareness (www.checkout.ie).

Another approach is to position the product for certain classes of *user* — Ribena fruit drink, for example, is positioned as the brand that children love and that mothers prefer to buy for their family, because it is rich in vitamin C and has a unique blackcurrant taste. People associate Ribena with health and childhood. As a result of effective advertising Ribena evokes a sense of well-being and goodness. Ribena is timeless and appeals to all generations; there is a sense that it is a tradition.

A product can also be positioned directly *against a competitor*, for example, Ryanair effectively positioning itself against Aer Lingus. It required simple but effective marketing from Ryanair to point out that the customer was paying a very high price for an assigned seat and 'free' meals. Given Ryanair's seat price, the lack of an assigned seat became a non-issue for the consumer and the availability of reasonably priced food and beverages dealt with that aspect of customer expectations.

Some organisations will find it easy to choose their positioning strategy. An organisation, for example, which is well known for low price in certain segments, will go for this position in a new segment if there are enough consumers who are price sensitive. In many cases, however, two or more organisations will go after the same position. Each organisation, therefore, will have to find other ways to set itself apart. An organisation will have to build a unique competitive advantage that appeals to a substantial group within the segment. A *competitive advantage* may be gained either by offering consumers lower prices or by providing more benefits to justify higher prices than competitors. The company, therefore, must do a better job than competitors at keeping costs and prices down or at offering better value to consumers. To the extent that it can do better than its competitors, it achieves a competitive advantage. Once a company has chosen a position, it must take strong steps to communicate and deliver it to target consumers. The company's positioning decisions determine who its competitors will be. When setting its positioning strategy, a company evaluates its competitive strengths and weaknesses in comparison with those of competitors and selects a position in which it can attain a strong competitive advantage.

EXAMPLE: IRISH CONSUMERS ARE WILLING TO PAY FOR QUALITY

Research by Glanbia Consumer Foods (2007) reports that one in every two shoppers is willing to pay a premium for quality Irish goods. The survey showed that:

- 58% of consumers will pay extra for homemade Irish goods
- 83% would prefer to buy brands with Irish traceability labels
- 86% said quality was the most important factor in judging value for money
- eight in ten would choose branded products over supermarket own-label goods.

The habits of 400 consumers were researched for the study. Consumers said that they chose where to shop on the basis of:

- good opening hours
- choice in products
- local ownership.

Nearly three-quarters of consumers would like access to more healthy 'foods on the go'. 'The Irish shopper in 2007 is someone who is focused on quality, is health-conscious and likes to buy local produced products,' said Glanbia's Colin Gordo.

Source: adapted from www.consumerconnect.ie

DEVELOPING THE MARKETING MIX

Once a company has decided on its positioning strategy, it is ready to begin planning the details of the marketing mix. The *marketing mix* consists of everything the organisation can do to influence the demand for its product or service. The marketing mix consists of four elements, known as the *four Ps*:

- *Product or service* —— the features, designs, brands and packaging offered, along with post-purchase benefits such as warranties and return policies.
- *Price* —— the amount of money consumers have to pay to obtain the product or service, including the list price, discount allowances and payment methods.
- *Place* —— the distribution activity of a company that make the product or service available through specific stores and non-store outlets to target consumers.
- *Promotion* —— the advertising, sales promotion, public relations and sales efforts designed to build awareness of and demand for the product or service.

An effective marketing strategy blends all the marketing mix elements into a co-ordinated programme designed to achieve the company's marketing objectives.

CONSUMER VALUE, SATISFACTION AND RETENTION

During the last decade, the digital revolution has enabled marketers to offer more products and services and distribute them more widely to more precisely targeted markets. This has resulted in an increasingly competitive marketplace. Marketers realise that in order to outperform competitors they must achieve the full profit potential from every consumer. They must make the consumer the core of the company's organisational culture, across all departments and functions, and ensure that every employee views any exchange with a consumer as part of a *customer relationship,* not as a *transaction.* Modern marketing strategies place an emphasis on building relationships with consumers and the nature of these relationships can vary. Some possible meanings a person might have with a product include:

- *Self-concept attachment* — the product helps to establish the user's identity.
- *Nostalgic attachment* — the product serves as a link with a past self.
- *Interdependence* — the product is part of the user's daily routine.
- *Love* — the product elicits emotional bonds of warmth, passion, or other strong emotion. (Fournier 1998)

Three drivers of successful relationships between marketers and consumers are *value, satisfaction* and *retention.*

Consumer value is defined as the ratio between the consumer's perceived benefits (economic, functional and psychological) and the *resources* (monetary, time, effort, psychological) *used to obtain those benefits* (Schiffman & Kanuk 2007). Some companies have grown steadily over many years by routinely providing total value to their consumers. Perceived value is relative and subjective. For example, Patrick Guilbaud, a two-star Michelin restaurant in Dublin city centre, which has been operating for twenty-five years, offers a dinner tasting menu for €130 (www.irelands-blue-book.ie).

During and after the consumption and use of a product or service, consumers develop feelings of satisfaction or dissatisfaction. *Consumer satisfaction* is the individual's perception of the performance of the product or service in relation to his or her expectations. Product expectations act as a standard against which the actual performance of the product is assessed. The concept of consumer satisfaction is a function of consumer expectations. The perceptions of product quality are compared to the consumer's expectations of the product's performance. Based on the comparison of expected quality to performance quality, consumers will experience positive, negative or neutral emotions depending on whether expectations were confirmed. These emotional responses then act as inputs to the overall satisfaction or dissatisfaction perception.

In the fast-moving competitive environment it is vital for organisations to provide satisfaction, otherwise they risk losing their consumers to competitors. Aer Lingus, for example, have been accused of failing to respond to the consumer need for low-cost, value for money, no-frills travel. It was having Ryanair as a competitor, however, that gave consumer satisfaction by providing services that were wanted. Ryanair redefined what consumers might expect and so were able to take consumers from other airlines and grow very rapidly.

The overall objective of providing value to consumers continuously and more effectively than competitors is to retain highly satisfied consumers. This strategy of *retention* encourages consumers to stay with the company rather than switch to another company. In almost all business situations, it is more expensive to win new consumers than to keep existing ones. A key goal for any marketer, therefore, should be consumer retention. A consumer-retention strategy attempts to build consumer commitment and loyalty by continually paying close attention to all aspects of consumer interaction, especially after-sales service.

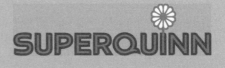

CASE STUDY: SUPERQUINN'S COMPETITIVE ADVANTAGE: 'THE CUSTOMER — FIRST, LAST AND ALWAYS'

What all businesses have in common, whether they admit it or not, is a total dependence on the customer for their success. A business is successful to the extent — and only to the extent — that it meets a customer need. Businesses depend on customers, not the other way round. According to Feargal Quinn, founder of Superquinn, 'My business philosophy has always been to find ways of satisfying our customers' needs, better than anyone else in the marketplace. Building on that idea, I have always believed that what is good for the customer is good for my business. Nowhere is this truer than in retailing.'

In order to sell successfully to people, those people have to be able to buy from you. If they don't have money, they can't do that. Therefore, retailers have a vested interest in customers having as much money as possible that they can spend with them and the best way for that to happen is to promote employment. Even in today's Celtic Tiger economy, job promotion is important.

An ongoing effort at expanding employment opportunities drives Superquinn to favour products made here in Ireland. Quinn adds, 'We've never felt it was our job to tell our customers what they should buy with their money. But on the other hand, knowing the importance of jobs to the communities we serve, we go out of our way to stock Irish goods whenever those goods are available, so the customer has the choice'. This is why Superquinn flags the presence of Irish goods on their shelves with a Shamrock sign and why it highlights Irish items on the customer's till receipt, showing them the amount they spent on Irish goods. Quinn takes the approach that if you look after the customer, all the other elements of success will fall into place. His point is that if you as a businessperson stay focused on serving customers' needs, you very often end up doing good for the community — but you also do good for yourself as well.

Some examples of how Superquinn has focused on customer needs include recognising a need that older customers have: for example, a person living on their own may find the packages in which items are sold are too large for their needs. That is why, many years ago, Superquinn introduced a policy for older customers that they would split a package if it was too big for them. It didn't make financial sense for Superquinn to do this, but they didn't lose out by making the gesture because it created an enormous amount of goodwill for them among customers generally. In the end it made good business sense to meet that particular customer need.

An even better example of meeting a customer need is its playhouses for looking after customers' children while customers shop. By carefully listening to what customers told Superquinn, it found out that mothers of young children had huge problem when they brought children into the shop with them. In response, it provided special places outside its shops where parents could leave their youngsters for an hour or two. According to Quinn, 'Of course it cost us a small fortune to do that, but it was a good investment in the long run. To start with, we attracted customers that passed other supermarkets in order to get to us just so they could leave their children in our playhouses. Apart from that, we found that the young mothers who could concentrate on their shopping ended up spending more with us than they otherwise would, which helped us from a business point of view. And again, we found that the goodwill we created among all our customers by providing what they saw as valuable community service added greatly to our favourable public image.'

The other way of looking at these activities is to see them as a way in which the business can realise its own business mission more effectively by working together with the community it serves. In essence, doing good is good business. As Quinn often said to his colleagues, 'At the end of the month, it's not me who signs your salary cheque — it's the customer.'

Source: adapted from www.feargalquinn.ie

CASE STUDY: FÁILTE IRELAND TARGETING THE HEALTH AND WELLNESS VISITOR SEGMENT

There has been a huge growth in the number of health spas in Ireland since 2000. In 2006 alone, over thirty such facilities

Fáilte Ireland
National Tourism Development Authority

opened, offering different types of spa experience. Much of this growth is represented in the hotel or resort spa sector, where the trend is for properties to provide a wellness or spa facility as an additional service for their clients. The growth is not only a response to changing consumer expectations but also plays a key role in educating Irish consumers with regard to spa experiences. Within a short period of time, Ireland's health and wellness industry has grown from offering a few select, dedicated health farms and spas to offering a significant choice to many consumers. These services include purpose-built facilities or destination spas. These offer a comprehensive, full-service wellness spa experience for overnight or day guests.

People visit spas for a variety of reasons including pampering, relaxation, fitness, health and spirituality. Internal and external treatments are equally important to spa-goers. What unites all customer groups is the desire to feel better, but it is how they seek to feel better that varies. The specific motivations of those who visit spas include:

• A desire to feel better by being pampered and indulged. Outer beauty is a key draw for the majority of Irish spa-goers, who assume that cosmetic treatments, e.g. facials and manicures, will be available at all spa facilities.
• A means of escape. Consumers generally feel better when removed from normal day-to-day environments and circumstances. Many people visit spa facilities to relieve or reduce stress or simply to indulge their senses.
• A desire to gain a holistic approach to well-being — for those who are looking for serenity, understanding and self-acceptance.
• A desire for improved wellness, to feel better by changing one's spirit or body — for those who want to discover how lifestyle choices can lead to optimal health.
• Rehabilitation — for those who need to recover after an illness.
• Expert advice on skin care and diet, and products and techniques to use at home to recreate the spa experience.
• A way to achieve fitness, for people who want to get in shape by attending fitness classes, or adopting a healthier lifestyle.

The primary target segments that have been selected for marketing investment purposes by Fáilte Ireland are as follows:

Pamperers. Taking time out for a spot of pampering is one way to temporarily escape daily hassles while also rewarding oneself for the hard hours put in. The treatments are luxurious — and the fact that people look and feel great afterwards is a bonus. The quality of treatments they receive is important, but so are the surroundings in which they are enjoyed. Pamperers are more likely to select a resort or destination whose reputation for excellence and pampering fits their requirements.

Relaxers. Their primary need is to take time out — to feel free from the pressures of everyday life. Visiting a spa allows relaxers to take time out, gives them a chance to reflect, to reconnect and to emerge with a renewed sense of purpose. The treatments enjoyed are important, but taking time out is the primary aim.

Fun-seekers. Fun-seekers love to get away with the girls or guys. Taking a spa break is a secondary consideration to the enjoyment they derive from being with friends. Fun seekers are unlikely to be experts in spa therapies and treatments but view spa breaks as just another activity to enjoy on a fun-filled activity weekend with friends or significant others.

Domestic Market. There are approximately 140,000 'wellness tourists' in Ireland. Irish spa-goers have two main reasons for visiting spas: to pamper and indulge themselves; and to escape. Indulgence is the entry point for most consumers, especially females. The level of experience of Irish spa-goers varies from 'committed' (14 per cent), to 'occasional' users (22 per cent), to 'dippers', or those who infrequently visit a spa (64 per cent).

Beauty Queens. Sometimes characterised as 'ladies who lunch' or more recently 'Ryder Cup wives', health and wellness for Beauty Queens is all about looking good. Exfoliated, manicured, wrapped and waxed, they feel they could grace the pages of a magazine cover.

Many factors are driving the health-conscious consumer to seek wellness tourism experiences, including changing demographics, an increasing desire across cultures to live longer and live well and the seemingly insatiable appetite for new and different leisure experiences. Fáilte Ireland aims to educate the primary target segments on products that are available in Ireland, for example by supporting the growing 'spa culture' that has developed in primary target markets.

Health and wellness tourism has several unique advantages, including a lack of seasonality, independence from weather conditions, an average length of stay that is longer when compared with other tourism sectors and regional diversity. Recent years have seen an exponential growth in the quality and variety of health and wellness facilities in Ireland. The unique combination of a diverse and professional supplier base with Ireland's unique destination attributes delivers a compelling proposition to consumers, positioning Ireland as a leading spa and wellness destination.

As the Irish market becomes more sophisticated, Irish consumers should become more demanding and the demand for more sophisticated, high-quality product and discreet spa experiences, isolated from other hotel activities, will increase. As the international market continues to mature, Ireland's uniqueness will be vital to providing such services with a compelling point of difference from other markets also trying to develop their wellness propositions and to attract high-spending visitors in this sector. Fáilte Ireland's research reveals that the British and domestic markets represent the greatest immediate growth opportunity, followed by the United States and German markets. Its focus will be on promoting Ireland as a health and wellness destination, particularly suited to short breaks, by emphasising the range and quality of product available. This positioning will require an increased focus on the inspiring and natural aspects of the health and wellness brand. The spotlight will be on 'feeling connected to a historic culture', 'regaining a balance of life' and 'getting away from it all'. Fáilte Ireland's primary focus will continue to be on the core markets of Britain, the United States and Germany, but a number of potential new markets — Italy, France and Scandinavia — have been identified for investment. Initial market intelligence suggests potential interest in Irish wellness products and markets will be targeted to develop potential visitor numbers.

In order to position Ireland as a world-class health and wellness destination and to create awareness of the expanding and superior product offered, Fáilte Ireland is committed to:

- Attracting a greater number of international spa and wellness tourists, particularly from British and other short-break markets.
- Encouraging international tourists already planning to visit Ireland to use Ireland's spa and wellness facilities during their stay — promoting higher spend and yield.
- Driving demand for wellness breaks in the domestic market.

While some international statistics are available, there is no measurement system in place in Ireland, and official figures relating to health and wellness tourism do not currently exist. This makes it impossible to assess the value and ongoing growth of the sector. On an international level, different countries define the product in different ways and there is a lack of conformity on how data is collected, making it very difficult to compare market information. Given that the Irish health and wellness sector is emerging and will continue to evolve in the future, it will be necessary to identify international trends and changing consumer needs in order to position Ireland as a world-class spa and wellness destination. This will be achieved through ongoing research and performance monitoring and will include a benchmark study to measure Ireland's competitive position against other wellness destinations. Fáilte Ireland is committed to allocating long-term investment to improve and evolve the current product offering. In particular, it will focus on the development of indigenous products and experiences which are unique to Ireland.

Source: adapted from www.failteireland.ie

Questions for Review

1. What is meant by the concept of consumer behaviour?
2. How did consumer behaviour develop as a field of study?
3. How do companies segment the market? Illustrate your answer with products or services you are familiar with.
4. Compare various methods companies use to position their products.

2

Perception and Consumer Involvement

CHAPTER OBJECTIVES

After reading this chapter you should be able to:

- Recognise that different people can perceive the same stimulus in divergent ways.
- Understand how consumers perceive a stimulus.
- Discuss different types of consumer involvement in buying situations.
- Describe the buyer decision process for new products.
- Explain why companies differentiate their products or services.
- Recognise the importance of branding.

PERCEPTION

Perception is defined as '*the process by which an individual selects, organises, and interprets stimuli into a meaningful and coherent picture of the world*' (Schiffman & Kanuk 2007). It can be described as 'how we see the world around us'. A *stimulus* is any unit of input to any of the senses. Examples of stimuli (i.e. sensory input) include products, packages, brand names, advertisements and commercials. *Sensory receptors* are human organs (eyes, ears, nose, mouth, skin) that receive sensory inputs. Perception is a process through which individuals are exposed to information, attend to the information, and comprehend the information. Individuals act and react on the basis of their perceptions, not on the basis of objective reality. For each individual, *reality* is a totally personal phenomenon, based on that person's personal experiences. Two individuals may be exposed to the same stimuli under the same apparent conditions, but how each person recognises, selects, organises, and interprets these stimuli is a highly individual process based on each person's own needs, values and expectations.

Before any type of marketing stimulus can affect consumers, they must be exposed to it. *Exposure* reflects the process by which the consumer comes into physical contact with a stimulus. *Marketing stimuli* are messages and information about products or brands communicated by either the marketer (e.g. advertisements, brand symbols, packages, price, etc.) or by non-marketing sources (e.g. word of mouth). Consumers can be exposed to marketing stimuli at the buying, using or disposing stages of consumption. Because exposure is critical to consumers' subsequent processing of any stimulus, marketers need to make sure that consumers are exposed to marketing stimuli. The consumer's 'selection' of stimuli from the environment is based on the interaction of expectations and motives with the stimulus itself. These factors give rise to three important concepts concerning perception: *selective exposure*, *selective distortion* and *selective retention*.

Selective Exposure

People are exposed to a great amount of stimuli every day. Individuals are exposed to advertisements in magazines and newspapers, on radio and television, on the Internet, and in their geographic environment on signs and billboards. It is impossible for a person to pay attention to all these stimuli; most will be automatically screened out. Otherwise, the vast amount of different stimuli to which people are constantly exposed might merely confuse and keep people perpetually disoriented in a constantly changing environment. *Selective exposure*, therefore, means that marketers have to work especially hard to attract the consumer's attention. Their message will be lost on most people who are not in the market for the product. Additionally, even people who are in the market may not notice the message unless it stands out from the surrounding of other advertisements.

While marketers can work hard to influence consumers' exposure to certain products and brands, ultimately consumers will control whether successful exposure occurs or not. Consumers can actively seek certain stimuli and avoid others. Readers of *Hello!* magazine selectively expose themselves to its fashion-oriented advertisements, whereas readers of *Business and Finance* choose to look at different kinds of advertisement. Some readers may ignore advertisements altogether.

Selective Distortion

Stimuli that consumers notice do not always come across in the intended way. Individuals try to fit incoming information into their existing mindset. *Selective distortion* describes the tendency of people to adapt information to personal meanings. People tend to interpret information in a way that will support what they already believe. Selective distortion, therefore, means that marketers must try to understand the mindsets of consumers and how they will affect interpretations of advertising and sales information.

Selective Retention

People forget much of what they learn. *Selective retention* is the tendency of people to retain only part of the information to which they are exposed, usually information that supports their attitudes and beliefs. Stimuli that make it through the attention filters are not always understood and remembered. Many stimuli are only transitory, which is why advertising is repeated. If a consumer did not notice or remember an advertisement the first time, he or she might pick it up on subsequent occasions. Jogging the memory, by repeating messages, or by producing familiar stimuli that the consumer can recognise (such as brand names, sounds, packaging, or logos) is, therefore, an important marketing task to reduce the reliance on the consumer's memory.

These three perceptual factors — selective exposure, selective distortion and selective retention — mean that marketers have to work hard to get their messages across to consumers. Consumer avoidance of marketing stimuli is a major problem for marketers. Consumers can simply leave the room or do something else when television commercials are aired. Zipping and zapping are two common avoidance practices. *Zipping* occurs when consumers videotape television programmes and fast-forward through the advertisements when viewing a show. *Zapping* occurs when consumers avoid advertisement exposure by using remote controls to switch to other channels during commercial breaks. Television channels often endeavour to coincide advertising times even between competing channels.

How Consumers Perceive a Stimulus

Consumers' senses are exposed to numerous inputs at any one time. To perceive each one would be overwhelming and extremely difficult. Sensory processing, however, is simplified by the fact that many stimuli do not enter conscious awareness. For people to perceive something, it must be sufficiently intense. *Perception* occurs when stimuli are registered by one of our five senses: vision, hearing, taste, smell or touch.

Perceiving through Vision

Marketers rely heavily on visual elements in advertising, store design, and packaging. Meanings are communicated through a product's colour, size and styling. Larger size attracts attention. When choosing among competing products, consumers tend to buy products in packages that appear taller. Colour is also an extremely important factor in visual perception. Evidence suggests that some colours (particularly red) create feelings of arousal and stimulate appetite, while others (such as blue) are more relaxing (Solomon 2002). Cool colours, therefore, are more appropriate in places such as spas or dentists' surgeries, where it is desirable for consumers to feel calm. In contrast, warm colours are more appropriate in environments such as health clubs and fast-food restaurants, where a high level of activity is desirable.

Perceiving through Hearing

Sound represents another form of sensory input. Consumers are more likely to notice loud music, voices and stark noises. Fast music, like that played at aerobics classes, tends to energise, while, in contrast, slow music can be soothing. The type of music played in a shop can have an interesting effect on consumer behaviour. A fast tempo creates a more rapid traffic flow and is more desirable in restaurants because consumers will eat faster, thereby allowing greater turnover and higher sales (Millman 1986). On the other hand, a slow tempo encourages leisurely shopping and can increase sales.

Music can also affect mood. Likeable and familiar music can induce a good mood, whereas music in a disliked style can induce a bad mood. Mood, in turn, may affect how people feel about products and consumption experiences, and can have a positive or negative effect on purchase intentions.

Perceiving through Taste

Food and drink marketers must stress taste perceptions in their marketing stimuli. A major challenge for marketers of light or low-calorie products is to provide healthier foods that still taste good. Yet what tastes good to one person may not taste good to another. Marketers often try to monitor consumer tastes through taste tests. Many food and drink products are thoroughly taste-tested before they are placed on the market.

Perceiving through Smell

Smells can invoke memories or relieve stress. Obviously, consumers like some products — perfumes and scented candles, for example — for the smell they produce. Retailers are aware that smell can attract consumers: they frequently position their bakery with its smell of freshly baked breads and cakes as the first food area consumers encounter in the shop.

Perceiving through Touch

Like the other senses, touch has important physiological and emotional effects. Depending on how people are touched, they can feel stimulated or relaxed. Research by Hornik (1992) showed that consumers who are touched by a salesperson are more likely to have positive feelings and are more likely to evaluate both the shop and salesperson positively.

Consumers also like some products because of their feel. Consumers buy skincare products because of their soothing effect on the skin. People go to massage therapists to experience tactile sensations and to feel relaxed. People associate the textures of fabrics and other surfaces with product qualities. The perceived richness or quality of the material in clothing is linked to its 'feel', whether rough or smooth, flexible or inflexible.

When Consumers Perceive a Stimulus

Stimulus intensity is measured in units. The intensity of a smell can be measured by the concentration of the stimulus in a substance or in the air. Stimulus intensity of sounds can be measured in decibels and frequencies, and stimulus intensity of colours can be measured by lightness and saturation. In the area of touch, stimulus intensity can be measured in terms of kilos and grams.

The *absolute threshold* is the minimum level of stimulus intensity needed for a stimulus to be perceived. In other words, the absolute threshold is the amount of intensity needed to detect a difference between something and nothing. Consumers will only consciously perceive a marketing stimulus when it is sufficiently high in intensity to be above the absolute threshold. If images or words in an advertisement are too small or the sound level is too low, consumer sensory receptors will not be activated and the stimulus will not be consciously perceived.

Whereas the absolute threshold deals with whether a stimulus can or cannot be perceived, the *differential threshold* refers to the intensity difference needed between two stimuli before people can perceive that the stimuli are different. The differential threshold, therefore, is a relative concept; it is often called the *just noticeable difference*. The differential threshold has important marketing implications. Sometimes marketers do not want consumers to notice a difference between two stimuli. Marketers, for example, might not want consumers to notice that they have decreased the size of the product or increased the price. In other instances marketers want consumers to perceive a difference between two stimuli. If, for example, a product is improved in some way, the changes must be above the differential threshold for the consumer to notice. Marketers hope that consumers can tell the difference between an old and an improved product. Sometimes, however, consumers cannot make the distinction because differential thresholds vary from sense to sense.

The concept of the perceptual threshold is important for another phenomenon — *subliminal perception*. The term subliminal means below the threshold of consciousness. People are *stimulated* below their level of conscious awareness: that is, they can perceive stimuli without being consciously aware that they are doing so. This process is called *subliminal perception* because the stimulus is beneath the threshold of conscious awareness.

Many apparent examples of subliminal perception, however, are not strictly speaking subliminal, since they are quite visible. It is important to recognise that if a consumer can see or hear a stimulus, it is not subliminal, because the stimulus is above the level of conscious awareness. Subliminal messages supposedly can be sent on both visual and aural channels. Three different types of subliminal stimulation have been identified: visual stimuli; accelerated speech in low-volume auditory messages; and embedding or hiding sexual imagery or words in print advertisements (Moore 1982).

CONSUMER INVOLVEMENT

One of the central questions in consumer behaviour is the understanding of how consumers respond to the various marketing stimuli that a company might use. A company that understands how consumers will respond to different product features, prices, and advertising has an advantage over its competitors. *Consumer involvement* is the perceived importance and/or interest consumers attach to the acquisition, consumption and disposition of a good, a service or an idea.

There are different types of consumer involvement, including *situational involvement* and *enduring involvement*. *Situational involvement* occurs over a short time period and is associated with a specific situation, such as the need to replace a product that has broken down (e.g. a car). In contrast, *enduring involvement* occurs when consumers show a consistently high level of interest in a product and frequently spend time thinking about the product. It is the combination of situational and enduring involvement that determines the consumer's *involvement responses* — that is, the complexity of information processing and the extent of decision making by the consumer.

EXAMPLE: FIFTY PER CENT OF IRISH CONSUMERS ARE WILLING TO CHANGE SHOPPING DESTINATION FOR IMPROVED FARM ANIMAL WELFARE

There is a growing interest among Irish consumers in the protection and welfare of farm animals. According to a 2007 study published by the European Commission, 72 per cent of Irish consumers report the protection of the welfare of farm animals as important to them. Fifty-seven per cent say they would like to be more informed about the conditions under which animals are farmed in Ireland. One third of consumers, however, report difficulties finding information on products sourced from animal-welfare-friendly production systems. More than half of the Irish consumers surveyed state that television is their preferred source of information on the topic. Thirty-six per cent say they would also use their daily newspaper, and twenty-six per cent add that radio is a useful source of information. Twenty-one per cent note that they would use the Internet as a source of information on the welfare of farm  animals. Only thirteen per cent report that they would not be interested in sourcing such information. The study also shows that 50 per cent of Irish consumers would be willing to change their usual place of shopping in order to buy more animal-welfare-friendly food products.

Source: adapted from www.ucd.ie/news/May07

The most important factors influencing a consumer's involvement level include:

- the type of product under consideration
- the characteristics of the communication the consumer receives
- the characteristics of the situation in which the consumer is operating
- the consumer's personality.

Consumer involvement generally increases when the product or service under consideration is more expensive, socially visible, and risky to purchase.

Involvement can be viewed as the motivation to process information. When there is a perceived linkage between a consumer's needs, goals or values and product knowledge, the consumer will be motivated to pay attention to product information. When relevant knowledge is activated in memory, a motivational state is created that drives behaviour (e.g. shopping). As involvement with a product increases, the consumer devotes more attention to advertisements related to the product, exerts more effort to understand these advertisements, and focuses attention on the product-related information in the advertisements (Celsi & Olson 1988).

The type of information processing that will occur depends on the consumer's level of involvement with a service or product. A person's degree of involvement can range from absolute lack of interest in a marketing stimulus at one end to obsession at the other end. Consumption at the low end of involvement is characterised by *inertia*, in which decisions are made out of habit because the consumer lacks the motivation to consider alternatives. At the high end of involvement, a consumer can display passionate intensity for people and objects that carry great meaning for him or her.

High Involvement

Consumers undertake *complex buying behaviour* when they are highly involved in a purchase and perceive significant differences between brands, or when the product is expensive, risky, purchased infrequently or highly self-expressive. Typically, the consumer has much to learn about the product category. In higher levels of involvement, consumers begin to process information in more depth. This means that consumers are more likely to think hard about a decision when it is made under high-involvement circumstances. In addition, higher levels of involvement are likely to lead consumers to engage in a more extended decision process and to move through each of the decision stages in a more thorough manner (see Chapter 7). Involvement also has multiple dimensions. The following factors increase a consumer's level of involvement with a purchase:

- *Self-expressive importance*: products that help people to express their self-concept to others.
- *Hedonic importance*: products that are pleasurable, interesting, fun, fascinating or exciting.
- *Practical relevance*: products that are essential or beneficial for utilitarian reasons.
- *Purchase risk*: products that create uncertainty because a poor choice could disappoint the buyer (Jain & Srinivasan 1990).

Marketers of high-involvement products should endeavour to understand the information-gathering and evaluation needs of high-involvement consumers. Marketers should help consumers learn about product-class attributes and their relative importance, and about what the company's brand offers on the product's important attributes.

Low Involvement

Habitual buying behaviour occurs under conditions of low consumer involvement and little significant brand difference. Some products will be of relatively low importance to consumers in terms of risk, or personal involvement, with the product. Typically, this would include frequent purchasing of grocery items. These types of goods are known as fast-moving consumer goods (FMCG). The consumer is faced with a very wide choice and, as there is little risk associated with any such purchase, he or she may be tempted to try out different products each week.

Consumers of these goods do not search extensively for information about the brands, nor do they evaluate brand characteristics or make weighty decisions about which brands to buy. Instead, they passively receive information as they watch television or read magazines. Advertisement repetition creates *brand familiarity* rather than *brand conviction*. Consumers do not form strong attitudes towards a brand; they select the brand because it is familiar, and may not evaluate the choice even after purchase.

Under these circumstances, companies try to make their product stand out from the others and often use the attraction of special offers, free gifts or free trials to entice consumers. The overall goal of a company developing a product in this area is to win consumers and then to keep them. Consumer loyalty is therefore an important objective for the producers of low-involvement products. In advertising for a low-involvement product, advertisements should stress only a few key points. Visual symbols and imagery are important because they can be remembered easily and associated with the brand. Television is usually more effective than print media because it is a low-involvement medium suitable for passive learning. Advertising planning should be based on classical conditioning theory, in which buyers learn to identify a certain product by a symbol repeatedly attached to it. (See Chapter 5.)

Consumers often undertake *variety-seeking buying behaviour* in situations characterised by low consumer involvement even where brand differences are perceived to be significant. When purchasing biscuits, for example, a consumer may hold some beliefs, choose a biscuit without much evaluation, then evaluate that brand during consumption. But the next time, the consumer might pick another brand out of boredom or simply to try something different. Brand switching occurs for the sake of variety rather than because of dissatisfaction.

In such product categories, the marketing strategy may differ for the market leader and for minor brands. The market leader will try to encourage habitual buying behaviour by dominating shelf space, avoiding out-of-stock situations, and running frequent reminder advertising. Challenger companies will encourage variety seeking by offering lower prices, deals, coupons, free samples and advertising that presents reasons for trying something new.

Table 1.1: Consumer decision processes for high- and low-involvement purchase decisions

	Low-involvement purchase decisions	High-involvement purchase decisions
Problem recognition	Trivial to minor	Important and personally meaningful
Information search	Internal to limited external search	Extensive internal and external search
Alternative evaluation and selection	Few alternatives evaluated on few performance criteria	Many alternatives evaluated on many performance criteria
Store choice and purchase	One-stop shopping with substitution very likely	Multiple store visits with substitution less likely
Post-purchase processes	Simple evaluation of performance	Extensive performance evaluation, use, and eventual disposal

Source: P. Lancaster in Doole *et al.* (2005).

EXAMPLE: HALIFAX BANK IDENTIFIES STRONG INERTIA AMONG IRISH BANK CONSUMERS

Before the launch of Halifax Bank in Ireland in November 2006, it had been twenty years since anyone had tried to launch a new consumer bank with a branch network in Ireland. Halifax is the retail brand of Bank of Scotland (Ireland), part of Britain's HBOS Group. The bank had been trading under the Bank of Scotland brand in Ireland since 1989 and its business arm still does so. Customer confusion as to whether Bank of Scotland was a retail bank or a business bank prompted the re-brand to Halifax. Establishing a new brand is not cheap. HBOS

spent €15 million on marketing and communications in 2006, and that was sustained into 2007 with a spend of €8 million from January to June 2007. Another €15 million was set aside for 2008.

Research has been central to Halifax's product launches and marketing. Strong inertia among bank customers was one of the key findings of the research, with few people interested in switching banks unless their bank did something bad to them. At the same time, consumers view all banks as much the same and there is little inherent brand loyalty. Patricia Byrne, senior marketing manager, Bank of Scotland (Ireland), says getting 'cut through' is not all about the size of the campaign, but to establish a point of difference to cut through competing advertising. To this end, Halifax's advertising does a lot of rate comparison between itself and its rivals. This tactic is widely used in Britain, but it was not widely practised by Irish banks.

Before Halifax was launched here, Irish consumers had some familiarity with the brand through spillover television advertisements from Britain, so they knew that Halifax was a British bank. This issue is one of the main reasons why Halifax is sponsoring the *Late Late Show* for two years. In a first for any *Late Late Show* sponsor, Halifax secured permission from RTÉ to use the show's famous owl motif in its television advertisement stings around the show, and there are plans to use it in further promotional activity in 2008.

Source: adapted from Siobhán O'Connell, Irish Times, 18 October 2007, p.19.

COMPULSIVE BUYING

Some consumers buy compulsively, purchasing excessive quantities of items they do not need and sometimes cannot afford. Unlike materialism, *compulsive consumption* is in the realm of abnormal behaviour — an example of the dark side of consumption. The activity is compulsive rather than pleasurable or functional. Individuals who buy compulsively gain satisfaction from *buying*, not from *owning*. Consumers who are compulsive buyers have an *addiction*; in some respects they are out of control, and their actions may have damaging consequences for themselves and for those around them.

Compulsive buying has a strong emotional component, and may be a response to tension or anxiety. Some research has found a relationship between compulsive buying and eating disorders such as binge eating. These consumers turn to shopping in the way other addicts use alcohol or drugs. Like other addicts, they seek the experience to protect their self-image, but when they end the experience they feel more self-loathing and are subject to the disapproval of others. Compulsive buyers feel anxious on days when they do not buy. When in a shop, compulsive buyers may experience great emotional arousal at the stimulation evoked by the store's atmosphere. The act of buying, in turn, brings an immediate emotional high and often a feeling of loss of control. This emotional high, however, is often followed by feelings of remorse, guilt, shame, or even depression. Compulsive buyers think that others would be horrified if they knew about these spending habits, and some even hide their purchases (Hoyer & MacInnis 2004).

THE BUYER DECISION PROCESS FOR NEW PRODUCTS

A *new product* is a good, a service or an idea that is perceived by some potential consumers as new, even though it may have been around for a while. Marketers are interested in investigating how consumers learn about products for the first time and how they make decisions on whether to adopt them or not. The *adoption process* has been defined as 'the mental process through which an individual passes from first learning about an innovation to final adoption' (Rogers 1983), and *adoption* as the decision by an individual to become a regular user of the product. Consumers go through five stages in the process of adopting a new product:

1. *Awareness.* The consumer becomes aware of the new product, but lacks information about it.
2. *Interest.* The consumer seeks information about the new product.
3. *Evaluation.* The consumer considers whether trying the new product makes sense.
4. *Trial.* The consumer tries the new product on a small scale to improve his or her estimate of its value.
5. *Adoption.* The consumer decides to make full and regular use of the new product.

Consumers differ greatly in their readiness to try new products. In each product area, there are 'consumption pioneers' and early adopters. Other consumers adopt new products much later. This has led to a classification of people into the following adopter categories.

* *Innovators* are adventurous; they try new ideas at some risk.
* *Early adopters* are opinion leaders in their community and adopt new ideas early but carefully.
* *Early majority* are deliberate; although they are rarely leaders, they adopt new ideas before the average person.

- *Late majority* are sceptical; they adopt an innovation only after most people have tried it.
- *Laggards* are tradition-bound; they are suspicious of changes and adopt the innovation only when it has become something of a tradition itself. (Kotler *et al.* 1999)

This adopter classification suggests that companies should research the characteristics of innovators and early adopters and should direct marketing efforts towards them.

DIFFERENTIATION

Consumers often perceive many products as similar, fulfilling the same basic functions. This does not apply only to fast-moving consumer goods. Products like cars, for example, can be quite indistinguishable from each other. Branding is a way for manufacturers to separate their products from those of competitors. This is called *differentiation*. In order to succeed, a company must offer something to the consumer that the consumer values and which is different from its competitor products. This differentiation is usually defined in terms of better performance, better design, or a better fit with consumer needs.

Differentiation aims to create an edge over competitors, and to have a differentiation package that is sustainable over time. This can be 'real' (e.g. a product design feature) or 'imaginary' (e.g. a strong brand image or advertising campaign). Consumers, however, really do have to believe that there is a difference. One of the advantages of differentiation is that it takes the focus away from price and may therefore lead to the possibility of charging a premium price. It might also generate buyer loyalty, reducing tendencies towards product substitution or switching.

EXAMPLE: DIFFERENTIATING CREDIT UNIONS IN TODAY'S MARKETPLACE

In our consumer-driven world, every product must differentiate itself from its competitors in order to capture market share. Financial institutions are no different from soft drink brands or airline companies in this regard. In today's world, many consumers have a choice of financial institutions. Some lure customers by having a national presence. Others attract customers with free gifts or services.

As a result, credit unions face a daunting challenge in this competitive marketplace.

Despite the competitive nature of today's marketplace, credit unions have continually grown across the world because of their ability to differentiate themselves through their services and community focus. Credit unions are fundamentally different from other financial institutions because they are not-for-profit entities and members have equal rights, regardless of their financial standing. Increasingly, credit unions worldwide place an emphasis on or actively market this difference.

Irish credit unions, for example, target rural and disadvantaged areas with their services. In many of these locations, the Money Advice and Budgeting Service, an independent organisation, offers advice to people experiencing financial difficulty. Credit unions then offer loans at competitive rates to low-income people, including loans to people with poor credit scores. Credit unions also differentiate their services by offering innovative products and by focusing on the community. Interest rates on loans, for instance, are on a product, not a risk, basis. Credit unions also market to the younger population through the National Youth Policy, realising how vital it is to maintain a strong youth base and to encourage the development of lifelong involvement in the movement.

Source: www.woccu.org

A company can differentiate its offering from those of competitors through its product, services, personnel, or image.

Product Differentiation

An organisation can differentiate its physical product. It can offer a variety of standard or optional *features* not provided by competitors. The *core product* represents the basic reason why the product is purchased in the first place. This defines not only what the product is used for, but how it meets more specific needs and how it differs from other products in the same category. A Renault Clio and a Lamborghini, for example, represent two quite different core products. One provides practical, economical, everyday motoring, while the other provides 'head-turning looks', race-bred engineering and high-speed performance.

Services Differentiation

In addition to differentiating its physical product, an organisation can also differentiate the service that accompanies the product. Some organisations gain competitive advantage through fast delivery, installation, speed of service or customer training. Given the importance of customer service as a marketing tool, many companies have set up strong customer service departments to handle complaints, credit service, technical service, and information provision. Some companies and providers have set up hotlines to handle consumer complaints and requests for information; for example the Free Legal Advice Centres (FLAC) operates a lo-call information hotline.

Personnel Differentiation

Companies can gain a strong competitive advantage through hiring and training better people than their competitors. Personnel differentiation requires that a company should select its customer-contact people carefully and train them well. These personnel must serve consumers with consistency and accuracy. They must make an effort to understand consumers, to communicate clearly with them, and to respond quickly to consumer requests and problems.

Image Differentiation

When competing products look the same, consumers may perceive a difference based on company or brand images. Companies therefore work to establish *images* that differentiate them from competitors. *Symbols* can provide strong company or brand recognition and image differentiation. Companies design signs and logos that provide instant recognition. A company brand or image should convey a singular and distinctive message that communicates the product's main benefits and positioning.

Differentiating Products through Branding

There is no formula for developing a strong brand and most good brands have developed over time. Much of their success lies in how consumers perceive them and the 'personality' consumers attach to them (see Chapter 4). Consumers view a brand as an important part of a product, and branding can add value to a product. In order to develop and maintain strong brands, a company must understand what the values of the brand are and must continue to communicate these as much as possible.

A *brand* is a name, term, sign, symbol, design or a combination of these, which is used to identify the goods or services of one seller or group of sellers to differentiate them from those of competitors (Bennett 1988).

A *brand name* is the verbal part of the brand, for example, Maxol, Statoil, Shell, but by itself it has no legal status. A *trademark*, on the other hand, is a legally protected brand name, logo (the name of the company written in a particular way), or symbol. The owners of trademarks have exclusive rights to their use. A brand conveys a specific set of features, benefits and services to buyers. It is a mark, a tangible emblem, that says something about the product. Powerful brand names command strong consumer loyalty. This means that a sufficient number of consumers demand these brands and refuse substitutes, even if the substitutes are offered at lower prices. In order to maintain strong brands, an organisation must understand what the values of the brand are and continue to communicate these as much as possible. This can entail advertising, sponsorship, good public relations, associations with celebrities, etc. The owners of many successful brands go to great lengths to protect them. One of the biggest threats is counterfeits, which illegally trade on the success of a brand with a usually cheap and inferior product.

EXAMPLE: DUNNES STORES TOP A 'DIRECT COPY' OF KAREN MILLEN DESIGN?

An Irish fashion designer told a court that a Dunnes Stores garment top was 'a direct copy' of a Karen Millen sweater, in a landmark legal case over the protection of design rights, in October 2007. It was the first case to be taken in Ireland, and the first case in Europe involving fashion items under a new EU regulation meant to protect design rights and prevent their unauthorised copying. Mosaic-owned brands Whistles and Coast are also involved in the case. The companies involved claim that Dunnes produced women's clothing items almost identical to a number of their tops, and that this infringed design rights protected by a 2001 European regulation on Unregistered Community Designs.

Helen McAlinden, who told the court that she had been in the fashion industry for twenty-five years, said in evidence that she had examined both the Karen Millen 'cami vest with a full shrug', and a Savida sweater sold by Dunnes Stores. 'I look at the Dunnes Stores garment as a direct copy. There is a slight difference in the shade of the black but I think any consumer would see these garments as the same,' she added. The expert witness, called by Mosaic, said the Karen Millen top featured a number of distinctive features. She told the court she had also examined a Karen Millen shirt, which had a number of distinctive features, and a similar Savida shirt from Dunnes Stores. 'It's almost the same. If two women walked into the room, my initial impression would be that they are wearing the same shirt.' Dunnes Stores have denied the claims.

Source: adapted from V. Kilfeather, Irish Examiner, 4 October 2007, p.2.

Many companies differentiate their products through branding, particularly, in a complex and crowded market-place. In a supermarket, for example, brand names and images make it easier to locate and identify required products. Brand names also tell the consumer something about product quality. Consumers who always buy the same brand know that they will get the same quality each time they buy.

EXAMPLE: TAYTO — ONE OF IRELAND'S FAVOURITE GROCERY BRANDS

Tayto rides high once again in the *Checkout* Top 100 Brands, hitting the top ten list yet another year in a row and reconfirming Tayto's position as one of Ireland's favourite grocery brands. As always, Tayto remains leader in the crisps and snacks category of the Checkout Top 100, beating off all competition and claiming the No. 1 spot yet again. Loved by Irish fans for that distinctive Tayto taste, Tayto crisps are preferred by three out of four people as part of a healthy balanced diet. Tayto's continued presence in the *Checkout* Top 100 Top 10 listing confirms that Tayto listens to consumers and responds with ongoing innovation, new product development and consistent great taste across all product ranges.

Source: adapted from www.checkout.ie

The issue of whether to brand or not to brand is still a hotly contested debate. Manufacturers' brands have long dominated the retail scene. In recent years, however, an increasing number of supermarkets, department stores, discount stores and appliance dealers have developed their own private brands. Private brands give consumers exclusive products that cannot be bought from competitors, which results in higher store loyalty. Examples of retailers that have created and maintained successful private brands are Dunnes Stores and Marks and Spencer.

Controversy has arisen over *manufacturers' brands*, when manufacturers such as Kellogg's or Coca-Cola have accused retailers of copying their brands by adopting similar packaging or brand names. Shops' own brands have been very successful. One of the reasons for this is that groceries fall into the low-involvement category, so consumers are willing to try out different things. Manufacturers have to decide whether to make products for the supermarkets to sell under the shop's own brand, or continue to be independent. Kellogg's, for example, have refused to make shops' own-brand products. They have developed the strap line 'If it doesn't say Kellogg's *on* the box, it isn't Kellogg's *in* the box.'

The top ten brands for fast moving consumer goods in Ireland in 2006 were:

1.   Coca-Cola (carbonated drinks)
2.   Lucozade (sports and energy drinks)
3.   Avonmore (milk)
4.   Jacobs (biscuits)
5.   7UP (carbonated drinks)
6.   Cadbury's Dairy Milk (confectionery)
7.   Brennan's (packaged bread)
8.   Tayto (crisps and snacks)
9.   Danone (yogurt and yogurt drinks)
10. Denny (prepared sliced meats).

Source: www.checkout.ie

The competition between manufacturers' and private brands is often called the *battle of the brands*. In this battle, retailers have many advantages. Retailers control what products they stock, where products go on the shelf, and which they will feature in promotion literature. Retailers can give their own store brands better display space and make certain they are better stocked. They can price store brands lower than comparable manufacturers' brands, thereby appealing to budget-conscious consumers. As store brands improve in quality and as consumers gain confidence in their store chains, store brands are posing a strong challenge to manufacturers' brands (Kotler *et al.* 1999). Those favouring branding suggest that branding leads to higher and more consistent product quality. Branding also increases innovation by giving producers an incentive to look for new features that can be protected against imitating competitors. Overall, branding is believed to encourage more product variety and choice for consumers.

CASE STUDY: THE ALTERNATIVE PIZZA COMPANY CHANGES NEGATIVE PERCEPTIONS ASSOCIATED WITH PIZZA

The Alternative Pizza Company, an artisan Irish producer of handmade pizzas based in Cork, has succeeded in achieving a product listing in the world-famous food hall in Harrods of London. Harrods is the second British retailer to list the Alternative Pizza Company's products, following on from Fresh and Wild, the upmarket British multiple fresh-food specialist retailer which has stocked the company's products since November 2006. Harrods food hall will carry four of the Alternative Pizza Company's innovative products, including a spelt hot chilli pizza and the award-winning Four Irish Cheeses pizza.

Harrods opened in 1849 as a small shop in Knightsbridge, London, and has grown to the renowned department store it is today. Shoppers have over 330 departments to browse through including the world famous 'food hall', which comprises several

different food halls with fish, meat, and pastry counters. Mohamed Al Fayed purchased Harrods in 1985, investing £400m in refurbishing the store. Harrods prides itself on selling only the best quality merchandise and giving customers exemplary service.

The Alternative Pizza Company was established in 2004 by David Flynn, a chef who loved cooking food with simple natural ingredients. In 2006 the company had sales of over €1.1 million. Their products are available in Superquinn, Dunnes Stores, Supervalu, Centra, Spar and other leading independents, as well as upmarket food shops. The Alternative Pizza Company product range is diverse and innovative. It includes: spicy pepperoni; wholemeal vegetarian; crispy bacon; hot chilli; organic smoked salmon and fennel; four Irish cheeses; bacon and cabbage; and black pudding and provençale sauce.

The company also produces a pizza-style garlic bread product with garlic butter and mozzarella cheese. Recipes for the range are developed by Chef Dave Flynn, production director and founder, whose four Irish cheeses pizza and organic smoked salmon and fennel pizza have both been nominated for a Great Taste Award.

Pizza is not the first food that comes to mind when thinking of innovative new products that meet consumer demands for high-quality, natural ingredients, but Martin Hanan from the Alternative Pizza Company begs to differ. Hanan and his colleagues are fast changing negative perceptions associated with pizza, in both Ireland and Britain, with an extensive range of handmade, premium pizzas. The Alternative Pizza Company offers a fresh perspective on the traditional frozen pizza. Moving away from thick-based, doughy pizzas with sparse toppings, the Alternative Pizza is a 100 per cent natural product that markets itself as a gourmet choice, with a light and crispy base, liberal toppings, and no artificial additives. Packaged in a brown cardboard box with minimum design, Hanan says that it is easily distinguished in the freezer among the usual sea of processed colours favoured by other pizza brands.

As Hanan explains, the Alternative Pizza tackles the mindset that frozen pizza is a cheap product of low nutritional value. 'We promote the Alternative Pizza as a food with "no nasties". We use only the finest Irish ingredients with no artificial preservatives, colourings or additives, and no GMO ingredients. People care about what they are eating today and we have positioned ourselves in the super premium market in response to this trend.'

Conscious of the need to innovate in order to remain competitive, the Alternative Pizza Company has already invested in new product developments, which include a gluten-free pizza and a spelt pizza; two recipes that are clearly in line with the brand's target audience of the health-conscious consumer. According to Hanan, 'Many people are unable to tolerate the protein called gluten in wheat, oats, barley or rye. For these people gluten can cause severe indigestion, and result in destruction of the villi that absorb food from the small intestine. We see an opportunity here to offer a convenient and healthy pizza for this sector.'

Currently the company is turning over €1,100,000 — a relatively small figure in the world of the leading frozen pizza companies — however, this figure represents growth of over 200 per cent on 2005 sales. Hanan sees huge potential for growth in the coming years: 'In Ireland, the total frozen pizza market is estimated to be worth €66.2 million annually. In 2004/2005 the pizza category grew by 3.4 per cent and the frozen pizza category is placed twenty-second out of the top 100 retail grocery categories. The top five brands make up 92.9 per cent value share of all pizza sales in the category, which proves that it is a very strong branded category and the latest trend is away from deep pan pizza in favour of thinner premium crusts.' He adds that figures from the British Frozen Food Federation show that a quarter of a billion frozen pizzas are sold each year in Britain. 'We see a gap in the market for a super premium pizza product and we intend to fill it.'

Source: adapted from www.pressreleasesireland.com/2007/02/22

CASE STUDY: BULMERS REVERSE NEGATIVE PERCEPTIONS ASSOCIATED WITH CIDER

Bulmers Ltd is the only Irish cider producer and can boast of being the fastest growing drinks brand in Ireland since the mid-1990s. In the late 1980s, consumers developed negative perceptions towards cider, which was seen as cheap and unsophisticated. The Bulmers pint bottle, however, now sells

better than any competitor in Ireland. And, as a result of this growth, per capita consumption of cider in Ireland is now the highest in the world. Bulmers is an Irish success story, having grown its share of the beer market from 2.8 per cent to over 10 per cent in under ten years, and the brand continues to grow. Through a successful marketing campaign, infusing a mature intellectual appeal into the brand, Bulmers has changed attitudes to cider and recovered a brand that had been subject to declining sales, low pricing and low profits.

The repositioning of the brand relied on a new creative message: 'Nothing added but time'. This was a move away from traditional beer and cider advertising, and as a consequence a new creative and media campaign had to appeal to and target males in the 18 to 34 age bracket. Developing this challenge became a long-term strategy. Television was chosen as the lead medium for the repositioning of Bulmers. The initial buying strategy was aimed at opinion leaders among television viewers. Programmes such as the *Late Late Show, Six One News* and *Primetime* were selected as being among the types of shows during which consumers would not expect to see a Bulmers advertisement. Hence, this type of programming was important to the brand. Bulmers made a heavy investment in ensuring that the 'first-class ticket' to which the brand aspired included the kind of people who wanted to see these commercials. The expenditure on television has consistently seen the brand in the top three beers and ciders sold.

Throughout the repositioning period the TV strategy developed into two distinct streams. First, the 'corporate' campaigns targeted premium programming across all main stations. High ratings and strong coverage, coupled with high-impact emotive commercials, have embedded the Bulmers values of tradition, respect and nature with an entire generation. Secondary to the strategy have been sporting programmes. Bulmers identified several key sports which would fit the brand's new persona — golf, soccer, GAA games and rugby. Golf and rugby were seen as particularly important when the age and social profile of typical consumers is taken into consideration.

The press played an extremely important role in the initial repositioning of Bulmers and is now an ongoing presence through its sponsorship activity. As with television, the press was initially used to position Bulmers where you would least expect to find it. *The Irish Times, Phoenix* magazine and the *Sunday Tribune* were all part of the mix in challenging consumer perceptions of where cider should traditionally have been advertised. The use of cinema has also played an important role in the Bulmers communication mix. Innovation has always played a strong role in the development of the Bulmers marketing platform. In an increasingly competitive marketplace the onus is on the advertiser to ensure that their brand is perceived in a unique and distinctive manner.

The intention of any Bulmers media activity is to reach the target 18–34 customer age group in a distinctive and relevant manner. The beer and cider market in Ireland is still extremely busy and competitive. As a result, advertising cut-through is essential in order for the Bulmers brand to stand out. New and innovative media solutions are constantly being included in the media mix to keep reinforcing the core messages of the brand. Communicating naturalness, tradition, heritage and craft was the beginning of a new journey. The vats and the slogan 'Nothing added but time' presented a new image of quality and maturity, which was not previously associated with a cider brand. Over the years, the brand continued to emphasise that quality and craftsmanship and the emphasis on 'Time' became evident in the communication of 'All in its own good time' and more recently 'Time dedicated to you'. Through repositioning, and the ongoing work with the Cider Industry Council to promote a responsible attitude to the consumption of cider, Bulmers has been a catalyst in displacing the negative image once associated with cider.

Source: adapted from www.bulmers.ie

Questions for Review

1. Explain the perceptual processes which cause people to form different perceptions of the same stimulus.
2. Discuss the concept of consumer involvement. Give examples of when consumers are in a high-involvement state, and when they are in a low-involvement state.
3. Describe the buyer decision process for new products.
4. What are the advantages of differentiation?
5. What are the advantages and disadvantages of branding?

3

Consumer Motivation

CHAPTER OBJECTIVES

After reading this chapter you should be able to:

- Describe motivation in a consumer behaviour context.
- Understand consumer needs, wants, and demands.
- Explain the impact of goals on consumer behaviour and motivation.
- Recognise that motivation can be positive or negative.
- Distinguish between rational and emotional motives in buyer behaviour.
- Identify the importance of individual differences in consumer motivation.

MOTIVATION AS A PSYCHOLOGICAL FORCE

In a consumer behaviour context, *motivation* refers to an activated state within a person that leads to goal-directed behaviour (Hilgard *et al.* 1975). It is the driving force within individuals that impels them to action. This driving force is produced by a state of tension, which exists as the result of an unfulfilled need. Individuals strive both consciously and subconsciously to reduce this tension through behaviour that they anticipate will fulfil their needs and thus relieve them of the stress they feel. This need may be *utilitarian*, i.e. a desire to achieve a functional or practical benefit, for example by eating organic vegetables for nutritional reasons. Alternatively, the need may be *hedonic*, i.e. considered in terms of pleasant sensations. Hedonic needs are subjective and experiential, and consumers might rely on a product to meet their needs for excitement, self-confidence, fantasy, and so on. Another type of hedonic consumption is the desire to engage in leisure activities, i.e. those activities that occur in 'free time' or 'non-work' time. Leisure, however, is an experience; therefore what one person defines as leisure another person may define as work (Fontenella & Zinkhan 1992).

Whether the need is utilitarian or hedonic, a discrepancy exists between the consumer's present state and some ideal state. The consumer's *goal* is the desired end state. The specific consumer selects the patterns of action he or she undertakes to achieve their goals as a result of individual thinking and learning. Marketers try to create products and services that will provide the desired benefits and permit the consumer to reduce this tension. Whether gratification is actually achieved depends on the course of action pursued. The specific goals that consumers wish to achieve and the courses of action they take to attain these goals are selected on the basis of their thinking processes (cognition) and previous learning (e.g. experience). Marketers must therefore view motivation as the force that induces consumption and, through consumption experiences, the process of consumer learning (see Chapter 5).

NEEDS

Human needs — i.e. consumer needs — are the basis of all modern marketing. Needs are the essence of the marketing concept. The key to a company's survival, profitability and growth in a highly competitive marketplace is its ability to identify and satisfy unfulfilled consumer needs better and earlier than the competition. Successful companies define their missions in terms of the consumer needs they satisfy rather than the products they produce and sell. Because consumers' basic needs do not change but the products that satisfy them do, a focus on developing products that will satisfy consumers' needs ensures that a company stays in the forefront of the search for new and effective solutions.

Every individual has needs; some are innate, others are acquired. A *need* is an internal state of tension caused by disequilibrium from an ideal or desired state (Hoyer & MacInnis 2004). As this definition indicates, each need has an equilibrium level at which it is in a state of satisfaction. The individual feels tension when there is any departure from this equilibrium and is motivated to find some way of fulfilling the need.

Innate needs are physiological; they include the needs for food, water, air, clothing and shelter. Because they are needed to sustain biological life, they are considered *primary needs* or motives. At certain times of the day, for example, an individual begins to feel hungry, and he or she realises it is time to get something to eat. The individual is motivated to direct behaviour towards certain outcomes (e.g. going to a restaurant, getting a takeaway, or heading for the fridge). Eating satisfies the need and removes the tension — in this case, hunger.

Acquired needs are needs that individuals learn in response to their culture or environment. These may include needs for self-esteem, prestige, affection, power and learning. Because acquired needs are generally psychological, they are considered *secondary needs* or motives. They result from the individual's subjective psychological state and from relationships with others. Acquired or secondary needs reflect the priorities of a culture. For example, an Irish consumer may desire to spend a large portion of his or her income on products that permit displays of wealth and status. A consumer's behaviour often fulfils more than one need, for example an individual may buy a luxury coat by Irish designer Paul Costelloe but which also provides protection from the cold. Thus, the coat fulfils a wider range of personal and social needs, such as acceptance or ego needs.

Specific Needs and Buying Behaviour

Based on the premise that consumers are not always aware of the reasons for their actions, motivational research attempts to discover underlying feelings, attitudes and emotions concerning product, service or brand use. A variety of needs can operate in a given situation. But what needs do consumers experience?

One well-known theory of needs is based on the research of psychologist Abraham Maslow. During the 1940s, Maslow, an American psychologist, was one of the first to classify human needs or motives. Maslow suggested that human needs may be classified into motivating factors that influence behaviour. He proposed that these needs are based on a hierarchical model, with basic needs at the bottom and higher needs at the top. Starting from the bottom of the hierarchy these needs are:

- *Physiological* — the need for food, water, sleep and air. Relevant products would include staple grocery items and medicines.
- *Safety* — the need for protection and security. Services would include insurance, alarm systems, investments, retirement plans.
- *Social* — the need for affection, friendship and acceptance. Items such as clothing, grooming products, drinks, and clubs would be included here.
- *Ego* — the need for prestige, success, accomplishment and self-esteem. Luxury cars, hand-crafted jewellery, original art work, credit cards, and membership of exclusive clubs would help satisfy these needs.
- *Self-actualisation* — the need for self-fulfilment and enriching experiences. Examples of products and services would include education, hobbies and travel.

Maslow's hierarchy of needs

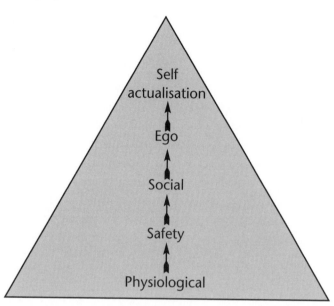

Maslow proposed that people tend to satisfy their needs systematically, beginning with the basic physiological needs and then moving up the hierarchy. Maslow further suggested that as long as physiological needs remain unsatisfied, an individual is motivated to fulfil those alone. Maslow's hierarchy of needs is adaptable to market segmentation and the development of advertisements because consumer goods are designed to satisfy each of the need levels and because most needs are shared by large segments of consumers (Schiffman & Kanuk 2007). Marketers may also use the hierarchy of needs to position their products, as the key to positioning is to find a niche — an unsatisfied need — that is not fulfilled by competing brands (see Chapter 1).

A common criticism of Maslow's theory is that needs are not always ordered exactly as in this hierarchy. Some consumers, for example, temporarily place a higher priority on buying lottery tickets than on acquiring necessities such as food and clothing.

EXAMPLE: NATIONAL LOTTERY

The National Lottery began gaming operations on 23 March 1987. The scratch card was the first game introduced and proved to be an instant hit. A year later, the Lotto draw was introduced. The game has changed somewhat in twenty years. Whereas players once picked six numbers from a total of 36, today they choose from a total of 45. The player has a one in 8,145,060 chance of winning the top prize. The move by the National Lottery into EuroMillions has also proved popular, as every week over 50,000 players win cash prizes in this draw.

The commercial success of the National Lottery has allowed it to innovate in terms of its core objectives: to operate a world-class lottery for the people of Ireland and to raise funds for beneficiaries on behalf of the Government. In 2006, a total amount of €217 million was raised for good causes, up €14.3 million from €203.2 million in 2005. Since its introduction twenty years ago, the National Lottery has raised over €2.6 billion for worthwhile causes. This money has been allocated across various categories: youth, sport, recreation and amenities, health and welfare, arts, culture and national heritage, and Irish language. The company's involvement in television game shows such as *Winning Streak, Fame and Fortune, Trump Card* and *Tellybingo* has brought the National Lottery into homes across the country, regularly appealing to over 60 per cent of the adult population. National Lottery game shows are frequently placed in the top five most watched programmes in Irish television ratings.

Source: adapted from 'Great Irish Brands', Irish Independent special supplement, 17 November 2007, pp. 30-31.

Most human needs are never fully or permanently satisfied. At fairly regular intervals throughout the day, for example, individuals experience hunger needs that must be satisfied; most people regularly seek companionship and approval from others to satisfy their social needs. Additionally, new needs emerge as old needs are satisfied, for example, as individuals move through various lifestyle stages. An individual, for example, may buy a two-seater sports car; but if at a later stage he or she has children a new need emerges for a family car.

Other motivational approaches have focused on specific needs and their influence on buying behaviour. Research conducted by McClelland (1955) stresses the importance of individual differences in motivation. His research findings suggest that individuals possess three basic motivational needs:

Need for achievement — individuals with a high need for achievement strongly value personal accomplishment. They place a premium on products and services that signify success because these consumption items provide feedback about the realisation of their goals. These consumers are good for buying products that provide evidence of their achievement.

Need for affiliation — individuals with a high need for affiliation strongly value being in the company of other people. This need is relevant to products and services that are 'consumed' in groups in order to alleviate loneliness. These consumers are good for buying products in shopping centres, consuming products in bars and clubs and becoming members of leisure centres.

Need for power — individuals with a high need for power want to control their environment. They strongly value goods that allow them to believe that they have influence over their surroundings. These consumers purchase items such as cars with loud boom boxes (large portable music equipment) together with exceptional accessories for their cars. Other consumers with a need for power may take luxury holidays or cruises that promise to respond to their every whim.

Because needs influence motivation and its effects, marketers are keenly interested in identifying and measuring them. Consumers' needs, wants, demands and goals have some important implications for marketers, for example, segmenting markets based on needs. Marketers can also identify currently unfulfilled needs or develop better need-satisfying alternatives. Indeed, this type of research is often essential to the development of new products or services. Needs, for example, that relate to how consumers perceive themselves, how they are perceived by others, and the esteem in which they are held by others are categorised as *symbolic needs*. Achievement, independence, and self-control are symbolic needs because they are connected to a sense of self. Similarly, a consumer's need for uniqueness is symbolic because it drives consumption decisions about how he or she expresses their identity (Tian *et al.* 2001). The need to avoid rejection and the need for achievement, status, affiliation and belonging are symbolic because they reflect a consumer's social position or role.

EXAMPLE: SATISFYING SYMBOLIC NEEDS AT BOODLES IRELAND

Boodles, the top-end jeweller situated on Grafton Street in Dublin, is a luxurious and contemporary venue which includes a spectacular glass staircase and quartz marble wall. Boodles opened in 2006, after spending almost €1 million on the luxurious interior, and they pay a rent of more than €520,000 per annum for 71 Grafton Street. According to Jody Wainwright, Managing Director of Boodles Ireland, 'High rents are usually good for us, as they tend to put us in a place where we do best.' Wainwright acknowledged that Grafton Street does not have the same high-end shops as Bond Street or Sloane Square in London, but said it was still a lucrative market, in the main luxury shopping thoroughfare.

Boodles offer an appropriate setting where bankers, developers and brokers spend an average of €10,000 on a purchase. According to Wainwright, the spending power of Ireland celebrities is a constant. Boodles Ireland is set to have a turnover of €8 million in the year to February 2008. Wainwright said the jeweller 'clocked up sales of €2 million over the two-week Christmas period of 2006 alone'. He admits, for example, selling a diamond necklace for €320,000 to an Irish celebrity during August 2007. While that was the biggest purchase to date, Wainwright said that about a dozen items have sold for more than €100,000.

Wainwright explains, 'We are not aiming to achieve a really high volume of sale. We're clearly dealing with something more specialised.' Boodles has a cocktail bar with a 'mixerologist' (barman) and a flat screen television to entertain you while you peruse the collection. Unsurprisingly, Boodles customers tend to come from Dublin's more affluent suburbs. According to Wainwright, however, 'We get lots of bankers and developers, but we also get plenty of farmers and builders who are doing well. The tourist trade is also particularly strong here and we get a lot of customers from Cork.' Apparently, the level of business generated by customers from the south has prompted Boodles to consider opening in Cork.

Everything in Boodles is designed in-house and made in one of their two workshops in London, which means that all their products are unique and they maintain good quality control. The cheapest offering at Boodles is a pair of pearl earrings for €150. The most expensive is a diamond ring costing €485,000. 'We have pendants for €435 — which is one of the cheapest popular offerings — and plenty at the €2,000 mark, but we probably play our strongest card with our raindance ring at €13,800,' said Wainwright.

*Source: adapted from S. Mitchell, 'Boosting Boodles', Sunday Business Post,
30 September 2007, p. 16.*

Schiffman and Kanuk (2007) summarise that individuals with specific psychological needs tend to be receptive to advertising appeals directed at those needs. They also tend to be receptive to certain kinds of products. Thus, knowledge of motivational theory provides marketers with key bases for segmenting markets and developing promotional strategies.

Some critics accuse marketers of creating new needs and manipulating consumers into buying goods they do not need, but most people agree that marketers cannot create needs; however, they can awaken latent needs and encourage consumers to engage in unwholesome behaviours. Aspects of drinking, smoking and gambling are often promoted as enticing and socially acceptable pastimes, while the addictive health aspects of these are downplayed (Schiffman & Kanuk 2007).

WANTS AND DEMANDS

Another basic concept in marketing is that of *human wants*. Wants are described in terms of products and services that satisfy needs. Human wants are shaped by culture and individual personality. A hungry person in Ireland, for example, may want potatoes in their meal, whereas a hungry person in Pakistan may want rice as part of their meal. In essence, consumer behaviour is about giving consumers what they want. All marketing activities of an organisation should be geared towards this. It implies a focus towards the consumer by satisfying their wants through the provision of a product or service.

As a society evolves, the wants of its members expand. As people are exposed to more objects that arouse their interest and desire, producers try to provide more want-satisfying products and services. People may have narrow, basic needs (e.g. for food or shelter), but almost unlimited wants. They also, however, have limited resources. Thus, they want to choose products that provide the most satisfaction for their money. Consumers view products as bundles of benefits and choose products that give them the best bundle for their money. When backed by an ability to pay — that is, buying power — wants become *demands*. The demand by Irish consumers for handmade Hermès handbags, for example, is so great that consumers have to join a waiting list. The bags cost between €5,000 and €12,000, but can cost up to €70,000. A frilly matching scarf on sale for €89 which can be tied to the bag or worn around the wrist is also being demanded (Daly 2005).

Companies go to great lengths to learn about and understand their consumers' needs, wants and demands. They conduct consumer research, focus groups and consumer clinics. They analyse complaint books, warranties and service data. They observe consumers using their own and competing products, and interview them in depth about their likes and dislikes. Understanding consumer needs, wants and demands in detail provides important input for designing marketing strategies. Wants and demands, however, are influenced not only by marketers, but also by family, peer groups, religion, ethnic background and education (see Chapter 10).

GOALS

Another factor affecting consumer behaviour and motivation is goals. A *goal* is a particular end state or outcome that a person would like to achieve (Hoyer & MacInnis 2004). Goals can be either *generic* or *product-specific*. Generic goals are the general classes or categories of goals that consumers see as a means to fulfil their needs. A product-specific goal is the attainment of the specifically branded product or service that consumers select for goal fulfilment. Marketers are particularly interested in product-specific goals.

Goals are the sought-after results of motivated behaviour. When a need is aroused, it produces a drive state. A *drive* is an affective state in which emotions and physiological arousal are experienced (Mowen 1995). The drive state activates an individual to engage in goal-directed action to obtain the product or service.

Goal-directed behaviour consists of the actions taken to relieve the need state, such as searching for information, talking to others, shopping for the best bargains, and purchasing products and services. Whether goals are situational and concrete or enduring and abstract, individuals are likely to be motivated to engage in behaviours that are relevant to achieving personal goals.

EXAMPLE: SURGERY IN THE SUN

Have the vacation of a lifetime in an exotic country, with sun, sea, and pristine white beaches.

'Your personal assistant awaits you at the airport, accompanied by car and driver. You are whisked away to a luxury beach hotel where you are warmly greeted and everything has been made "just right" for your arrival. Sound great so far? Now add world-class plastic surgery abroad. Got your interest?'

This is a marketing paragraph from one of the leading cosmetic holiday tour operators, promising sun, sea, sand and stitches. Companies such as Gorgeous Getaways, Surgical Attractions, and Surgery Safaris all promise high-quality procedures performed in exotic locations, so you can relax and recuperate in style, not to mention at a fraction of the price you would pay at home. Cosmetic surgery is one of the fastest-growing industries in Ireland, according to Voluntary Health Insurance. Every year, many more people choose to aesthetically enhance themselves through popular cosmetic procedures such as breast implants, Botox injections, nose reshaping and liposuction. While the Irish public has become more accepting of cosmetic surgery, the industry remains largely unregulated.

Most operators offer packages based on a stay of between ten and fourteen days. This includes a pre-operative consultation, the procedure itself, and a five-day recuperation period. So why would someone considering a cosmetic procedure choose to travel? According to Gorgeous Getaways, for the same price as the procedure at home, patients can get a five-star hotel, full service, and a relaxing holiday. However, medical tourism raises many issues for consumer rights: for example, if something goes wrong it will not be covered by their standard medical insurance. A spokesperson for the VHI says cosmetic surgery is not covered at all by insurance and it can only insure against unplanned operations that would be needed abroad. Due to an increase in personal income and changing attitudes in relation to ageing and beauty, more Irish people now consider going under the cosmetic knife. An MRBI poll (2005) showed that one in ten Irish men said they would consider cosmetic surgery, in particular eye-bag removal or a tummy tuck. One in five women said they would consider a breast uplift or enlargement, liposuction or a tummy tuck.

Source: adapted from N. Matthews, Sunday Business Post 'Agenda' section, 17 September 2006, p. A3.

For any given need, there are many different and appropriate goals. The goals selected by individuals depend on their personal experiences, physical capacity, prevailing cultural norms and values, and the goal's accessibility in the physical and social environment. Needs and goals are interdependent; neither exists without the other. People, however, are often not as aware of their needs as they are of their goals. Individuals are usually more aware of their *physiological* needs than they are of their *psychological* needs. Most people know when they are hungry, thirsty, or cold, and they take appropriate steps to satisfy these needs. The same people may not consciously be aware of their needs for acceptance, self-esteem or status. They may, however, subconsciously engage in behaviour that satisfies their psychological (or acquired) needs.

POSITIVE AND NEGATIVE MOTIVATION

Motivation can be *positive* or *negative*. Individuals may experience a driving force *towards* some object or condition or a driving force *away* from some object or condition. Psychologists refer to positive drives as needs, wants or desires and to negative drives as fears or aversions. Both positive and negative motivations serve to initiate and sustain human behaviour. *Fear appeals* emphasise the negative consequences that can occur unless the consumer changes behaviour. A fear-appeal strategy is often used in marketing communications, though more commonly in social marketing contexts in which organisations encourage people to, for example, convert to a healthier lifestyle by giving up smoking, or if they are going drinking to designate a driver who will not be drinking during the outing. A key reason why fear appeals can be successful is that they create emotional responses. These emotions then focus a person's attention on how to cope with the problem. The increased attention on coping responses makes it more likely that the person will be motivated to respond to the threat (Tanner *et al.* 1991).

EXAMPLE: SHOCK-STYLE ADS DRIVE MESSAGE HOME

TV road safety ads are about more than just shocking viewers: they use a deep psychological strategy to get their message across too. There is a swift grab for the remote control in many homes when a road safety ad begins. Few want to watch bodies being crushed and lives irrevocably changed after a serious crash. For many, the thought is too shocking, and too close.

Behind these adverts is Belfast-based Lyle Bailie International, which has designed all TV road safety ads shown in the Republic for more than ten years. The company says the adverts are about more than just shocking viewers.

According to Chief Executive David Lyle, 'There is a deep psychological strategy behind this. We are encoding people's long-term emotional memory with a sense of the awfulness of what can happen. We do this to influence decision making. Viewers will associate the act of drinking and driving, or not wearing seat belts, with taking you to a terrible place.' He agrees the ads are shocking and that they do prompt many people to switch over. This does not mean, however, that people are avoiding the adverts. Quite the contrary — it is a sign of their success. Millward Brown researched reactions to an advert about seat belt wearing which shows the damage an unrestrained body can cause in a crash. They found fifty per cent of people switched channels when the ad began. Only three per cent of these, however, said they were both unaware of and uninfluenced by the message. So when someone flicks it is because they have seen the ad and it has already succeeded in convincing them. The ads are designed to have a fairly immediate impact.

They are heavily reliant on 'visual narrative' (advertising jargon for letting the pictures tell the story). In part, this is because there is a high proportion of people with poor literacy skills among the 17–49-year-old male target audience. To reach this group, advertisers try to buy slots around men's favourite programmes — sport and movies. Road safety adverts must compete with contrary messages, such as car ads highlighting speed or power as a selling point and ads for alcoholic drinks. Road safety ads also try to contradict films that glamorise dangerous driving.

During 2006, €4.5 million, from sponsorship and Road Safety Authority (RSA) funding, was spent buying road safety media advertising. Designing a road safety advertisement can take up to six months and cost up to €650,000. An important part of the process is testing it on focus groups of different ages, genders and backgrounds. Relatives of crash victims are included in this process. The aim of an advert is not to just to raise awareness, that is not enough. Awareness is an immensely important first step but the ad has to do much more. It has to shift attitudes.

Source: adapted from D. Labanyi, Irish Times, *24 January 2007, p. 41.*

Needs, wants or desires may lead to goals that can be positive or negative. A goal has *valence,* which means that it can be positive or negative. A positively valued goal is one towards which consumers direct their behaviour; they are motivated to *approach* the goal and will seek out products that should be instrumental in attaining it. A positive goal is one towards which behaviour is directed; thus, it is often referred to as an *approach object.* A negative goal is one from which behaviour is directed away and is referred to as an *avoidance object.* Products such as deodorants and mouthwash frequently rely on consumers' negative motivation by depicting the onerous social consequences of underarm odour or bad breath. Because both the approach and avoidance goals are the results of motivated behaviour, both are simply referred to as *goals.*

Because a purchase decision can involve more than one source of motivation, consumers often find themselves in situations in which different motives, both positive and negative, conflict with one another. Because marketers are attempting to satisfy consumers' needs, they can also attempt to provide possible solutions to these dilemmas.

The *theory of cognitive dissonance* is based on the premise that people have a need for order and consistency in their lives and that a state of tension is created when beliefs or behaviours conflict with one another. A state of dissonance occurs when a consumer must make a choice between two products, each of which usually possesses both good and bad qualities. By choosing one product and not the other, the person gets the bad qualities of the chosen product and loses out on the good qualities of the other product. This loss creates an unpleasant, dissonant state that the person is motivated to reduce. People tend to convince themselves, after the transaction, that the choice they made was the smart one by finding additional reasons to support the choice they made, or perhaps by highlighting any flaws associated with the option they did not select.

A marketer can resolve this conflict by bundling several benefits together. In 2004, for example, Tayto launched its 'Honest' brand of crisps and popcorn in response to consumer needs for healthier snack products without compromising on taste. Honest crisps are 40 per cent lower in fat and Honest popcorn contains 30 per cent less fat; salt is also reduced by 30 per cent in both products. More recently, in April 2007 Tayto launched 'Velvet Crunch' to the Irish market, with just 83 calories per pack and 70 per cent less fat. Products such as these allow the consumer to reduce conflicts they may have experienced.

Perceived risk is another factor affecting motivation. *Perceived risk* reflects the extent to which the consumer is uncertain about the consequences of buying, using or disposing of a product or service. If negative outcomes are likely, or positive outcomes are unlikely, perceived risk is high. Consumers are more likely to pay attention to and carefully process marketing communications when perceived risk is high. In addition, when perceived risk increases, consumers tend to collect more information and evaluate it carefully. Perceived risk can be associated with any product or service, but it tends to be higher when:

- little information is available about the product or service
- the product or service is new
- the product or service has a high price
- the product is technologically complex
- there are fairly substantial quality differences between brands, so the consumer might make an inferior choice
- opinions of others are important, and the consumer is likely to be judged by the acquisition, usage or disposition decision. (Bettman, 1973)

As noted in Chapter 2, products can be described as either high- or low-involvement products. In general, consumers find high risk uncomfortable. As a result, they are usually motivated to engage in a number of behaviours and information-processing activities to reduce or resolve risk. To reduce the uncertainty component of risk, consumers can collect additional information by conducting online research, reading consumer magazines, or talking to salespeople or family or friends. Consumers also reduce uncertainty by being brand loyal, ensuring that the product should be at least as satisfactory as the last purchase.

The lack of money also constrains consumers who might otherwise have the motivation to engage in a behaviour that involves purchasing a product or service. However, motivated consumers who lack sufficient money can still process information and make buying decisions, though they might be currently constrained in their immediate ability to purchase.

Limitations on consumers' time is another factor that impacts on whether motivation results in transaction. Many consumers believe they are more pressed for time than ever before, a feeling called *time poverty*. The sense of time poverty has made consumers very responsive to marketing innovations that allow them to save time. Another aspect of time is the psychological dimension — how it is actually experienced — which is an important factor in queuing theory (the mathematical study of waiting queues). A consumer's experience of waiting can radically influence his or her perceptions of service quality. Although people may assume that something must be pretty good if they have to wait for it, the negative feelings aroused by long waits can quickly turn off consumers (Taylor 1994).

EXAMPLE: ONLINE ORDERING HELPS LUNCH DELIVERIES TAKE OFF

In our 'cash-rich, time-poor' society, hungry workers in isolated business parks are turning to new web-based lunch delivery services to avoid queues or long walks for food. There are so many food service companies branching into the online order-delivery business that this has become one of the fastest growing areas in the Irish food industry. The catalyst for the new services, offered by companies such as Manna, Munchies, and others, has been the mass relocation of businesses from the Dublin city centre and suburban business districts to large, satellite business campuses in Dublin suburbs such as Sandyford, Stillorgan, Park West and City West, where demand for online ordering is escalating. For now, it appears that the majority of online order takers are based in Dublin, though other companies are now partaking in the trend around the country. The office delivery trade is, mostly, a recent sideline to companies' original business models. The usual model is that a café or restaurant sets up a lunch delivery service which takes telephone orders, and this then spawns a website that allows internet ordering.

Dublin-based café and sandwich-bar chain Café Sol started a lunch delivery service in 2004 when it began taking lunch orders by phone for delivery to offices in the Dublin 2 area. This limited the delivery distance from its production site. Café Sol began actively attempting to expand its delivery business earlier in 2007 by emailing and calling prospective clients. By going online, it succeeded in drawing customers with free trial offers. The company now services many locations along the length of the M50 and is hoping to expand to cover the whole of the greater Dublin area. The launch of its website in September 2007 was a crucial step in growing the business. Marketing co-ordinator Tara McIntyre says, 'You need a powerful website to represent your brand, so moving the whole service online will be the most important step for us now.' The necessity of providing an efficient online ordering system is now widely acknowledged by companies aspiring to enter the lunch business in a serious way. With demand on the increase and Irish broadband continually improving, the online lunch delivery industry has huge potential.

Source: adapted from www.techcentral.ie

RATIONAL VERSUS EMOTIONAL MOTIVES

Motives can be further divided into *rational motives* and *emotional motives*. In a marketing context, the term *rationality* implies that consumers select goals based on totally objective criteria, such as size, weight, price, or miles per litre of petrol.

Emotional motives imply the selection of goals according to personal or subjective criteria (e.g. pride, fear, affection, status). The assumption underlying this distinction is that subjective or emotional criteria do not maximise utility or satisfaction. It is reasonable to assume, however, that consumers always attempt to select alternatives that, in their view, serve to best satisfy their needs. The assessment of satisfaction is a very personal process based on the individual's own need structure, as well as on past behavioural and social (or learned) experiences (Schiffman & Kanuk 2007). What may appear irrational to an outside observer may be perfectly rational in the context of the consumer's own psychological field.

Consumers may seek to experience a variety of emotions, such as love, hate, fear, grief or anger. It may seem unusual that people would seek out negative experiences, but amusement parks, for example, are built in part to create fear; and horror films are created to frighten and even disgust people. In general, consumers go to the cinema and theatre to experience second hand the emotions of love, hate and anger. In 2006, Irish consumers spent €17.8 million at the cinema box office — an increase of 8.9 per cent on 2005 figures. Almost 350,000 Irish people go to the cinema each week (Kennedy 2007).

An important point made by hedonic consumption theorists is that emotional motives sometimes dominate utilitarian motives in choosing products (Hirschman & Holbrook 1982). Hedonic products are intrinsically more emotionally involving than, for example, using a particular mouthwash or shampoo. The choice of a hedonically relevant product tends to be based on its symbolic value and on the likely emotion that it is anticipated to elicit in the consumer.

EXAMPLE: BROWN THOMAS SERVING EMOTIONAL MOTIVES

Brown Thomas was first opened on Dublin's Grafton Street in 1849 by haberdashers and general drapers Hugh Brown and James Thomas. In 1971, under threat of closure, the store was bought by Galen and Hilary Weston. In 1995, Brown Thomas merged with Switzers and the brand was extended to Cork, Limerick, and Galway.

Today, Brown Thomas has grown to become a splendid showcase for major Irish and international designers from all over the world. Each store carries a range of world-class brands such as Alexander McQueen, Balenciaga, Dolce and Gabbana, Gucci, Lanvin and Prada. There are also luxury boutiques in the Dublin store, bringing the consumer the best of Chanel, Dior, Fendi, Hermès, and Louis Vuitton, alongside other exclusive collections from a carefully selected range of designers.

There is a strong emphasis on service at Brown Thomas. The sales consultants don't just sell. They understand that sometimes consumers have an idea in their mind but would like a helping hand to bring it to life. After all, as most consumers have experienced, shopping isn't always about knowing what one is looking for. The range of services on offer includes the complimentary personal shopping and corporate gifting service, which means that help is on hand whenever and wherever it is needed.

There is also the made-to-measure service, complete with personal tailor, for today's time-pressed businessman. From floor to ceiling and everything in between, Brown Thomas aims to present itself with élan, flair and dash. Brown Thomas prides itself in being Ireland's pre-eminent retailer, continuously innovating and looking at ways to delight both the Irish and international consumer. The store environments are benchmarked against the best in the world. Recent innovations include the designer and shoe rooms in Brown Thomas Dublin as well as the Vera Wang bridal boutique exclusive to Brown Thomas in Ireland.

Through its internationally acclaimed fashion shows and charity initiatives (such as the Fashion Targets Breast Cancer Campaign in Ireland), its exclusive product launches, unique boutiques and award-winning window displays, Brown Thomas has remained one of the top destinations for the glitterati from the worlds of fashion, sport and film. Just some of the names that have visited the stores over the years include Elle McPherson, Elizabeth Hurley, Pamela Anderson, Paris Hilton, Stella McCartney and footballer Pelé.

Source: adapted from 'Great Irish Brands', Irish Independent special supplement, 17 November 2007, p. 10-11.

Motives are hypothetical constructs — that is, they cannot be seen or touched, handled, smelled or otherwise tangibly observed. For this reason, no single measurement method can be considered a reliable index. A number of different attempts have been made to identify various emotions that people experience in relation to their buying behaviour. Psychologists have attempted to measure ten emotions: interest, joy, surprise, sadness, anger, disgust, contempt, fear, shame and guilt. The results revealed that pleasant surprise and interest were associated with satisfied consumers. In contrast, those who were dissatisfied revealed a general pattern of anger, disgust, contempt, guilt and sadness, which combined to create a generally hostile consumer (Westbrook & Oliver 1991).

Motivational research, however, is still regarded as an important tool by marketers who want to gain deeper insights into the *whys* of consumer behaviour than conventional marketing research techniques can yield. Since motivational research often reveals unsuspected consumer motivations concerning product or brand usage, its principal use today is in the development of new ideas for promotional campaigns, ideas that can penetrate the consumer's conscious awareness by appealing to unrecognised needs (Schiffman & Kanuk 2007). Motivational research also provides marketers with a basic orientation for new product categories and enables them to explore consumer reactions to ideas and advertising at an early stage to avoid costly mistakes. Furthermore, as with all qualitative research techniques, motivational research findings provide consumer researchers with basic insights that enable them to design structured quantitative marketing research studies to be conducted on larger, more representative samples of consumers.

CASE STUDY: FOCUS IRELAND SATISFYING BASIC MOTIVATIONAL NEEDS

Focus Ireland was founded by Sr Stanislaus Kennedy as a result of research findings into the needs of homeless women in Dublin. Through listening to the experiences of the women, the research team realised the importance of involving people who were experiencing or had experienced homelessness, in the development of services for people out-of-home. In 1985, two years after the initial research, Focus Point (now Focus Ireland) opened its doors in Eustace Street, Dublin. The agency provides various services to young people, such

as advice, advocacy, information, help with finding a home, and a warm and welcoming place to meet and have a low-cost meal. Since 1985, Focus Ireland has continued to grow and expand its services. In 1988, the organisation opened its first development of low-rent, good-quality long-term and short-term housing in Dublin. Focus Ireland now has additional housing and service projects in Dublin as well as housing developments in both Limerick and Waterford.

In 2005, more than 4,000 people presented as homeless to Focus Ireland. Single adults remain the largest homeless group. As part of Focus Ireland's five-year strategy, the association aims to acquire 800 new homes by 2010.

Focus Ireland has identified three different stages of homelessness and provides services that will help people move on whatever their stage. Not everyone who comes to Focus Ireland will experience all three stages.

First, those in crisis are either already homeless or threatened with homelessness. At this stage Focus Ireland provides them with a place to go and someone to support them and help them plan a way forward. Typically, the second stage is a stage of transition and focuses on stabilisation, whether it is in short-term accommodation, participation in transitional programmes or participating in training or education programmes. The third stage concentrates on settlement; it is at this stage that Focus Ireland customers are offered a long-term home, whether it is with Focus Ireland, the local authority or in the private rented sector.

Focus Ireland believe that if people are to move out of homelessness they need help and support at each stage, whether they are homeless, at risk of becoming homeless, or if they need help to maintain a home for the long term. Support is often key to the successful transition from homelessness to home. All Focus Ireland tenants are provided with support in their housing projects. Customers who are housed in local authority or private rented accommodation are linked in with Focus Ireland Tenancy Support and Settlement Teams who provide them with the emotional and practical support they need to help them to settle into their new homes and communities. The team also supports households who are finding it difficult to sustain their tenancy.

Sr Stanislaus believes that home is a place in which a person should feel safe and secure, warm and dry; a place to rest, eat, sleep, entertain, find solitude, pray, love, laugh, argue and cry. A place to read a book, share a meal, watch a television programme, play an instrument, do a bit of gardening, play with the children, get the housework done and the bills paid, be at ease with oneself and with friends and family, in safety and security, without fear of interference or intrusion. Sr Stanislaus suggests that, 'The need for a place like that is deep and urgent in all of us. The desire for a place called home is the deepest need in every human heart and perhaps the least recognised. And yet for many people, home is elusive, unattainable, beyond their grasp, because something has happened in their lives, some catastrophic event has separated them from home and they find it impossible to come home again, to secure a place of their own.'

People who find themselves homeless are people who are going through a transition in their lives. Perhaps they are moving from one home to another and have somehow got stranded in between; perhaps they are in transition from family home to independence, and something has gone wrong for them; perhaps they have been mentally ill and are in transition to healing but they haven't yet found their new place in the community; perhaps they are fleeing violence or abuse and are trying a place in the community where they can be safe and secure. The danger is that people can sometimes get trapped in this transition state and never get to the other side, the place they set out for. What began as a phase in their lives, an unfortunate event, when they managed to slip through the net of provision for people at risk, can quickly develop into a state of life, a way of being in the world; homeless, friendless, isolated, marginalised, and insecure. If there is no one to give them a helping hand at this crucial time in their lives, they can slip into a whole way of life that is without hope. Those who are weak can be destroyed; those who are mentally insecure can slip into insanity; those who are young can easily get sucked into a life of crime and violence; those who are sexually vulnerable can be exploited and end up living a life of prostitution and degradation.

People who are homeless have no possessions or security. Before long they have no self-respect either and if they are not helped to come home they can end up bitter and resentful, maybe destructive towards themselves and others. Sr Stanislaus noted, 'It is with people who are out of home that we in Focus Ireland have the privilege to work. All of them have something beautiful in their hearts, they may be a good bit troubled but they can be made whole again if someone looks, notices, pays attention to them and helps them.'

Source: adapted from www.focusireland.ie

CASE STUDY: UNISLIM MOTIVATING IRISH CONSUMERS TOWARDS HEALTH

We are constantly bombarded and inundated with diet tips and nutritional advice, but back in the 1970s dieting and healthy eating were concepts that were virtually unheard of. With more than thirty-

five years of nutrition experience, Unislim is Ireland's longest-running slimming and health organisation. It was set up by Agnes McCourt in the early 1970s after she struggled to lose post-baby weight; her daughter Fiona Gratzer took over the reins in 2001 and today the organisation holds 600 weekly meetings across Ireland. When Agnes McCourt (a former PE teacher) tried to lose weight she found there was nothing on offer in 1960s Ireland. She had gone to her local GP, who suggested that she take diet pills. Unimpressed by this advice and aware that there weren't any exercise or slimming classes for women in Ireland, she got a core group of people together and went to the local parish hall to set up a class. These classes were confessional in nature: people would reveal what they had eaten that week and in return receive basic nutritional information.

People lost weight and news of the concept spread rapidly. Realising that there was a gap in the market McCourt and her husband left their teaching jobs to open up Ireland's first provincial gym in Newry. Unfortunately it coincided with the start of the troubles in the north in 1969. When the building next door to their gym was blown up they saw the devastation first hand and decided against starting that business. At the same time McCourt continued to run weight reduction classes. Eventually she realised that if she trained other people to spread the word rather than trying to do all the classes herself she would not only be in a position to change more people's lives, but would also be able to grow the business further. In 1972 the business was franchised out, evolving into what it is now widely known as Unislim.

A completely new concept, Unislim was seen as a revolutionary idea at the time because nothing like this existed. Not even their main competitors, Weight Watchers, had come into the market. Nowadays, as there is an abundance of dietary information in the public domain, it does not necessarily mean that people really need to go to a Unislim class. So what is it that makes the concept so compelling? According to Gratzer it is not enough for people to be equipped with dietary information; they must be educated and shown how they can incorporate healthy eating into their lifestyles. 'We use a unit system for people to record a food diary but what Unislim has, which is unique, is the ability to motivate people to make a change. Lots of members, who have been longstanding members, go to maintain their weight loss because they feel being answerable to somebody every week and picking up or renewing information is the only way to achieve that goal,' she says.

Unislim also regard themselves as nutritional educators and the approach they have taken over the past thirty-five years has clearly stood the test of time. Gratzer attributes the success of Unislim to a strong brand and to the positive benefits the classes have on people's lives. She also says that Unislim food products are performing extremely well in a declining market. Gratzer adds, 'There are a few things that we haven't revealed yet but there are ways we are planning on capitalising on the Unislim brand and building on our reputation of building solid, sound, healthy nutritional advice which has always had the respect of the medical profession.' Gratzer hopes to maintain the ethos that Unislim is an Irish company, a unique point of difference from their competitors. 'Our plans are written by Irish people, we employ Irish people and our plans are made with the Irish person in mind. People like to support an Irish-grown company; all our foods are made in Ireland so I think people are proud to support Irish products and Irish services if they are given the choice,' she added.

Source: adapted from www.irishentrepreneur.com

Questions for Review

1. Consumer needs are the basis of all modern marketing. Discuss.
2. Examine Maslow's hierarchy of needs theory and outline the relevance of this theory for consumer behaviour.
3. How can needs, wants or desires lead to goals that can be positive or negative?
4. Distinguish between rational and emotional motives. Illustrate your answer with examples of how consumers attempt to satisfy these motives.

4

Personality, Lifestyles and Psychographics

CHAPTER OBJECTIVES
After reading this chapter you should be able to:

- Discuss the concept of personality.
- Understand various research approaches to personality.
- Explain self-concept and self-esteem.
- Describe brand personality.
- Understand the connection between personality and consumer lifestyles.
- Explain the importance of psychographics for market segmentation.

WHAT IS PERSONALITY?

Personality, lifestyles and values are the basic components of *psychographics*, the description of consumers based on their psychological and behavioural characteristics. Traditionally, psychographics measured consumer lifestyles, but more modern applications have broadened the approach to include concepts such as the psychological makeup of consumers, their values and personality, and the way they behave in relation to specific products (their usage patterns, attitudes and emotions). Marketers use psychographics to gain a more detailed understanding of consumer behaviour than they could ascertain from demographic variables such as ethnicity, social class, age, gender and religion.

Although individuals with comparable backgrounds tend to hold similar values, it is important to remember that people do not always behave the same way even when they hold the same values. Consumers vary in terms of their personality and the way in which they respond to particular situations.

The word 'personality' comes from the Latin term persona, which means an actor's face mask. One's personality can therefore be described as the 'mask' worn as a person moves from situation to situation during a lifetime (Mowen 1995). Personality consists of the distinctive patterns of behaviours, tendencies, qualities or personal dispositions that make one individual different from another, leading to a consistent response to environmental stimuli (Hoyer & MacInnis 2004). These patterns are internal characteristics that individuals are born with or that result from the way people have been raised. Personality helps marketers understand why people behave differently in different situations.

The concept of personality has a number of characteristics. First, to be called personality, a person's behaviour should show some degree of consistency — that is, behaviours must show a consistency that distinguishes them from a person's random responses to different stimuli. Personality characteristics are relatively stable across time rather than of short-term duration. Second, typical behaviours should distinguish one person from another. This means that a personality characteristic cannot be shared by all consumers. A third characteristic of personality is that it interacts with particular situations. Consumer situations refer to those temporary environmental factors that form a context in which consumer activity occurs. One type of situation is the social context in which purchases occur. A fourth aspect of the study of personality is that it cannot be expected to accurately predict an individual's behaviour on one specific occasion from a single measure of personality (Kassarjian & Sheffet 1975). Personality characteristics are not rigidly connected with specific types of behaviour. Marketers, for example, cannot predict how many packets of biscuits a person will buy or the type of car a person will own by looking at specific personality characteristics. The choice of a particular brand depends on the interaction of personality, the situation and the product. Within each of these categories, a variety of interacting forces may operate. The consumer may, for example, buy a gift for a friend, may be pressed for time, or may be in a happy mood.

A person's personality is usually described in terms of traits such as:

- self-confidence
- ascendancy
- emotional stability
- dominance
- sociability
- achievement
- autonomy
- defensiveness
- order

- change
- affiliation
- adaptability
- deference
- aggressiveness (Horton 1979).

Under certain circumstances, however, personalities can change. An individual's personality, for example, may be altered by major life events, such as marriage, the birth of a child, the death of a parent or partner, or a change of job or profession. An individual's personality may change not only in response to abrupt events but also as part of a gradual growing-up or maturing process. Aspects of personality, however, continue to be included in marketing strategies. These dimensions are usually used in conjunction with a person's choice of leisure activities, political outlook, and other individual factors to segment consumers in terms of *lifestyles*.

RESEARCH APPROACHES TO PERSONALITY

Psychoanalytic Approaches

According to psychoanalytic theories, personality arises from a set of dynamic, unconscious internal struggles within the mind (Freud 1959). Freud's *psychoanalytic theory of personality* is a cornerstone of modern psychology. This theory was built on the premise that *unconscious needs* or *drives,* especially sexual and other biological drives, are at the heart of human motivation and personality. Freud constructed his theory on the basis of patients' recollections of early childhood experiences, analysis of their dreams, and the specific nature of their mental and physical adjustment problems.

Freud suggested that individuals pass through several developmental stages in forming their personalities. In the first stage, the oral stage, the infant is entirely dependent on others for need satisfaction, and receives oral gratification from sucking, eating and biting. At the anal stage, the child is confronted with the problem of toilet training. Then in the phallic stage the youth becomes aware of his or her genitals and must deal with desires for the opposite-sex parent.

Freud believed that the failure to resolve the conflicts from each stage could influence one's personality. The individual, for example, who received insufficient oral stimulation as an infant may reveal this crisis in adulthood through oral-stimulation activities like chewing gum, smoking and over-eating, or by distrusting others' motives (including those of marketers). At the anal stage, an individual whose toilet training was too restrictive may become obsessed with control and be overly orderly, stubborn or mean, resulting in an excessive need for neatness, and in excessive saving. These individuals may also engage in extensive information search and deliberation when making purchasing decisions. On the other hand, those whose training was overly lenient may become messy, disorganised adults. According to Freudian theory, an adult's personality is determined by how well he or she deals with the crises that are experienced while passing through each of these stages. Researchers who apply Freud's psychoanalytic theory to the study of consumer personality believe that human drives are largely *unconscious* and that consumers are primarily unaware of their true reasons for buying what they buy.

EXAMPLE: MAGNUM ICE CREAM APPEALS TO THE 'INDULGENT SOUL' OF CONSUMERS

Magnum ice cream, first launched in Ireland in 1990, is marketed to appeal to the senses in adult consumers. Magnum promotes itself as having its own ritual — biting into the cool luxurious Magnum chocolate and then encountering a smooth contrast of delicious vanilla ice cream. Its producer HB claims that 'everyone knows that eating a Magnum isn't an ordinary experience!' In 2006, HB relaunched Magnum with a new look and feel that reflected a premium brand. The relaunch was a huge success and resulted in a nine per cent increase in the impulse singles market for Magnum. Magnum classic is the third best-selling handheld ice cream in Ireland. In 2004, HB sold thirteen million Magnums in Ireland. Magnum is the world's best-selling impulse ice cream in most of the forty-plus national markets in which it is available, and prides itself in being 'the pinnacle of indulgence in ice cream'.

Source: adapted from www.unilever.ie

Trait Theory

Trait theorists propose that personality is composed of characteristics that describe and differentiate individuals (Cattell 1965). Trait theory focuses on the measurement of personality in terms of specific psychological characteristics, called traits. A *trait* is defined as 'any distinguishing, relatively enduring way in which one individual differs from another' (Guilford 1959). People might be described as aggressive, easygoing, quiet, moody or shy. Psychologist Carl Jung developed one of the most basic trait-theory schemes, suggesting that individuals could be categorised according to their levels of introversion and extroversion (Jung 1964). Introverts are shy, prefer to be alone, and are anxious in the presence of others. Introverts tend to avoid social situations and therefore may not find out about new products from others. They are less motivated by social pressure and more likely to do things that please themselves. In contrast, extroverts are outgoing and sociable.

Trait theorists are concerned with the construction of personality tests that enable them to pinpoint individual differences in terms of specific traits. Selected *single-trait personality tests* (which measure just one trait, such as self-confidence) are often developed specifically for use in consumer behaviour studies. These personality tests measure such traits as *consumer innovativeness* (how receptive a person is to new experiences), *consumer materialism* (the degree of the consumer's attachment to possessions), and *consumer ethnocentrism* (the consumer's likelihood to accept or reject foreign-made products). Trait researchers have found that it is generally more realistic to expect personality to be linked to how consumers *make their choices* and to the purchase or consumption of a *broad product category* rather than a specific brand. In general, however, marketing researchers have not been able to predict consumers' behaviours on the basis of measured personality traits (Solomon 2002).

Social-Psychological Theory

Another group of theories focuses on social rather than biological explanations of personality. These theories propose that individuals act in social situations in order to meet their needs. Horney (1945) believed that behaviour can be characterised by three major orientations. *Compliant* individuals are dependent on others and are humble, trusting and tied to a group. They desire to be loved, wanted, and appreciated. *Aggressive* individuals need power, move away from others, and are outgoing, assertive, self-confident and tough-minded. They desire to excel and win admiration. *Detached* individuals are independent and self-sufficient but suspicious and introverted. They desire independence, self-reliance, self-sufficiency and individualism or freedom from obligations. Richins (1983) found that assertiveness and aggressiveness were significantly related to styles of interaction with companies. Highly assertive and aggressive people, in particular, were likely to perceive complaining as acceptable and to enjoy doing it.

Companies often use social-psychological theory to position their products or services. If a company, for example, wants to target consumers who have a desire to be non-conformist or individualistic they would be guided by the characterisation of the *detached* individual. Essence of Ireland, for example, is a company which designs tailor-made holidays for individual needs in West Cork. The range of activities include diving, garden trails, a gourmet food holiday, arts and crafts, golf and a discovery week, which combines morning life-coaching sessions with afternoon activities (www.essenceofireland.ie).

Behavioural Approaches

In contrast to other explanations of personality, behavioural approaches propose that differences in personality are a function of how individuals have been rewarded or punished in the past. According to behavioural approaches, individuals are more likely to have traits, or engage in behaviours, for which they have received positive reinforcement. *Reinforcement* increases the likelihood that a specific response will occur in the future as a result of particular stimuli. They are less likely to maintain characteristics and behaviours for which they have been punished (Skinner 1974). Behavioural approaches to personality involve the principles of operant conditioning (see Chapter 5).

PERSONALITY AND SELF-CONCEPT

Many marketers use an idea related to personality — a person's self-concept. The *self-concept* represents the 'totality of the individual's thoughts and feelings having reference to himself as an object' (Rosenberg 1979). This suggests that individuals evaluate themselves in an objective fashion regarding just who and what they are. Because people have a need to behave consistently with their self-concept, this perception of themselves forms part of the basis for the personality. Self-consistent behaviour helps a person to maintain his or her self-esteem and gives the person predictability in interactions with others. *Self-esteem* refers to the positivity of a person's self-concept. People with low self-esteem expect that they will not perform very well, and they will try to avoid embarrassment, failure or rejection.

EXAMPLE: ANOREXIA NERVOSA AND LOW SELF-ESTEEM

Although no one knows exactly why some people develop eating disorders, research indicates that it is probably due to a combination of several factors. These include certain personality traits (among other things, anorexics tend to be perfectionists and to have low self-esteem) and the nature of the family and home environment (they frequently come from families that place a lot of emphasis on looks, demand perfection, or don't allow the expression of negative feelings such as anger in the home). Societal forces, including the enormous pressure on women to be thin or even underweight, are also thought to play a role. Even though they might appear to be outgoing and happy, people with anorexia typically have low self-esteem. Their low self-esteem drives them to struggle for perfection. They may feel powerless and unable to control their own lives, often because of family dynamics. A young person who doesn't have some control over his or her life, who is discouraged from expressing anger or sadness, who doesn't have the chance to set normal interpersonal boundaries, and who is exposed to unrealistically high expectations is in an environment that may contribute to the development of an eating disorder. That person might find that denying himself or herself food becomes an expression of power and control and in many cases she/he believes that the 'perfect body' will bring the perfect life.

Source: adapted from www.vhi.ie

According to Sirgy (1982), people have more than one self-concept. At least eight types of self-concept have been identified, which have been summarised as follows:

1. *Actual self* — how a person *actually* perceives himself or herself.
2. *Ideal self* — how a person *would like* to perceive himself or herself.
3. *Social self* — how a person thinks *others* perceive him or her.
4. *Ideal social self* — how a person *would like others* to perceive him or her.
5. *Expected self* — an image of self somewhere in between the actual and ideal selves.
6. *Situational self* — a person's self-image in a specific situation.
7. *Extended self* — a person's self-concept that includes the impact of personal possessions on self-image.
8. *Possible selves* – what a person would like to become, could become, or is afraid of becoming.

The self-concept, therefore, is a very complex structure. It is composed of many attributes, some of which are given greater emphasis when the overall self is evaluated. Marketing communications can influence a consumer's level of self-esteem by exposure to advertisements in which a person tries to evaluate his or her self by comparing it to people depicted in artificial images. This form of comparison appears to rely on a basic human motive, and many marketers have tapped into this need by supplying idealised images of happy, attractive people who just happen to be using their products. Car manufacturers, for example, now promote their cars as a means to greater happiness, either by ownership or by simply by driving the car. Various manufacturers of SUVs market them as increasing self-concept, resulting in a 30 per cent increase in sales during 2007.

A Behaviour and Attitudes (2007) survey conducted with 1,003 Irish women illustrated that 49 per cent of women agree that women in paid employment have a higher standing in society. Fifty-five per cent of the women surveyed agree that those working in paid employment have higher self-esteem than homemakers. Over half the women said they were working in paid employment by choice (O'Brien 2007).

EXAMPLE: IRELAND A BOTOX NATION

Welcome to Ireland 2007, the Botox nation, where everything is for sale, everyone has their price and nothing is quite what it seems. During 2006, 20,000 Irish people used Botox and another 86,000 used other fillers, and the market is rising here at 28 per cent per year. The most likely candidates for the treatment are women in their early forties. Botox, the world's fastest growing drug, is made from minuscule amounts of the botulinum toxin and is manufactured in Westport. There are 800 people employed in the Allergan factory in Westport which manufactures the world's most loved cosmetic treatment, and the factory's turnover is over €1 billion a year. The factory has expanded to keep up with global demand, and generates about €80 million in taxes for the area. The cosmetic industry is one of Ireland's biggest sources of tax revenue. As the early-forty-year-olds get older, they are obsessed with feeling and looking younger. They live with an obsessive fear of crow's feet and consume large amounts of pharmaceutical drugs, cosmetics, and pills and potions of every sort. They are also Ireland's biggest customers. Without them, the Botox nation would have no pharmaceutical industry — the biggest exporter in the country.

Source: McWilliams (2007)

Self-esteem advertising attempts to change product attributes by stimulating positive feelings about the self. One strategy is to challenge the consumer's self-esteem and then show a linkage to a product that will provide a remedy.

Conspicuous consumption is an attempt to offset deficiencies or a lack of esteem by devoting attention to consumption. Conspicuously consumed items are important to their owners because of what they tell others. The visibility of these goods and services is critical because their message can be communicated only if others can see them. Conspicuous consumption can be observed in most social classes, as individuals at all levels try to 'keep up with the Joneses', acquiring and displaying products that are characteristic of a respected member of their class. Strongly related to conspicuous consumption is the notion that people often judge others on the basis of what they possess. Thus, products or services become *status symbols* to indicate their owner's place in the social hierarchy. Consumers will endeavour, therefore, to acquire items that reflect not only their current social class; and their class aspirations can explain some acquisitions and consumption behaviour. Belk (1988) suggested that possessions play a major role in establishing a person's identity. As such, possessions become part of ourselves and form an *extended self.* His findings may be summarised in his statement that 'we are what we have ... which may be the most basic and powerful fact of consumer behaviour'.

EXAMPLE: BONFIRE OF THE BRANDS — BATTLING AN OBSESSION WITH BRANDED GOODS

Neil Boorman, author of *Bonfire of the Brands* (2007), used to be obsessed with labels, but in 2006 he burned all his branded possessions in order to cleanse himself of what he believed was an addiction. Boorman tried the impossible: to live a brand-free existence. Disposing of everything from television to toilet paper and starting a life without logos was difficult, but taught him much about consumerism. 'I knew it was virtually impossible, but in a way I did it partially to prove that point.' Brands are supposed to offer choice, and they do: choice between products. The one choice that isn't really available to us is to live a brand-free lifestyle. In order to avoid buying branded toilet paper, for example, Boorman was forced to buy in bulk from a janitorial supplier and ended up with a kind of shiny, tough paper. As a journalist and author he still had to write, but how to do so without a branded computer? Boorman paid a company several hundred pounds to customise his laptop and remove its logos.

'I did start to get a little out of control,' he says. 'I was completely obsessed by brands beforehand. They occupied my thoughts all the time. So, surprise, surprise, after the bonfire I was living this crazy, self-regulated lifestyle — and I was being just as obsessive.' It is Boorman's self-confessed addiction to brands that makes his project more interesting: 'I was getting into debt and yet I spent all my money on a pair of €300 Gucci flip-flops.' As a follower of fashion Boorman was also a keen reader of the signals given out by other people's branded goods: trainers; sunglasses; haircuts; even what department store bag they chose to carry their gym gear in. 'We all do it to a certain extent. The things that we buy indicate what kind of lifestyles we enjoy, and our lifestyles indicate what kind of people we are. Naturally, we look for those things to work out whether that person is someone I could be friends with or have a relationship with or have sex with. If someone asked me I'd have to be honest and say I probably did pass up a few relationships, platonic or otherwise, on the basis of bad shoes.'

'When I saw adverts I did think, boy, if I buy those Prada sunglasses, perhaps I'll be more attractive and successful. I expected those things to come true, and because I'm quite gullible I kept on believing. But after twenty years of buying into those dreams, eventually I did start to think, well, why are those things not happening? Far from being much happier than I was, I was much more miserable … You could say that I'm just particularly gullible, but if that's the case, then why is the UK advertising industry worth €28 billion?'

Source: adapted from Boorman (2007)

PERSONALITY AND CONSUMER BEHAVIOUR

Because the inner characteristics that constitute an individual's personality are a unique combination of factors, no two individuals are exactly alike. Each person's distinct personality, therefore, will influence his or her buying behaviour. Marketers cannot change consumers' personalities to conform to their products; however, if they know which personality characteristics influence specific consumer responses, they can attempt to appeal to the relevant traits inherent in their target group of consumers.

Much of the consumer-related personality research to date has followed the trait approach and focused on identifying specific personality traits that explain differences in consumers' purchase, use and disposition behaviour. A number of studies have attempted to find a relationship between personality and consumer behaviour, but reviews of this research generally conclude that personality is not a good predictor of consumer behaviour (Kassarjian 1971). One major problem is that researchers developed many of the trait measurement instruments for identifying personality disorders in clinical settings, so these instruments may not be appropriate for identifying traits related to consumer behaviours.

Although personality has not been shown to be strongly related to consumer behaviour, some researchers believe that more reliable measures of traits, developed in a consumer context, would reveal a relationship (Lastovicka & Joachimsthaler 1988). The association between personality and consumer behaviour may be stronger for some types of consumer behaviour than for others. Although personality, for example, may not be very useful in understanding brand choice, it may help marketers to understand why some people are more susceptible to persuasion, particularly like a certain advertisement, or engage in more decision-making processes. An example is the selection of a greeting card, which represents a personal message and therefore is an extension of the sender's personality.

BRAND PERSONALITY

Marketers are keenly interested in understanding how people think about brands. Consumers subscribe to the notion of *brand personality*; that is, they attribute various descriptive personality-like traits or characteristics to different brands in a wide variety of product categories. Some personality dimensions that can be used to compare and contrast the perceived characteristics of brands in various product categories include:

- old-fashioned, wholesome, traditional
- surprising, lively, with it
- serious, intelligent, efficient
- glamorous, romantic, sexy
- rugged, outdoorsy, tough, athletic (Aaker 1997).

As these dimensions reveal, a brand's personality can be either functional or symbolic. Brand personality can also be enhanced by the use of an associated logo to reinforce the name, or through the particular style in which the name is presented. The classic example of this is the Coca-Cola brand name, where the visual impact of the written name is so strong that an individual recognises the design rather than reads the words. Coca-Cola is therefore instantly identifiable whether the name is written in English, Russian, Chinese or Arabic because it always somehow *looks* the same. Coca-Cola was again the top brand in Ireland in 2006 as it is across the world. Coca-Cola means a lot more to people than a fizzy drink in a bottle or can. It is the world's biggest brand, and is more recognisable than any other person or thing on the planet. Consumers not only ascribe personality traits to products and services, but they also tend to associate personality factors with specific colours. Coca-Cola is associated with red, which suggests excitement. In 2006, *Business Week* came up with its annual valuation of the brand, $67 billion, which is impressive given that the next biggest brand in the world, Microsoft, is worth $59 billion. Coca-Cola is the ultimate globalised brand. It is, and seeks to be, everywhere (www.checkout.ie).

EXAMPLE: BAILEYS CONVEYS ITS BRAND'S IRISH PERSONALITY

Launched in 1974, Baileys is the world's top-selling liqueur brand. In each and every country, the idea that sells Baileys is its Irishness. 'It's hugely important,' says Baileys' external affairs director Peter O'Connor. 'We could produce Baileys more cheaply in New Zealand or Australia, but whenever we've researched the idea consumers say "over my dead body".' The production site is Irish, the farms supplying the milk are Irish; the cows — all 40,000 of them — are Irish. Then there is the brand's identity: a flowing handwritten signature, R. A. Bailey, underlined with a flourish, as if to scupper any doubts about the author's existence. There is also the name itself, credibly Irish without being clichéd. And the signature? 'There's no Mr or Mrs Bailey,' admits O'Connor. 'We wanted a name that was Irish, but not "show" Irish. The R. A. Bailey was a way of putting a name behind the factory, a way of getting across that the product comes from Ireland.' But Baileys' success isn't just down to taste. Like many brands that conquer the world, 'R. A. Bailey' is self-made, dreamed up to fill a gap in the market, in this case for a spirit that would appeal to younger consumers, particularly women. Inventing a product category gave Baileys the freedom to create the image it wanted, without reference to established rivals.

Strong design and good judgement have helped Baileys make the most of its assumed identity. The packaging, like the name, has strong Irish associations, but the allusions are made sparingly through the use of Celtic symbols and the colour palette. The bottle's retro look has been carefully managed too. The biggest change came in 2003, when the rolling fields on the label were dropped for an abstract swirl of amber and browns, referencing the liqueur rather than its origins.

Source: adapted from www.brandchannel.com

CONSUMER LIFESTYLES

Lifestyle has been defined simply as 'how one lives' (Hawkins *et al.* 1995). Each person chooses products, services, and activities that help define a unique *lifestyle*. An individual's choice of goods and services makes a statement about who one is and about the types of people with whom one desires to identify — and even those to avoid. *Lifestyle* refers to a pattern of consumption reflecting a person's choices of how he or she spends time and money. Lifestyle is more than the allocation of discretionary income. It is a statement about who one is in society and who one is *not*. What people do in their spare time is often a good indicator of their lifestyle. Consumers who engage in different activities and have differing opinions and interests may represent distinct lifestyle segments for marketers. People coming from the same subculture, social class and even occupation may have quite different lifestyles.

Lifestyle and personality can be closely related. A consumer who has a personality categorised as low risk will probably not indulge in a lifestyle that includes property speculating or engage in hobbies such as deep sea diving or rock climbing. Lifestyle and personality, however, should be distinguished. Personality refers more to the internal characteristics of a person, whereas lifestyle refers more to the external characteristics of how a person lives. Although both concepts describe the person, they describe different aspects of the individual (Mowen 1995).

A lifestyle marketing perspective recognises that people sort themselves into groups on the basis of the things they like to do, how they like to spend their leisure time, and how they choose to spend their disposable income. The lifestyle marketing perspective means that marketers have to look at *patterns of behaviour* in order to understand consumers. A goal of lifestyle marketing is to allow consumers to pursue their chosen ways of enjoying their lives and to express their social identities by focusing on product usage in desirable social settings. A Behaviour and Attitudes survey (2007) conducted with Irish women revealed that, of the nineteen issues researched, financial independence is their most valued goal. Younger women tend to spend the most on themselves, while the cost of rent, mortgage, and family expenses place additional financial burdens on those aged 35 years and older (McShane 2007).

Lifestyles change over time and people change the goods and services they buy over their lifetimes. Buying is also shaped by the stage of the *family life cycle* — the stages through which families might pass as they mature over time. Tastes in clothes, furniture, and recreation are all age-related. New lifestyle trends are always emerging and many of these changes are driven by young consumers who are continually redefining what is 'hot' and what is 'cold'.

EXAMPLE: FOOD IS THE NEW FASHION

If you hadn't already realised it, food is the new fashion! We no longer 'eat to live', but rather we 'live to eat', or at least food has become integral to our lifestyle and somewhat an extension of our personality. We buy food the same way we buy clothes: our mood influences what we choose. Smart casual to hang out with friends, exotic to impress, relaxed to chill out at home. No matter what type of food shop you have, you can't ignore this consumer trend.

Every retailer has to understand the fast pace of life today and it is no longer about 'what you sell' but rather the 'benefit of what you sell'. Retailers must constantly appraise how food is relevant to the way consumers live their lives. Long gone are the days when Irish consumers were stereotyped as unimaginative, conservative and uncomplaining. Men especially have become a lot more confident experimenting in the kitchen, whether it is with the lads or trying to impress the girlfriend. We are moving to a 'cool' food decade. It is now trendy to be able to cook and to know about food. Food as fashion is an indicator of how Irish living is changing today. Irish consumers have evolved from defining themselves by the brand of car they drive or the clothes they wear. Certain Irish consumers are increasingly discerning and now we set ourselves apart by what we eat and where we eat. Food is an expression of individuality. It is not the product that we aspire to buy. It is the benefit we gain from the purchase. The perception of food as being fashionable is more an emotional value and little to do with the food itself. For example, Green and Black's premium chocolate is not only organic and fair trade, it is fashionable too. The challenge for all food retailers is to realise that they are not selling food products any more. They are selling attitude. And today's attitude is unlikely to be relevant tomorrow.

Source: adapted from www.bradleymcgurk.com (brand consultants)

PSYCHOGRAPHICS

Consumers can share the same demographic characteristics and still be very different people. Marketers, therefore, need to investigate demographic data to really identify, understand, and target consumer segments that will share a set of preferences for particular products and services. *Demographics* allow marketers to describe *who* buys, but psychographics allow marketers to understand *why* they buy. When personality variables are combined with knowledge of lifestyle preferences, marketers can then decide which consumer segments they should focus on. This tool is known as psychographics. This form of applied consumer research is commonly referred to as lifestyle analysis.

The term *psychographics* comes from the idea of describing or writing about (graph) the psychological (psycho) makeup of consumers. Psychographics is used to assess consumers' activities, interests and opinions (AIOs). In turn, AIOs are used to measure consumer lifestyles. Generally, researchers tend to equate psychographics with the study of lifestyles. Psychographic research is used by marketers to describe a consumer segment in order to help a company to better reach and understand its consumers. Psychographic studies usually include questions to assess a target market's lifestyle and the personality characteristics of its members that distinguish them from other groups. Psychographics, therefore, can help a marketer to fine-tune its products or services to meet the needs of different segments.

Psychographic segmentation can be used in a variety of ways:

- *To define the target market.* This information allows the marketer to go beyond simple demographic or product descriptions (e.g. college students or frequent users).
- *To create a new view of the market.* Sometimes marketers create their strategies with a 'typical' consumer in mind. This stereotype may not be correct because the actual consumer may not match these assumptions.
- *To position the product.* Psychographic information can allow marketers to emphasise features of the product that fit in with a person's lifestyle.
- *To better communicate product attributes.* Psychographic information can offer useful input to brand designers, who must communicate something about the product.
- *To develop overall strategy.* Understanding how a product fits, or does not fit, into consumers' lifestyles allows marketers to identify new product opportunities, and create environments most consistent with these consumption patterns.
- *To market social and political issues.* Psychographic segmentation can be an important tool in political campaigns and can also be used to find commonalities among types of consumers who engage in destructive behaviours such as drug use. (Solomon 2002)

Psychographic research differs from more traditional research approaches in the use of these *AIO statements*. AIO statements attempt to describe the lifestyle of the consumer through his or her activities and the personality of the consumer through his or her interests and opinions. Activity questions ask consumers to indicate what they do, what they buy and how they spend their time. Interest questions focus on what the consumers' preferences and priorities are. Opinion questions ask for consumers' views and feelings on such things as world, local, moral, economic and social affairs. There are no strict rules for developing AIO items (Mowen 1995). Using data from large samples of AIO statements, marketers create profiles of consumers who resemble each other in terms of their activities and patterns of product usage. The dimensions used to assess lifestyle are shown in the table.

Table 4.1: Lifestyle dimensions

Activities	Interests	Opinions	Demographics
Work	Family	Themselves	Age
Hobbies	Home	Social Issues	Education
Social events	Job	Politics	Income
Holidays	Community	Business	Occupation
Entertainment	Recreation	Economics	Family size
Club membership	Fashion	Education	House type
Community	Food	Products	Geography
Shopping	Media	Future	City/town size
Sports	Achievements	Culture	Stage in life cycle

Source: Plummer (1974)

AIO studies may be general or specific. In general studies, marketers seek to classify the consumer population into groups based on general lifestyle characteristics, with the understanding that consumers within each group have similar lifestyles. One of the problems with the general approach is stereotyping and generalisation. On the other hand, however, stereotyping serves the purpose of highlighting certain behaviours that may help the marketer. The specific approach seeks to understand consumer behaviour in relation to a particular product or service. The AIO questions must be tailored to make them more product-specific. The advantage of this method is that groups emerge which are much more sharply defined in terms of their usage of a particular product or service. In either type of study, consumers are usually presented with *Likert scales* in which respondents are asked if they strongly agree, agree, are neutral, disagree, or strongly disagree with the statements in the questionnaire.

Psychographic analysis also allows better positioning of new products within that segment, due to its ability to look beyond simple demographics and to position the product in line with the hopes, fears, activities and dreams of the products' consumers. The overall objective of psychographic segmentation is to develop strategies that are consistent in all their elements with the AIOs of the target market. Hence advertising often stresses lifestyle elements rather than product attributes and uses models consistent with that lifestyle when viewed by consumers.

Typically, the first step in conducting psychographic analysis is to determine which lifestyle segments are producing the majority of consumers for a particular product. According to the *80/20 principle*, frequently used in marketing research, only 20 per cent of a product's users account for 80 per cent of the volume of product sold (Solomon 2002). Researchers continually attempt to determine who uses particular brands and try to distinguish heavy, moderate and light users. They also look for patterns of usage and attitudes towards the product. In many cases, just a few lifestyle segments account for the majority of brand users (Kassarjian 1971). Marketers primarily target these heavy users, even though they may constitute a relatively small number of total users. After the heavy users are identified and understood, the brand's relationship to them is considered. Heavy users may have quite different reasons for using the product; they can be further subdivided in terms of the *benefits* they derive from using the product or service.

One of the most widely known psychographic tools is the Values and Lifestyle Survey (VALS), developed in the United States in the 1970s. The VALS study surveyed a broad section of Unites States consumers on several demographic, value, attitude and lifestyle variables. Although VALS was widely used to identify potential target markets and to understand how to communicate with consumers, by the late 1980s researchers were criticising it for being outdated and for not predicting behaviour adequately. In response to these criticisms, VALS2 was developed. Because the VALS2 survey includes only items related to consumer behaviour, it is much more closely related to consumption than VALS was. VALS2 incorporates the behaviour of United States consumers in 170 product categories, creating segments based on two factors:

1. consumers' resources: including income, education, self-confidence, health, eagerness to buy, intelligence, and energy level
2. consumers' self-orientation, or what motivates them, including their activities and values.

VALS2 describes three self-orientations.

1. *Principle-oriented* consumers are guided by intellectual aspects rather than by feelings or by other people's opinions.
2. *Status-oriented* individuals base their views on the actions and opinions of others and strive to win their approval.
3. *Action-oriented* consumers desire social or physical action, variety, activity and risk.

Hoyer and MacInnis (2004) conclude that VALS2 works best with products and services that are related to the ego, such as clothes and cars, and for which involvement is likely to be high. If you would like to see what VALS type you would be classified as, you can take the survey at www.sric-bi.com/VALS/presurvey.shtml.

CASE STUDY: CULLY AND SULLY PRODUCT BRANDING

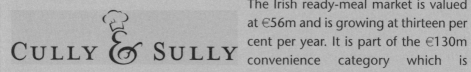

The Irish ready-meal market is valued at €56m and is growing at thirteen per cent per year. It is part of the €130m convenience category which is currently one of the most strategic categories for retailers worldwide responding to changing consumer habits. The market is dominated by retailer private-label products, and there are relatively few brands in the category. The strongest is Tesco with its Value, Ethnic, Finest and Balanced brands. Research, however, showed that consumers are not satisfied with current retailer and food manufacturer offerings. Although the new chilled ready-meals should have changed perception, consumers were still in a 'frozen ready-meal' state of mind which perceives ready-meals as poor in taste and quality. Competitive pack analysis demonstrated that the messages used on chilled convenience products did not differ from those in the frozen category. Chilled products, therefore, missed the opportunity to communicate the added value of their fresh offer.

Changing consumer purchasing and eating patterns have provided significant opportunity in the Irish ready-meals sector for tasty, nutritious and enjoyable meal solutions. Young entrepreneurs Colum O'Sullivan (Sully) and Cullen Allen (Cully) from Ballymaloe House set about developing a range of gourmet ready-to-cook meals to target this category. Their initial challenge was to create a brand proposition, name, identity and packaging design for the new range. It was also essential to communicate Colum and Cullen's passion for fine food so that consumers would trust the products. The brand also aimed for fun and quirky connotations to convey the founders' youthfulness. At the same time food is a serious business, so the brand could not be too playful.

Colum and Cullen worked with a brand consultant, who developed the brand by focusing on the personalities of both owners, and the fun approach they have to selecting ingredients, recipes and preparing meals. The consultant worked closely with them in developing the market positioning, brand personality, and brand name. The name Cully and Sully associates directly with the two founders who are the manifestation of the brand and it would be central to adding authenticity and originality to the sell-in to trade and with consumers in taste demonstrations. The creative team built a unique look and feel based on the duo's personalities and passion for good food, and created a style that reflected real food values through the blackboard menu idea, which was unlike any other ready-meals packaging on the market. This allowed Cully and Sully to have a friendly and informal voice to the consumer on their packs, while their brandmark reflected a serious attitude towards real food.

Cully and Sully launched their pies in September 2004. Two years later, they launched their range of five soups, which are sold through SuperValu, Centra, Superquinn, Spar and Mace stores. "We were told that we'd have to discount our prices at the start, but we believed that people who appreciated good food would not be influenced by this — and, anyway, we couldn't afford it,' said Sully. 'So we bought a camper van, which we use for promotions.' The two do all the marketing themselves. 'Every week, we're in supermarkets doing tastings,' said Cully. 'We meet between 100 and 300 people a day, and this gave us the feedback which drove the development of the new recipes. We also had support from food critics, which meant a lot.' Cully and Sully were nominated in the Ernst and Young Entrepreneur of the Year Awards in 2006. Cully and Sully's turnover in their first year was €400,000. In 2005, it was €700,000 and in 2006 it reached €1.6 million. In January 2007, they moved into the British market, selling in Budgens and Londis stores.

Source: adapted from www.gdba.ie and Kieron Wood, Sunday Business Post,
7 January 2007.

CASE STUDY: KITTENSOFT — DEVELOPING A BRAND PERSONALITY THAT SELLS

In the last few years, the toilet tissue category has experienced growth across many European markets. Several markets are seeing the benefit from the support of added value innovations and effective category segmentation that drives a range of differentiated products. Equally, in some countries, category development has stalled with the proliferation of traditional low-cost products, value has either declined or seen little growth, and commoditisation looms as a very real threat. Conversely, the value growth of the more progressive markets is almost entirely driven by the introduction and further differentiation of premium toilet tissue.

Irish-made KittenSoft bathroom tissue is one of the leading bathroom tissue brands in the country. KittenSoft has now been relaunched with its softest ever paper. In the premium category, softness is the most important product attribute. With new softer cushions, KittenSoft feels thicker, stronger and softer than ever. KittenSoft packaging has been redesigned with a new cuter kitten and softer cushions, which communicates the luxurious softness of the new embossed tissue. The KittenSoft 'Escape' television advertisement invites consumers to 'escape into a world of softness with KittenSoft'. Equally important is the newly defined clear brand personality depicting KittenSoft as likeable, appealing, familiar, Irish, warm-hearted, soft and protective, yet big and strong. The toilet tissue market has also benefited from the 'cash rich, time poor' consumers. They now perceive the toilet tissue category as personal care and are therefore willing to pay a higher premium for a more luxurious offering.

The many recent innovations in toilet tissue have given consumers what they want and continue to result in an ever-increasing market share for the premium and super-premium types of toilet papers. The pace of innovation and differentiation has accelerated and toilet tissue offerings are now thicker, stronger, moister, quilted, fragranced, skin friendlier, coloured, embossed and branded, and consumers appreciate the wide range of comfort and style they find in the category. Today's consumers are willing to spend more money for a higher quality toilet tissue, and are more loyal to these differentiated products.

Source: adapted from www.retailnews.ie and www.iapi.ie

Questions for Review

1. Discuss the various research approaches to personality.
2. Explain what is meant by self-concept and self-esteem and their relationship to consumer buying behaviour.
3. What is meant by brand personality? Highlight your answer with an example of a product which you consider has brand personality.
4. What would a company hope to gain by analysing consumer lifestyles?
5. Discuss the benefits of psychographic segmentation for marketers.

5

Consumer Learning

CHAPTER OBJECTIVES

After reading this chapter you should be able to:

- Discuss the elements of learning relevant to consumer behaviour.
- Explain cognitive, behavioural, and observational learning theories.
- Understand the role of memory in learning.
- Examine methods used to measure consumer learning.
- Recognise why people forget.

THE ELEMENTS OF CONSUMER LEARNING

While learning is all-pervasive in the lives of consumers, there is no single theory of how people learn. Because learning theorists differ on how learning takes place, it is difficult to come up with a generally accepted definition of learning. From a marketing perspective, however, 'consumer learning can be thought of as the process by which individuals acquire the purchase and consumption knowledge and experience that apply to future related behaviour' (Schiffman & Kanuk 2007). From this definition, it is clear that learning is a *process*; that is, it continually evolves and changes as a result of newly acquired *knowledge* (which may be gained from newspapers, the Internet, by word of mouth, etc.) or from *experience*. Learning is a relatively permanent change in behaviour caused by experience. The learner need not have the experience directly: an individual can also learn by observing events that affect others (Baron 1989). Individuals also learn when they are not trying: consumers recognise many brand names and can hum many product jingles, for example, for products they themselves do not use. This casual, unintentional acquisition of knowledge is known as *incidental learning*.

The term *learning* encompasses the total range of learning, from simple, almost reflexive responses to the learning of abstract concepts and complex problem solving. Most learning theorists recognise the existence of different types of learning and explain the differences through the use of distinctive models of learning. When analysing the topic of learning, consumer researchers typically discuss two types — *cognitive* learning and *behavioural* learning. Although these theories differ markedly in a number of essentials, each theory offers insights to marketers on how to shape their messages to consumers in order to bring about desired purchase behaviour.

Cognitive learning theorists focus on relatively complex forms of learning, such as how people retain verbal material (e.g. advertising messages), how people have insights, and how people plan. As such, most cognitively oriented theorists view learning as occurring through *information processing*, which is the process through which consumers are exposed to information, attend to it, comprehend it, place it in memory, and retrieve that information for later use.

Behavioural learning has been defined as a process in which experience with the environment leads to a relatively permanent change in behaviour or the potential for a change in behaviour (Mowen 1995). This suggests that behaviour is primarily made in response to environmental stimuli.

Despite their different viewpoints, learning theorists in general agree that in order for learning to occur, certain basic elements must be present. The four elements included in most learning theories are *motivation*, *cues*, *response*, and *reinforcement*.

Motivation

The concept of motivation is important to learning theory. As discussed in Chapter 3, motivation is based on needs and goals. Motivation acts as a spur to learning. It is the motive that arouses individuals and thereby increases their readiness to respond. This arousal is essential as it activates the energy necessary to engage in learning activity. Any success in achieving the motivating goal, however, tends to reduce arousal. This is reinforcement, and will create a tendency for the same behaviour to occur again in a similar situation. This is why companies attempt to have their products or their names available when consumers' motives are aroused — when it is hoped that consumers will learn a connection between the product and the motive. Flahavan's hot Irish breakfast cereal, for example, is promoted during winter months, whereas HB ice cream is heavily promoted during the summer.

Cues

If motives serve to stimulate learning, cues are the stimuli that give direction to these motives. Cues can influence the manner in which consumers respond to a motive. An advertisement is the cue or *stimulus* that suggests a specific way to satisfy a motive. Marketers use place, price, styling, packaging and store displays as cues to help consumers fulfil their needs in product-specific ways. Cues serve to direct consumer drives when they are consistent with consumer expectations. Marketers must be careful to provide cues that do not upset those expectations. Consumers, for example, expect designer clothes to be expensive and to be sold in upscale retail stores and to advertise only in upscale fashion magazines. The Design Centre at

Powerscourt Shopping Centre, Dublin, for example, promotes itself as being home to leading contemporary Irish and international labels. The Design Centre focuses on 'youthful looks with an eclectic mix of lines from sophistication to funky wear' (www.powerscourtcentre.com). Each aspect of the marketing mix, therefore, must reinforce the others if cues are to serve as the stimuli that guide consumer actions in the direction desired by marketers.

Response

This is the mental or physical activity consumers make in reaction to a drive or a cue. Appropriate responses to particular situations are learned over time through experience: for example, if a prior experience of a particular store has not been good, the consumer will tend to ignore the store in future. This means that there is no observable behaviour; the consumer just did not go into the shop. To an observer it looks as though there was no response, yet learning has taken place, as the consumer has chosen not to shop there. Cues provide some direction, but there are many cues competing for the consumer's attention. Whichever response the consumer makes depends on previous learning, and that, in turn, depends on how related responses have been reinforced.

Reinforcement

Reinforcement increases the likelihood that a specific response will occur in the future as a result of particular cues or stimuli. When marketers provide *positive reinforcement* in the form of an award, the response is strengthened, and appropriate repeat behaviour is learned. When Boots' No. 7 Protect and Perfect anti-wrinkle serum was launched in 2007, for example, it sold out in days after independent scientists said it was as effective at combating sun damage as other products available on prescription from a doctor.

Negative reinforcement also strengthens responses so that appropriate behaviour is learned. Marketers can attempt to provide reinforcement by reducing motive arousal. They can achieve this by removing a negative reinforcer: for example, Benylin cough mixture, which stresses fast relief, is removing the negative reinforcer, an unpleasant cough. Benylin is the market leader in the grocery cough remedy market in Ireland (www.checkout.ie).

Overall, understanding cognitive and behavioural learning theories is important to marketers because learning principles are at the heart of many consumer purchase decisions. One of the reasons marketers are concerned with how individuals learn is that they are interested in teaching them as consumers about products, product attributes, and their potential benefits; where to buy them, how to use them, how to maintain them, and how to dispose of them. They are also interested in how effectively they have taught consumers to choose their brands and to differentiate their products from those of their competitors. Marketing strategies are based on communicating with the consumer — directly, through advertisements, and indirectly, through product appearance, price, packaging, and distribution channels. Marketers want their communications to be noted, believed, remembered and recalled. For these reasons, they are interested in every aspect of the learning process.

COGNITIVE LEARNING THEORY

Cognitive learning theory approaches focus on the importance of internal mental processes. A considerable amount of learning takes place as the result of consumer thinking and problem solving. Cognitive learning theory holds that the kind of learning most characteristic of human beings is *problem solving*, which enables individuals to gain some control over their environment. Cognitive learning also focuses on mental activities such as thinking, remembering, developing insight, forming concepts and learning ideas. Thus, cognitive learning is an active process in which consumers seek to control the information obtained.

How people learn in the consumer environment is an important issue for marketers. It has been suggested that consumers learn through *education* and through *experience* (Hoch & Deighton 1989). *Learning through education* involves obtaining information from companies in the form of advertising, sales personnel and the consumer's own directed efforts to seek the data. The consumer then has to process the information he or she receives. Information processing is related to both the consumer's cognitive ability and the complexity of the information to be processed. Consumers process product information by attributes, brands, comparisons between brands, or a combination of these factors. Although the attributes included in the brand's message and the numbers of available alternatives will influence the intensity or degree of information processing, consumers with higher cognitive ability apparently acquire more product information and are more capable of integrating information on several product attributes than consumers with lesser ability (Schiffman & Kanuk 2007). Individuals also differ in terms of *imagery* — their ability to form mental images — and these differences influence their ability to recall information. Tourism Ireland, for example, the organisation responsible for marketing the island of Ireland overseas, uses images of beautiful scenery, the warmth of the people, and the living and historic culture in its advertising campaign. The more experience a consumer has with a product category, the greater is his or her ability to make use of product information. Greater familiarity with the product category also increases cognitive ability and learning during a new purchase decision, particularly regarding technical information.

Learning through experience involves the process of gaining knowledge through direct contact with products. Overall, learning from experience is a more effective means of gaining consumer knowledge. It promotes better retrieval and recall because the consumer is involved in the learning experience and the information obtained is more vivid, concrete and salient. The more experience a consumer has with a product category, the greater is his or her ability to make use of product information. Greater familiarity with the product category also increases cognitive ability and learning during a new purchase decision, particularly with regard to technical information. Some consumers learn by analogy; that is, they transfer knowledge about products they are familiar with to new or unfamiliar products in order to enhance their understanding.

EXAMPLE: LEARNING FREE OF CHARGE AS LIBRARIES GO WI-FI

Computer-savvy consumers will be able to access Wi-Fi Internet free at their local library using their own laptops. In May 2007, the Government announced the provision of grants totalling over €700,000 to enable public libraries to provide this service. The change is part of an ongoing scheme called Changing Libraries, which has been in place since October 2005, that aims to create and deliver online content in conjunction with public library authorities. The aim is to reinforce the role of the library service as a key provider of information for all users. Along with a variety of material available from different public library websites (e.g., www.clarelibrary.ie, www.corkpastandpresent.ie, etc.), more general online content available to library users includes:

- askaboutireland.ie, providing information on various aspects of Irish interest, including history, sport and nature.

- culturenet.ie, a gateway to Irish cultural resources online.
- lifesteps.ie, consisting of seventeen guides on how to use the Internet to achieve various life steps (such as buying a home or starting a business).
- borrowbooks.ie, allowing consumers to search for books not just in their local authority area, but in the catalogues of any library in the country.

Source: adapted from Consumer Choice, *May 2007, p. 196.*

BEHAVIOURAL LEARNING THEORIES

Researchers have identified three major approaches to behavioural learning: classical conditioning, operant conditioning and vicarious learning. In *classical conditioning*, behaviour is influenced by a stimulus that occurs prior to the behaviour and elicits it in a manner that has the appearance of being a reflex. In *operant conditioning*, behaviour is influenced by the consequences of the behaviour. *Vicarious learning* occurs when individuals observe the actions of others and model or imitate their actions. Behavioural learning theories are sometimes referred to as *stimulus–response theories* because they are based on the premise that observable responses to specific external stimuli signal that learning has taken place. When an individual responds in a predictable way to a known stimulus, he or she is said to have learned. Behavioural theorists are not so much concerned with the *process* of learning as they are with the *inputs* and *outcomes* of learning, that is, the stimuli that consumers select from the environment and the observable behaviours that result.

Classical Conditioning

Classical conditioning is also called *respondent conditioning.* In the process of classical conditioning a neutral stimulus is paired with a stimulus that elicits a response. Through a repetition of the pairing, the neutral stimulus takes on the ability to elicit the response. Classical conditioning theorists regard all organisms (both human and animal) as relatively passive entities that can be taught certain behaviours through repetition (i.e. conditioning). In everyday speech, the word *conditioning* refers to the automatic response(s) to a situation, built up through repeated exposure.

Ivan Pavlov, a Russian physiologist working in the 1920s, was the first to describe conditioning and to propose it as a general model of how learning occurs. According to Pavlovian theory, conditioned learning results when a stimulus that is paired with another stimulus that elicits a known response serves to produce the same response when used alone. Pavlov demonstrated what he meant by *conditioned learning* in his studies with dogs. The dogs were hungry and highly motivated to eat. In his experiments, Pavlov sounded a bell and then immediately applied a meat paste to the dogs' tongues, which caused them to salivate. Learning (conditioning) occurred when, after a sufficient number of repetitions of the bell sound followed almost immediately by the food, the sound of the bell alone caused the dogs to salivate. The dogs associated the bell sound (the *conditioned* stimulus) with the meat paste (the *unconditioned* stimulus) and, after a number of pairings, gave the same unconditioned response (salivation) to the bell alone as they did to the meat paste. The unconditioned response to the meat paste became the conditioned response to the bell.

When classical conditioning occurs, a previously neutral stimulus (the conditioned stimulus) is repeatedly paired with the eliciting stimulus (the unconditioned stimulus). In the pairing, the conditioned stimulus needs to occur prior to the unconditioned stimulus, so that it predicts the unconditioned stimulus. After a number of such pairings, the ability to elicit a response is transferred to the conditioned stimulus. The response elicited by the conditioned stimulus is called the *conditioned response*.

Marketers are particularly interested in the study of classical conditioning. They attempt to identify stimuli (e.g. messages, sights, sounds) that will elicit positive reactions from consumers. Their goal is to associate their product or service with the positive stimulus, so that the product will elicit a similar positive reaction when the consumer thinks about or encounters it. The basic form of classical conditioning demonstrated by Pavlov focuses on cues that induce hunger, thirst and other basic drives. In a consumer behaviour context, when these cues are consistently paired with conditioned stimuli such as brand names, consumers may learn to feel hungry, thirsty or aroused when later exposed to the brand cues. Conditioning effects are more likely to occur after the conditioned stimulus and the unconditioned stimulus have been paired a number of times (Rescorla 1988). *Repetition* increases the strength of the association between a conditioned stimulus and an unconditioned stimulus and slows the process of forgetting. There is a limit, however, to the amount of repetition that will aid retention as an individual can at some point become satiated with numerous exposures and both attention and retention will decline. This effect, known as *advertising wearout*, can be moderated by varying the advertising message.

Marketers often prominently display credit card insignia in highly visible locations in stores to attract the consumers' attention so that the credit cards become paired with the buying act. For many consumers the buying act takes on the properties of an unconditioned stimulus that elicits the unconditioned response of positive feelings. Through many pairings of the credit card with the buying act, the credit card becomes a conditioned stimulus that elicits a conditioned response of positive feelings. The positive feelings elicited by the credit card in turn make it more likely that a person will spend money when their card symbol is present.

EXAMPLE: CREDIT CARDS ACT AS CONDITIONED STIMULI TO ELICIT BUYING BEHAVIOUR

The 'Credit Cards: A Nation in Debt' report published by Mintel Ireland in November 2007 showed that 39 per cent of Irish consumers aged fifteen and over now own a credit card and are using their cards to finance a lifestyle they could not otherwise afford. The report shows the number of credit cards issued to Irish consumers rose by 40 per cent since 2001. Figures released by the Central Bank showed that there were 2.1 million personal credit cards issued in Ireland at the end of September 2007, up from the September 2006 level of just under two million cards.

Mintel predicted that the number of credit cards issued to Irish consumers would increase by 53 per cent by 2012. The nation's credit card holders had an estimated €3.5 billion credit at their disposal for Christmas 2007, compared with a total of €1.25 billion of debit in December 2006. Transaction volumes have increased by 67 per cent in the last five years. Transaction values have also grown by a huge 112 per cent in the last five years. One in five credit card users admitted to buying on impulse without thinking of the consequences. Similarly, only one third of people admit to spending more money than normal while using a credit card. Owning luxury items is a top priority for Irish people and they are not afraid to get into debt to get the things they want.

Research from the Financial Regulator shows that consumers are increasingly using credit cards to live beyond their means, with €1bn added to credit card debt every month. In any given month €2.6bn is outstanding. Around €1bn gets paid off in the month, but another €1bn is added to the credit card debt. The research revealed that 45 per cent of card holders do not pay off their balance in full each month, incurring high interest charges. The Financial Regulator's research also showed that the majority of people have no idea what interest rate they are paying. One in ten people thought they were paying interest of less than five per cent when the average is around three times that figure.

The Mintel report showed that consumers are more concerned about their body weight than about their spiralling credit card debt. Mintel's head of research Julie Sloan said the trend of credit card dependence, and dangerously high levels of debt, is likely to continue. She cautioned, 'The rising cost of borrowing does not seem to have deterred credit card users and there may be a sense of denial here.'

Source: adapted from E. English, 'Christmas credit card spending may hit €3.5bn', Irish Examiner, 12 November 2007, p. 3; and C. Weston, 'Credit card culture fuels €2.6bn debt each month', Irish Independent, 29 March 2007, p. 4.

Overall, evidence is accumulating that consumers respond to a variety of stimuli in a manner consistent with a classical-conditioning interpretation. Because early experiments involved conditioning animals to salivate to bells and to reveal other assorted rudimentary behaviours, the tendency has been to view classical conditioning as a simple process in which organisms automatically react to stimuli. In contrast, contemporary behavioural scientists view classical conditioning as the learning of associations among events that allows the organism to anticipate and to cognitively represent its environment. Classical conditioning, then, rather than being a reflexive action, is seen as *cognitive associative learning* — not the acquisition of new reflexes, but the acquisition of new knowledge about the world (Mackintosh 1983). Although a great deal of consumer behaviour (e.g. the purchase of branded convenience goods) is influenced to some extent by repeated advertising messages stressing a unique competitive advantage, a significant amount of purchase behaviour results from careful evaluation of product choices. Consumers' assessments of products are often based on the degree of satisfaction or rewards that consumers experience as a result of making specific purchases; in other words, from *operant* or *instrumental conditioning*.

Operant Conditioning

Operant conditioning, also known as *instrumental conditioning*, occurs as the individual learns to perform behaviours that produce positive outcomes and to avoid those that yield negative outcomes. Like classical conditioning, operant conditioning requires a link between a stimulus and a response. In operant conditioning, however, the stimulus that results in the most satisfactory response is the one that is learned.

Operant learning theorists believe that learning occurs through a trial-and-error process, with habits formed as a result of rewards received for certain responses or behaviours. This model of learning applies to many situations in which consumers learn about products, services and retail stores. For example, consumers learn by shopping in a number of stores which stores carry the type of clothing they prefer at prices they can afford to pay. In contrast, responses in classical conditioning are involuntary and fairly simple, while those in operant conditioning are made deliberately to obtain a goal and may be more complex. Operant conditioning is, therefore, more helpful in explaining complex, goal-directed activities.

B. F. Skinner, an American psychologist, is closely associated with operant conditioning. According to Skinner, most individual learning occurs in a controlled environment in which individuals are 'rewarded' for choosing an appropriate behaviour. In consumer behaviour terms, operant conditioning suggests that some purchase behaviours will result in more favourable outcomes (rewards) than other purchase behaviour. A favourable experience is 'instrumental' in teaching the individual to repeat a specific behaviour.

Like Pavlov, Skinner developed his model of learning by working with animals. Small animals, such as rats and pigeons, were placed in his 'Skinner box'; if they made appropriate movements (e.g. depressing levers or pecking keys), they received food (a positive reinforcement). Skinner demonstrated the effects of operant conditioning by teaching pigeons and other animals to dance, play ping-pong, and perform other activities by systematically rewarding them for desired behaviours.

Skinner distinguished two types of reinforcement (or reward) that influence the likelihood of a response being repeated. The first type, *positive reinforcement*, consists of events that strengthen the likelihood of a specific response. Marketers of Head and Shoulders shampoo, for example, positively reinforce consumers by alleviating them of all signs of dandruff. *Negative reinforcement* is an unpleasant or negative outcome that also serves to encourage a specific behaviour. An advertisement that shows a model with wrinkled skin is meant to encourage consumers to buy and use the advertised skin cream. The Nivea Visage range, for example, shows advertisements that illustrate wrinkle prevention and visible wrinkle reduction. Either positive or negative reinforcement can be used to elicit a desired response. Negative reinforcement, however, should not be confused with punishment, which is designed to *discourage* behaviour. Car clamping, for example, is not negative reinforcement, it is a form of punishment, designed to discourage drivers from parking illegally.

Operant conditioning is useful for understanding consumer learning when the conscious choice results in positive or negative reinforcement. Favourable experiences resulting from the choice will lead to positive reinforcement of that particular choice. This is strong justification for the emphasis placed on satisfying consumers. Advertisements that depict satisfied consumers can also result in learning a connection between a brand and favourable experiences. Other types of promotion, such as cash rebates, free samples, low introductory prices or trial periods are forms of operant conditioning. The company's goal in these cases is to structure a situation so that consumers are given a reward as a consequence of having tried the product, service or new brand supplied by the company.

When a learned response is no longer reinforced, it diminishes to the point of *extinction*, that is, to the point at which the link between the stimulus and the expected reward is eliminated. If a consumer is no longer satisfied, for example, with service from a retail store, the link between the stimulus (the store) and the response (expected satisfaction) is no longer reinforced, and there is little likelihood that the consumer will return.

In summary, there are apparent differences between classical and operant conditioning:

- Classical conditioning is dependent on an already established response to another stimulus, while operant conditioning requires the learner to discover the appropriate response and therefore involves the learner at a more conscious level than classical conditioning would.
- While classical conditioning is not dependent on the learner's actions, in operant conditioning a particular response can change the learner's situation. The response is instrumental in producing reinforcement, hence the name instrumental or operant conditioning.

Because of these differences, each method is better suited to explaining different types of consumer learning. Adapting to and attempting to control one's environment is better explained by operant conditioning as it requires the learner to discover the correct response that will lead to reinforcement. Learning brand names or acquiring attitudes, tastes and opinions are probably better explained by classical conditioning because the material learned in such cases can be associated with stimuli that already elicit either favourable or unfavourable experiences.

Vicarious or Observational Learning

Another approach to learning examines how aspects of cognitive learning are linked to operant conditioning. *Observational learning*, also called *vicarious* or *social learning*, occurs when people watch the actions of others and note the reinforcements they receive for their behaviours — learning occurs as a result of vicarious rather than direct experience. Such actions can range from purchasing a product, to learning a skill, to avoiding buying drugs.

Consumers often observe how others behave in response to certain situations (stimuli) and the ensuing results (reinforcement) that occur, and they imitate (model) the positively reinforced behaviour when faced with similar situations. Social learning theorists emphasise the importance of models in transmitting information through observational learning. A *model* is someone whose behaviour a person attempts to emulate. Role models are usually people an individual admires because of traits such as appearance, accomplishment, skill and social class. Consumer models with which the target audience can identify are shown achieving positive outcomes to common problem situations through the use of the advertised product. In order for observational learning in the form of modelling to occur, four conditions must be met:

1. The consumer's attention must be directed to the appropriate model who, for reasons of attractiveness, competence, status, or similarity it is desirable to emulate.
2. The consumer must remember what is said or done by the model.
3. The consumer must convert this information into actions.
4. The consumer must be motivated to perform these actions. (Bandura 1986)

EXAMPLE: VICARIOUS LEARNING WITH ROLE MODEL PADRAIG HARRINGTON AND FLORA

Flora was created as a healthy alternative to butter, lard and hard margarine. Flora is a spread high in polyunsaturated fat and low in saturated fat. In Ireland today, Flora claims clear market leadership of the health spreads sector, with a 45 per cent share. Flora's stated long-term commitment is to promoting heart health in Ireland through positive lifestyle and dietary changes.

Flora Proactiv consists of a range of low-fat spreads, a semi-skimmed milk drink, one-a-day yogurt drinks, and low-fat yogurts enriched with substances called plant sterols that occur naturally at low concentration in vegetable oils. Plant sterols have been clinically proven to dramatically lower cholesterol when a person moves to a healthy diet. Cholesterol is a soft waxy substance found in the bloodstream and in all the cells of a body. It is normal to have cholesterol, and it is an important part of a healthy body; but problems arise if the level of cholesterol is too high when it builds up on artery walls. A person's body makes some cholesterol, but the remainder comes from cholesterol in foods containing high levels of saturated fats. Flora advertises that clinical trials prove that, gram for gram, no other spread is more effective at lowering cholesterol as part of a healthy diet than Flora Proactiv spread.

Flora Proactiv uses cholesterol-lowering plant sterols from vegetables, vegetable oils, fruit, nuts and grains. Flora Proactiv contains considerably more plant sterols than a person could eat as part of a normal diet. Flora claims that Proactiv, used as part of a healthy diet, can lower cholesterol by an average of ten to fifteen per cent in just three weeks.

The Flora Test the Nation campaign encouraged people all over the country to participate in an event which tested their blood pressure and cholesterol levels. This event helped people nationwide to know their cholesterol numbers and be advised on ways of maintaining a healthy heart lifestyle. Results of Test the Nation revealed that one third of the population in Ireland has higher than normal cholesterol and blood pressure. It was found that women are more likely to have high cholesterol than men; while above normal levels of blood pressure were more frequent in men than in women.

The brand's advertising campaign features celebrity golfer Padraig Harrington, who has also been taking the Flora Proactiv Challenge. Harrington, a fit and healthy sportsman in his thirties, discovered that he had a relatively high cholesterol level, so he took the challenge of using Flora Proactiv products to reduce his cholesterol. The key part of the plan was one Flora Proactiv mini-drink every day, or three portions of the other products from the Flora Proactiv cholesterol-reducing range. Harrington has now reduced his cholesterol from 6.5 to 5.5 and is continuing to use Flora Proactiv to maintain his heart-healthy diet.

Source: adapted from www.retailnews.ie/April06 and www.unilever.ie

The behaviour-modelling process is a powerful form of learning and is the basis of much of today's advertising. Children also learn much of their consumer behaviour by observing their parents or older siblings. They imitate the behaviour of those they see rewarded, expecting to be rewarded similarly if they adopt the same behaviour. On the other hand, television has the potential to teach violent behaviour to children. Children may be exposed to new methods of aggression by individuals they regard as models (e.g. cartoon heroes), and at some later stage, when a child becomes angry, these behaviours may be imitated.

Social learning theorists also argue that people can control their own behaviour by creating their own reinforcement structure. Consumers, for example, often reward themselves by making a purchase as a reward for themselves for doing something well. Overall, observational learning is a complex process because people store observations in their memory as they accumulate knowledge, perhaps using this information at a later point to guide their own behaviour (Solomon 2002).

THE ROLE OF MEMORY IN LEARNING

Although it is important for consumer researchers to understand how memory is structured, a basic concern for most cognitive scientists is discovering how information gets stored in memory, how it is retained, and how it is retrieved. *Memory* involves a process of acquiring information and storing it over time so that it will be available when needed. *Memory control processes* are methods of handling information that may operate consciously or unconsciously to influence the encoding, placement and retrieval of information (Bettman 1979). Just as a computer processes information it receives as input, the human mind also processes the information it receives as input. *Information processing* is related to both the consumer's cognitive ability and the complexity of the information to be processed. Consumers process product information by attributes, brands, comparisons between brands, or a combination of these factors.

Because information processing occurs in stages, it is generally believed that there are separate and sequential 'storehouses' in memory where information is kept temporarily before further processing. These are: *sensory memory*, *short-term memory* and *long-term memory*.

Sensory Memory

All data comes to individuals through their senses. The senses, however, do not transmit whole images as a camera does. Instead, each sense receives a fragmented piece of information (such as the smell, colour, shape and feel of a product) and transmits it to the brain in parallel, where the perceptions of a single instant are synchronised and perceived as a single image, in a single moment of time. The image of a sensory input lasts for just a second or two in the mind's *sensory store*. If it is not processed, it is lost immediately. As consumers are constantly bombarded with stimuli from the environment they subconsciously block out a great deal of information that they do not need or cannot use. For marketers, this means that although it may be relatively easy to get information into the consumer's sensory store, it is difficult to make a lasting impression. Furthermore, the brain automatically and subconsciously 'tags' all perceptions with a value, either positive or negative; this evaluation, added to the initial perception in the first microsecond of cognition, tends to remain unless further information is processed. This would explain why first impressions tend to last and why it is hazardous for a marketer to introduce a product prematurely into the marketplace.

Although the sensation would only last for a few seconds in the sensory memory, it would be sufficient to allow an individual to determine if he or she should investigate further. If the information is retained for further processing, it passes through an 'attentional gate' and is transferred to short-term memory.

Short-term Memory

The short-term memory also stores information for a limited period of time and its capacity is limited. *Working memory*, which is another term for short-term memory, implies that individuals actively process information in this memory stage. The amount of information that can be held in short-term memory is limited to about four or five items. Verbal input may be stored acoustically (in terms of how it sounds) or semantically (in terms of what it means). The information is stored by combining small pieces into larger ones in a process known as *chunking*. A chunk may be conceptualised as a single meaningful piece of information. A chunk could be a single letter, a syllable or an entire word. A brand name, for example, can be a chunk that summarises a great deal of detailed information about the brand.

The limited capacity characteristic of short-term memory means that it acts as a kind of 'bottleneck'. If more information is received than the consumer can handle, some of it will be lost. The term *information overload* is used to describe the situation in which more information is received than can be processed in short-term memory. In addition to being unable to process all the information, consumers may react to overload by becoming aroused and by more narrowly focusing attention on only certain aspects of the incoming stimuli (Kahneman 1973). The consumer may simply make a random choice, not buy anything, or focus on the wrong product qualities for his or her decision.

The amount of arousal felt by the consumer will influence the capacity of short-term memory (Kahneman 1973). In high-involvement situations, the consumer is likely to be more aroused and more attentive, thereby expanding the capacity of short-term memory to its maximal extent. In contrast, under low-involvement conditions, the consumer's arousal level is apt to be low, so the consumer applies relatively little memory capacity to the stimulus.

One of the functions of short-term memory is to assist in the transfer of information to *long-term memory*. As an individual allocates more capacity to a stimulus, the likelihood of it being transferred to long-term memory increases. If information in the short-term memory undergoes the process known as *rehearsal* (i.e. the silent, mental repetition of information) it is then transferred to the long-term memory. The transfer process takes from about two to ten seconds. If information is not rehearsed and transferred, it is lost in about thirty seconds or less.

Long-term Memory

In contrast to short-term memory, where information only lasts a few seconds, long-term memory retains information for relatively extended periods of time. Long-term memory has an essentially unlimited capacity to store information (Bettman 1979). Although it is possible to forget something within a few minutes after the information has reached the long-term memory, it is more common for data in long-term memory to last for days, weeks or even years.

The amount of information available for delivery from short-term storage to long-term storage depends on the amount of *rehearsal* it is given. The purpose of rehearsal is to hold information in short-term storage long enough for encoding to take place. The way information is mentally programmed or *encoded* helps to determine how it will be represented in memory. *Encoding* is the process by which an individual selects a word, a visual image or a jingle to represent a perceived object. Marketers help consumers to encode brands by using brand symbols. Homestead, for example, with its easily recognisable jingle 'Homestead, Homestead brings value home', has grown from the original twenty products into a brand with over 120 products. Homestead has products in areas as diverse as biscuits, spaghetti, kitchen towels and firelighters.

Marketers also realise that 'learning' a picture, for example, takes less time than learning verbal information, but both types of information are important in forming an overall mental image. A consumer may process a stimulus simply in terms of its sensory meaning, such as colour or shape. When this occurs, the meaning may be activated when the person sees a picture of the stimulus. Pictures also tend to be more memorable than their verbal counterparts, particularly under low-involvement circumstances (Childers and Houston 1984). Bord na Móna, manufacturers of peat briquettes, for example, uses television to best communicate the benefits consumers get from a 'real fire' with glowing faces reflecting the contentment afforded only by the 'real open fire'. The messages imply that nothing could take the place of a real fire and that a real fire is an essential ingredient in a relaxing, homely evening.

Information does not just sit in long-term memory waiting to be retrieved. Instead, information is constantly organised and re-organised as new links between chunks of information are forged. Many information-processing theorists view the long-term memory as a network consisting of nodes (i.e. concepts), with links between and among them. As individuals gain more knowledge about a subject they expand their network of relationships and sometimes their search for additional information. This process is known as *activation,* which involves relating new data to old to make the material more meaningful. Product information stored in memory tends to be brand-based, and consumers interpret new information in a manner consistent with the way in which it is already organised. Consumers are confronted with thousands of new products each year, and their information search is often dependent on how similar or dissimilar these products are to product categories already stored in memory. Consumers are therefore more likely to recall the information they receive on new products which bear a familiar brand name, while their memory is less affected by exposure to competitive advertisements.

Retrieval is the process by which individuals recover information from long-term memory. Individuals have a vast quantity of information stored in their heads that is not necessarily available on demand. Although most of the information entered in long-term memory does not go away, it may be difficult or impossible to retrieve unless the appropriate cues are present. When a person is unable to remember something with which he or she is very familiar, he or she is experiencing a failure of the retrieval system. Marketers maintain that consumers tend to remember the product's benefits rather than its attributes, suggesting that advertising messages are most effective when they link the product's attributes with the benefits that consumers seek from the product (Schiffman & Kanuk 2007). Consumers are likely to spend time interpreting and elaborating on information they find relevant to their needs and to activate such relevant knowledge from long-term memory.

Given the importance of retrieval, marketers need to understand how they can enhance the likelihood that consumers will remember something about specific brands. Retrieval can be facilitated by providing retrieval cues. A *retrieval cue* is a stimulus that facilitates the activation of memory (Pham & Johar 1997). One of the most important types of retrieval cues is the brand name. In addition to brand names, logos and packages can also act as retrieval cues. Retrieval cues have implications for buying decisions. Consumers remember very little advertising content when they are actually making a decision in the store (Cobb & Hoyer 1986). The reason is that advertising is typically seen or heard in a context completely different from the purchase environment. One way of overcoming this problem is to place a cue from the advertisement on the brand's package or on an in-store display (Keller 1987). Thus, packages are sometimes labelled 'As seen on TV'.

Retrieval may be hindered by interference: for example, a large number of competitive advertisements in a product category will lower the recall of a specific brand. Interference effects are caused by confusion with competing advertisements, and make information retrieval difficult. Advertisements can also act as retrieval cues for a competitive brand. The level of interference experienced can depend on a consumer's previous experience, prior knowledge of brand attribute information, and the amount of brand information available at the time of choice. Advertising that creates a distinctive brand image can assist in the retention and retrieval of message contents.

Mood can also affect retrieval of information. Being in a positive mood can enhance the recall of stimuli in general. Individuals are more likely to recall information that is consistent with their mood. In other words, if an individual is in a positive mood, he or she is more likely to recall positive information. Likewise, if an individual is in a negative mood, he or she will recall more negative information (Hoyer & MacInnis 2004). From a marketing perspective, if an advertisement can influence a consumer's mood in a positive direction, the recall of relevant information may be enhanced when the consumer is feeling good.

Overall, therefore, it is clear that retrieval is an important concept for marketers. The objective of marketing communications is often to increase retrieval of the brand name, brand benefit, logo, advertisement character, or package. Newer competitors in an established industry work particularly hard to increase consumers' awareness of their brand names. Although retrieval is an important objective for marketers, not all consumers can remember things equally well. In particular, elderly consumers have difficulty recognising and remembering brand names and advertisement claims. Research shows that elderly consumers' memory for information from advertising can be improved if they form a *mental image* of things in the advertisement. Imagery creates a greater number of associations in memory, which, in turn, enhances retrieval (Law *et al.* 1998).

MEASURES OF CONSUMER LEARNING

For many marketers, the dual goals of consumer learning are increased market share and brand-loyal consumers. These goals are interdependent: brand-loyal consumers provide the basis for a stable and growing market share, and brands with larger market shares have proportionately larger groups of loyal buyers. Marketers focus their promotional budgets on trying to teach consumers that their brands are best and that their products will best solve the consumers' problems and satisfy their needs. Thus, it is important for the marketer to measure how effectively consumers have 'learned' its message. Measures of consumer learning include *recognition, recall measures* and *comprehension*.

Recognition tests and *recall tests* are conducted to determine whether consumers remember seeing an advertisement, the extent to which they have read it or seen it and can recall its content, their resulting attitudes towards the product and the brand name, and their purchase intentions.

Recognition tests are based on *aided recall*, whereas recall tests use *unaided recall*. In recognition tests, the consumer is shown an advertisement and asked whether he or she remembers seeing it and can remember any of its salient points. Brand recognition is particularly important for in-store decisions because it helps individuals identify or locate the brands they want to buy. Logos on brands or packages may be fundamental in enhancing brand recognition. Grocery shopping frequently involves consumers in a recognition task.

Recall means that a consumer must retrieve the information from long-term memory. In recall tests, the consumer is asked whether he or she has read a specific magazine or watched a specific television show, and if so, whether they can recall any advertisements or commercials seen, the product advertised, the brand, and any significant points about the product. Introducing a surprise element in an advertisement can be particularly effective in aiding recall even if it is not relevant to the factual information being presented (Heckler & Childers 1992). In addition, mystery advertisements, in which the brand is not identified until the end of the advertisement, are more effective at building associations in memory between the product category and that brand — especially in the case of relatively unknown brands (Fazio *et al*. 1992).

EXAMPLE: THE GUARANTEED IRISH SYMBOL IS ONE OF THE MOST RECOGNISED LOGOS IN IRELAND

The Irish Goods Council originally launched the Buy Irish initiative in 1975. This was removed from government 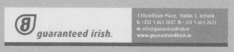 control in 1984 following a ruling by the European Court that individual countries were not allowed to promote their own products as being superior to those produced elsewhere within the European Union. As a result, Guaranteed Irish became a not-for-profit company and has continued in its aim of raising awareness and demand for Irish products and services with its own financing.

The Guaranteed Irish symbol has gone through many changes over the years. In the 1970s and 1980s, the Guaranteed Irish symbol was all about supporting the Irish economy in a time when Ireland had high unemployment levels. With the changing Irish economic landscape, Guaranteed Irish as a brand has had to move with the times. When the brand was set up, Ireland was an agricultural and embryonic manufacturing nation, with widespread unemployment. The symbol was then seen as a catalyst for creating jobs and revitalising the economy. Today, when employment is very high, consumers have new reasons for wishing to buy Irish. According to Tom Rea, director of Guaranteed Irish, 'People today have different concerns, such as wanting to know exactly where their food has come from and the distance it has travelled to get to them.' In a recent survey commissioned by Guaranteed Irish, 70 per cent of those surveyed agreed with the statement: 'I try to buy Irish foods whenever possible.'

The establishment of numerous multinational firms in Ireland has altered the more traditional economic landscape. In response, the Guaranteed Irish brand has successfully adapted to products and services of a highly skilled knowledge economy by successfully incorporating multinationals such as Wyeth and Pfizer into its portfolio. Both of these corporations now feature the Guaranteed Irish symbol on their Irish-made products. In 2003, to reflect the new, modern Ireland, Guaranteed Irish decided to rebrand, which involved the introduction of a new symbol, house style and brochure. The new logo retains the essence of the old (a lower case 'g' with an embedded 'i'), yet with a modern twist reflecting a changing Ireland that is professional, global, and style conscious. Market research strongly suggests this new symbol draws usefully on the original symbol's legacy; despite only being introduced in 2004 it is already extremely well recognised by the general public, with ninety per cent of those questioned in a recent survey recognising the symbol once prompted.

Source: adapted from 'Great Irish Brands', Irish Independent special supplement, 17 November 2007, pp. 16–17.

Another measure of consumer learning is the degree to which consumers accurately comprehend the intended advertising message. *Comprehension* is the process of using prior knowledge to understand more about what has been categorised. Comprehension is a function of the message characteristics, the consumer's opportunity and ability to process the information, and the consumer's motivation (or level of involvement). To ensure a high level of comprehension, many marketers conduct *pre-testing* before the advertising is actually run. Pre-tests are used to determine which, if any, elements of an advertising message should be revised before major media expenses are incurred. After the advertisement appears, marketers may use *post-testing* to evaluate the effectiveness of an advertisement and to identify which elements, if any, should be changed to improve the impact and memorability of future advertisements.

FORGETTING

One important area of memory research involves the question of why people forget. When information is placed in long-term memory it tends to stay there. It may be difficult, however, to retrieve. Early memory theorists assumed that memories simply fade away with the passage of time. In some cases, individuals forget things because memory links *decay* over time, often because they are not used. Forgetting also occurs due to interference: as additional information is learned, it displaces the earlier information. Two types of interference have been acknowledged: *proactive interference* and *retroactive interference*. In *proactive interference*, material learned prior to the new material interferes with the learning of new material (Hilgard *et al.* 1975). As new responses are learned, a stimulus loses its effectiveness in retrieving the old response. When *retroactive interference* occurs, new material presented after old material has been learned interferes with the recall of the old material. That is, the learning of new material interferes with the retrieval or the response generation of the old material from memory.

Forgetting, which results from proactive and retroactive interference, can create problems for marketers. With both kinds of interference, the problem is the similarity of old and new information. If consumers receive a series of commercials for products in which similar types of claims are made, confusion will result and learning will be impeded. Research on proactive and retroactive interference suggests that confusion grows proportionally to the degree that the competing commercials involve similar types of products, or that differing products use similar adjectives to describe their performance (e.g. high quality, low cost, etc.). Experiments have shown that a unique item in a series of relatively homogeneous items is recalled much more easily, because the effects of proactive and retroactive interference are minimised (Mowen 1995).

Because of the operation of proactive and retroactive interference, the recall of verbal information decreases over time. If a marketer wants to obtain rapid awareness of a product, a high frequency of advertisements over a short period of time will be most effective. Rapid forgetting, however, can occur immediately after the burst of advertisements. If the goal is to build long-term awareness of the advertisement, the commercials should be scheduled so that the advertisements are seen by consumers regularly over a long period of time. To maintain awareness, marketers will often combine the approaches and use a high-intensity campaign to bring out a product and then regularly schedule the advertisement after the introduction.

CASE STUDY: LEARNING ABOUT CONSUMER RIGHTS — THE CONSUMERS' ASSOCIATION OF IRELAND

The last forty years have seen extraordinary change for consumers, certainly as Irish citizens, but also as citizens of Europe and the world. Irish consumer legislation has radically altered since the 1960s. This is in no small way due to the statements made by American president John F. Kennedy in his address to the United States Congress on 25 March 1962, which, undoubtedly set in motion the demand for and provision of every single consumer right that we rely upon today. Kennedy outlined that 'Consumers, by definition, include us all. They are the largest economic group, affecting and affected by almost every public and private economic decision. Yet they are the only important group whose views are not often heard.'

Kennedy declared four fundamental consumer rights; in 1985 these were added to by the United Nations and endorsed as the now internationally recognised eight basic rights of consumers. They are:

- the right to *safety* — the right to be protected against products, production processes and services that are hazardous to health or life
- the right to be *informed* — to be given the facts and information you need to make your own choices
- the right to *choose* — to be able to choose from a range of products and services offered at competitive prices. As a consumer, you also have the right to expect satisfactory quality
- the right to *be heard* — to have your interests as a consumer represented in government policy
- the right to *redress* — to a fair settlement of consumer disputes, including compensation for misrepresentation, shoddy goods or unsatisfactory services
- the right to *education* — to learn the knowledge and skills you need to make informed and confident choices about goods and services
- the right to a *healthy environment* — to live and work in an environment which does not threaten the well-being of present and future generations
- the right to *satisfaction of basic needs* — to access basic essential goods and services such as adequate food, clothing, shelter, health care, education and sanitation.

What followed these, very much through the lobbying efforts of consumer associations across the world, are the many statutory instruments, legislative provisions, European Union directives, regulations, regulators, courts and arbitrators that provide the redress mechanisms that we rely upon as consumers of goods and services.

The Consumers' Association of Ireland Ltd (CAI) was set up in 1966 to protect and educate consumers. The aim of CAI is to represent consumers, making sure that their needs as consumers of goods and services are given higher priority. CAI is an independent, non-profit and non-government organisation. The association furthers its aim by:

- promoting action to safeguard the interests of consumers, ensuring that those who take decisions which will affect the consumer can have a balanced and authoritative view of the interests of consumers before them
- insisting that the interests of all consumers are taken into account

- making representations of the views of consumers on all matters of concern to them to local and central government, government agencies, industry and any other quarter where the company sees fit, including representation on the existing law and on proposed legislation
- making representations on the adequacy and availability to consumers of consumer advice services and on the needs of such services for supporting facilities
- representing the consumer on appropriate government and other bodies or international organisations including those that exist within the framework of the European Communities.

The means by which the association achieves its aims include:

- using research and information from *Consumer Choice* magazine to form policies which support and safeguard consumer interests
- promoting and seeking implementation of those policies, representing the consumer interest on appropriate bodies
- being available for consultation by those who seek a consumer view on policies and proposals
- keeping in touch with consumers' experiences and concerns
- working with other agencies to achieve beneficial change for consumers
- promoting the interests, experience and views of consumers through meetings, reports, interviews, exhibitions, letters and publications.

The association also concentrates on special areas. Through its monthly publication *Consumer Choice*, it reports on services and other areas of consumer interest, including: food and food safety; product performance; finance and financial products; environment and health issues; and consumer rights and how to safeguard these rights. Consumer protection remains an essential part of the work of consumer organisations. But consumer protection is essentially defensive and responsive. To be effective the consumer movement must also be dynamic — setting the agenda, defining solutions, shaping opportunities, and interacting in a positive and creative way with those who provide goods and services. In a modern and growing economy the consumer must be the driving force that requires innovation, forces change and growth, and accepts nothing less than real quality underpinned by genuine choice. The agenda for the Consumers' Association of Ireland is to continue to work for the protection of Irish consumers in the European Union. It will also proceed with its endeavours to improve consumer education. The consumer must become more assertive, sometimes in partnership with the producer, and sometimes taking the lead.

Source: adapted from D. Jewell, '40 Years of the CAI', Consumer Choice, September 2006, pp. 325–26; and www.thecai.ie

CASE STUDY: BLACKROCK CASTLE OBSERVATORY MAKING LEARNING FUN

Blackrock Castle is a sixteenth-century castle on the banks of the Lee estuary approximately 4km from the heart of Cork city. The inspirational Cosmos at the Castle project is a redevelopment of the castle as a centre for scientific research, outreach and communication. The project is a joint venture between Cork City Council, Cork Institute of Technology and a private benefactor. The vision of Blackrock Castle Observatory is to 'affect positive change in attitudes toward science, engineering, and technology in Ireland and be recognised and respected as a centre of excellence in scientific research, education, and outreach'.

The mission of Blackrock Castle Observatory is to provide the people of Ireland with a centre of excellence in science:

- by fostering interest in science, engineering and technology through the medium of astronomy
- by developing innovative programmes which increase awareness of science, engineering and technology
- in collaborating with governmental, professional, industrial and educational establishments on programmes which increase awareness of science, engineering and technology
- through research in astronomy, optics and imaging
- by exploring and developing applications for their research
- through consultative services to governmental, professional, industrial and educational establishments
- through activities and commitment, inspire people of all ages and from all walks of life to experience the wonder of science.

A unique feature of the facility is the manner in which children and adults are encouraged to interact with science. The primary objective of Blackrock Castle Observatory is to increase the level of awareness of, and interest in, science and technology through the delivery of the highest-quality educational experience. Blackrock Castle houses Ireland's first fully interactive astronomy centre. The idea of the facility is to be informative, intelligent and, most of all, fun.

Astronomy captivates and inspires people to question the world in which they live. This quality can be used to encourage students to develop an interest in science. The broad appeal of astronomy provides a unique medium through which key ideas in science can be communicated, and applications of engineering and technology can be simultaneously developed and demonstrated. Through the creation of an accessible, fun visitor centre, Blackrock Castle Observatory envisages sparking interest in students to continue learning science at third level, thereby fuelling the urgent Irish need for graduates for an economy ever more reliant on technology.

Cosmos at the Castle is an exploration of the origin of life, which includes a number of interactive exhibitions. A biometric hand-reading is required to gain access to the exhibition, meaning hands must be scanned before entry. The exhibition takes visitors through the timeline of events that have shaped the way the world is today. The timeline features a series of cataclysmic events that altered the course of life on earth, such as the asteroid that marked the extinction of the dinosaurs many millions of years ago. There are display areas teeming with galaxies which dissolve into chosen areas of discovery or argument: life on earth; DNA; evolution versus creation; the formation and constituents of stars and planets, and whatever else might be up there; the chance to send a message via radio telescope to a planet of your choice; tracking comets; and forecasting asteroids and eruptions. A gallery of cinema-sized high-definition digital video screens with proximity sensors allows visitors to interact with the process of the evolution of the entire universe and of life on earth. Importantly, because of the manner in which the facility was designed, it is possible for the content on all the screens to be changed as required to suit changing educational needs. The exhibition culminates in an interactive presentation called *Comet Chaser.* The audience uses touch-screen technology to determine the outcome of a scenario in which a comet is hurtling towards earth.

The castle also houses a team of astronomical researchers from Cork Institute of Technology who are currently working on a number of projects including the construction of Ireland's first robotic observatory. Dr Niall Smith, Head of Research at Cork Institute of Technology, explains, 'The telescopes and domes must operate without any human assistance. This means the observatory has to do some "thinking" for itself. The "thinking" is done by computers that have been programmed to take specific actions under certain conditions. It is not a simple task to get computers to "think", and researchers at the observatory have to write many new computer programmes themselves to do this. The two optical telescopes at Blackrock Castle Observatory are also linked in a robotic way. Normally, the two telescopes operate separately, looking at different objects in the sky, but if one of them finds something interesting it can automatically send a signal to the second telescope to tell it to stop what it is doing and switch its attention to the interesting object. This information can even be transmitted to telescopes abroad.'

Blackrock Castle Observatory is a unique Irish facility that promotes science, engineering and technology through the medium of astronomy; where a culture of innovation and creativity captures the imagination of students and the general public, encouraging them to explore and participate in science. The pivotal idea is that Cosmos at the Castle will encourage its young visitors, largely school groups and tourists, to take a greater interest in science, not just as a subject, but as an experience.

Source: adapted from www.bco.ie; and L. Roseingrave, Evening Echo, *14 June 2007, p. 14.*

Questions for Review

1. What basic elements must be present in order for learning to occur?
2. How can the principles of cognitive learning theory be applied to consumer behaviour?
3. Compare and contrast the three main approaches to behavioural learning.
4. What three types of memory have been proposed? How do they differ?
5. How do marketers measure consumer learning?
6. Why does forgetting occur?

6

Consumer Attitude Formation and Change

CHAPTER OBJECTIVES

After reading this chapter you should be able to:

- Recognise the importance of attitudes towards products and services.
- Discuss attitude formation.
- Explain how attitude change is achieved.
- Understand consumers' attitudes towards advertisements.
- Identify situations when attitudes predict behaviour.
- Describe factors which influence affective attitudes.

WHAT ARE ATTITUDES?

An *attitude* is a lasting, general evaluation of people, objects, advertisements or issues. An attitude is lasting because it tends to endure over time. Consumers have attitudes towards a wide range of products, services, advertisements, the Internet and retail stores. There is a general agreement that attitudes are *learned*. This means that attitudes relevant to purchase behaviour are formed from direct experience with the product, from word-of-mouth information acquired from others, the Internet, and various forms of direct marketing. As learned predispositions, attitudes have a motivational quality; that is, they might propel a consumer *towards* a particular behaviour or turn the consumer *away* from a particular behaviour.

Attitudes are important because they (a) guide the thoughts of consumers, (b) influence the feelings of consumers, and (c) affect the behaviour of consumers. Consumers decide which advertisements to read, whom to talk to, where to shop, and where to eat — depending on their attitudes. Attitudes also influence the three essentials of consumer buyer behaviour: acquisition, consumption and disposition of a product. Marketers, therefore, need to change consumers' attitudes in order to influence consumer decision making and to change consumer behaviour.

Attitudes can be described in terms of five main characteristics.

1. *Favourability* refers to how much a consumer likes or dislikes something.
2. *Attitude accessibility* refers to how easily and readily an attitude can be retrieved from memory.
3. *Attitude confidence* refers to how strongly a consumer holds an attitude. In some cases this can be very strong; in other cases a consumer may be less certain.
4. *Attitude persistence* refers to how long an attitude lasts. An attitude held with confidence may last for a long time, whereas others may last only a short time.
5. *Attitude resistance* refers to the difficulty of changing an attitude. Attitudes are likely to be more difficult to change when consumers are brand loyal.

Marketers can influence consumers' attitudes towards new products and novel behaviours when they understand how attitudes are formed. This understanding also helps marketers to plan strategies for changing consumer attitudes about existing products and established behaviours. During 2006, the Mintel International Group published a report about attitudes towards processed foods in the Irish market. The research revealed that the processed foods market is currently facing a series of challenges because of intense criticism from relevant health/government organisations in relation to obesity issues and food hygiene. These debates, and others, mean that the processed foods industry is at a critical stage in which manufacturers are making a concerted effort to cut back on the levels of salt, sugar and fat contained in food, following government pressure, and attempting to reposition their brands in order better to reflect changing attitudes towards food and nutrition generally in Ireland (www.foodandbeveragereports.com).

ATTITUDE FORMATION

Attitude formation can be divided into three areas: (a) how attitudes are learned; (b) the sources of influence on attitude formation; and (c) the impact of personality on attitude formation.

How Attitudes are Learned

Consumers often purchase new products that are associated with a favourably viewed brand name. Their favourable attitude towards the brand name is frequently the result of repeated satisfaction with other products produced by the same company. An EU-wide consumer survey has found that Irish shoppers are the most likely to stick to 'tried and tested' product brands. Two-thirds of Irish people aged over 40 and half of those aged between 25 and 40 consistently buy the same brand rather than shopping around. The research also found that Irish people in all age categories are far more likely than other Europeans to be brand-conscious when it comes to clothes (www.futurefoundation.net).

Sometimes attitudes *follow* the purchase and consumption of a product. A consumer, for example, may purchase a brand-name product *without* having a prior attitude towards it because it is the only product of its kind available (e.g. the last bottle of high-energy drink on the shelf). Consumers also make trial purchases of new brands from product categories in which they have little personal involvement. If they find the purchased brand to be satisfactory, then they are likely to develop a favourable attitude towards it.

In situations in which consumers seek to solve a problem or satisfy a need, they are likely to form attitudes (either positive or negative) about products on the basis of information exposure and their own knowledge and beliefs. In general, the more information consumers have about a product or service, the more likely they are to form attitudes about it, either positive or negative. Regardless of available information, however, consumers are not always willing to process *all* the information about a product and they often use only a limited amount of the information available.

Two or three important beliefs about a product are likely to dominate in the formation of attitudes, while less important beliefs provide little additional input to attitudes. Marketers, therefore, should not include *all* the features of their products and services in their advertisements, but should focus on the few key points that are at the heart of what distinguishes their product from the competition.

Sources of Influence on Attitude Formation

The formation of consumer attitudes is strongly influenced by *personal experience*, by the *influence* of family and friends, *direct marketing*, *mass media* and the *Internet*. A primary means by which attitudes towards goods and services are formed is through the consumer's direct experience in trying and evaluating them. Recognising the importance of direct experience, marketers frequently attempt to stimulate trial of new products by offering money-off coupons or even free samples. In such cases, the marketer's objective is to get consumers to try and evaluate the product. If a product proves to be to their liking, then it is likely that consumers will form a positive attitude and be more likely to purchase the product again. In addition, from consumer information added to coupons the marketer is able to create a database of interested consumers.

As individual consumers come in contact with others — especially family, close friends and admired individuals (e.g. a sports hero) — they form attitudes that influence their lives. The family is an extremely important source of influence on the formation of attitudes, as it is the family that provides individuals with many basic values and a wide range of less important beliefs.

Marketers are increasingly using highly focused direct-marketing programmes to target consumers with products and services that fit their interests and lifestyle. Marketers very carefully target consumers on the basis of their demographic, psychographic or geographic profiles with highly personalised product offerings and messages that show they understand their special needs and desires (e.g. mothers of newborn babies). Direct-marketing efforts can favourably influence the attitudes of target consumers, because selected products and services offered and the promotional messages conveyed are very carefully designed to address individual segment's needs and concerns, and therefore achieve higher success rates than mass marketing would.

In Ireland, data protection legislation takes the sending of unsolicited direct marketing ('junk mail' or 'spam') very seriously and it offers protection against this practice through the data protection commissioner. The application of data protection law varies depending on the medium through which the marketing is delivered. The traditional and oldest form of direct marketing is postal marketing. For mail received through an individual's letter box to be considered as direct marketing it must be addressed to a named person and promote a product or service. Unaddressed mail put into letter boxes or mail addressed to 'the occupant', 'the resident' or 'the householder' does not necessarily involve the use of personal data and consequently data protection legislation does not apply.

Mass-media communications also provide an important source of information that influences the formation of consumer attitudes. Newspapers and a variety of general and special-interest magazines and television channels constantly expose consumers to new ideas, products, opinions and advertisements. Research indicates that, for consumers who lack direct experience with a product, exposure to an emotionally appealing advertisement message is more likely to create an attitude towards the product than for consumers who previously had direct experience with the product category (Lee *et al.* 2000). It is important for marketers, therefore, to realise that emotional appeals are most effective with consumers who lack product experience.

EXAMPLE: AER LINGUS EMPHASISES EMOTIONAL APPEAL IN NEW ADVERTISEMENT

Aer Lingus would like its image in the airline industry to mirror Tesco's image in the supermarket business for 'very good service at a smart price' — according to the airline's marketing chief, Fintan Lonergan. 'We're not Aldi or Lidl, and we're definitely not Harrods, or even Marks and Spencer. Tesco is about right. It strikes a balance between low prices and the value to be had from how things are delivered,' said Lonergan.

Aer Lingus unveiled a fresh version of itself during September 2007. It launched its first television brand commercial since the 11 September 2001 crisis, which nearly pushed Aer Lingus into bankruptcy. The new commercial reintroduces a human face to the Aer Lingus brand, which had taken a deliberately functional approach to marketing in recent years. The new advertisement features several members of the airline's cabin crew delivering a standard of friendly care that Aer Lingus still sees as its primary point of differentiation from more unambiguously no-frills rivals such as Ryanair. The emotional appeal of the new advertisement, with its emphasis on warmth and friendliness, is a distinct novelty. According to Lonergan, 'I think it's very believable in terms of today's Aer Lingus. Our business is flying people from place to place. We've never forgotten that. In our view, low-fare air travel doesn't have to be a bad experience, and can be quite the opposite. I believe with this brand message, we are putting a clear space in our customers' minds between Aer Lingus and its rivals.'

Source: adapted from C. O'Mahony, 'Aer Lingus plans to build "Tesco-like" image',
Sunday Business Post, *30 September 2007, p. 25.*

Another issue when evaluating the impact of advertising messages on attitude formation is the level of apparent realism that advertising can provide. Attitudes that develop through direct experience (e.g. product usage) tend to be more confidently held and more enduring than attitudes developed through indirect experience (e.g. reading a printed advertisement). Television, for example, usually provides the consumer with more realism than would be possible through a radio or printed advertisement. Furthermore, the Internet has an even greater ability to provide telepresence, which is the simulated perception of direct experience.

Impact of Personality on Attitude Formation

Personality also plays a role in attitude formation. Consumers who, for example, like information and enjoy thinking are likely to form positive attitudes in response to advertisements or direct mail that are high in product-related information. This means that marketing messages must be credible to generate support arguments and to increase beliefs in the product or service.

On the other hand, consumers who do not require a lot of product-related information are more likely to form positive attitudes in response to advertisements that feature an attractive model or well-known celebrity. In many marketing messages, information is presented by a celebrity, an actor, a company representative, or a real consumer. The credibility of these sources, plus the credibility of the company, should influence consumer attitudes. When marketing communications do not feature an actual person, consumers judge credibility by the reputation of the company delivering the message. Consumers are more likely to believe and change their attitudes based on messages from companies that have a reputation for producing quality products, for dealing fairly with consumers, or for being trustworthy. The founder of Superquinn, Feargal Quinn, realised early in his food business career that the Irish are proud of their country, so he labelled all Irish-produced goods under the 'shamrock campaign' a label which is still used today.

ATTITUDE CHANGE

Social marketing refers to attempts to change consumer attitudes and behaviours in ways that are beneficial to society as a whole. Similar to attitude formation, attitude changes are *learned*; they are influenced by *personal experience* and other *sources of information*, and by *personality*. Marketers who are market leaders, however, want to maintain and strengthen prevailing positive attitudes of consumers to their products, in the hope that consumers will not succumb to competitors' special offers or to other inducements used to entice them. An effective strategy for changing consumer attitudes towards a product or brand is to make a particular need prominent. Just a few years ago the popularity of the Atkins diet raised very serious concerns about the possibility of a huge change in eating habits as people became obsessed with weight issues. The Atkins formula put a big emphasis on eating protein and vegetables at the expense of carbohydrates. Companies who produced large amounts of white flour-based breads and cakes were asking questions regarding the impact Atkins would have on global eating patterns. The Atkins diet fad, however, faded, illustrating how consumer attitudes can change very quickly.

EXAMPLE: CHANGING IRISH CONSUMER ATTITUDES TOWARDS PLASTIC BAGS

Plastic bag consumption increased alarmingly in Ireland in the 1990s. Retail outlets placed no limits on the amount of bags consumers could use when doing their shopping. One of the most significant side effects of this trend was the careless disposal of plastic bags by consumers after use — a significant proportion of which ended up as highly visible components of litter. Furthermore, because of their composition, nearly all plastic bags do not degrade. Thus, in addition to being highly visible because of the volumes being carelessly disposed of, they also became highly persistent pollutants in urban, rural and coastal settings. This trend was also undermining Ireland's clean, green image on which the Irish tourism industry depends so much.

The primary purpose of the plastic bag levy was to reduce the consumption of disposable plastic bags by influencing consumer behaviour. Since its introduction on 4 March 2002, the levy has been an outstanding success. Prior to the introduction of the levy it is estimated that over 1.2 billion plastic bags were dispensed free of charge at retail outlets annually, equating to roughly 328 bags per inhabitant per year. The fall in the consumption of plastic bags has been considerable, with the reduction being estimated at over 90 per cent. The plastic bag levy had an immediate effect on consumer behaviour — with plastic bag per capita usage decreasing overnight from an estimated 328 bags to 21. Recent data, however, indicated that plastic bag usage rose to 31 bags per capita during the course of 2006. The levy was therefore increased to 22 cent on 1 July 2007 in order to reduce the per capita usage at least to the level achieved in 2002.

Source: adapted from www.environ.ie

Changing consumer attitudes is a key strategy for most marketers. Consumers are constantly receiving messages inducing them to change their attitudes. *Attitude-change strategies* available to marketers include:

1. changing the consumer's basic motivational function
2. associating the product with an admired group or event
3. resolving two conflicting attitudes
4. altering components of the multi-attribute model
5. changing consumer beliefs about competitor brands.

Changing the consumer's basic motivational function. Consumers hold certain brand attitudes partly because of a brand's utility. When a product has been useful or helped consumers in the past, consumers' attitudes towards it tend to be favourable. One way of changing attitudes in favour of a product is by showing people that it can serve a utilitarian purpose that they may not have considered.

Attitudes are also an expression or reflection of a consumer's general values, lifestyle and outlook. If a consumer segment generally holds a positive attitude towards owning the latest and smallest mobile phone, then the attitudes of that segment towards new electronic devices are likely to reflect that orientation. Vodafone, for example, has introduced 'Internet on the move' which gives full mobile Internet access through a mobile phone, laptop or handheld PC without the need of a fixed phone line.

Associating the product with an admired group or event. Attitudes, in part, are related to certain groups, social events or causes. It is possible to change attitudes towards products, services and brands by pointing out their relationships to social groups, events or causes. Companies frequently  remind consumers of the civic and public acts they sponsor, to let the public know about the good that they are trying to do. SuperValu, for example, have been national sponsors of Ireland's Tidy Towns and Villages competition since 1992, making it one of the longest running sponsorships in the country. As a company, SuperValu believes that its organisation is a 'good fit' with tidy towns, as both celebrate the achievements of real people making a real difference in their community.

Resolving two conflicting attitudes. Attitude-change strategies can sometimes resolve actual or potential conflict between two attitudes. Specifically, if consumers can be made to see that their negative attitude towards a product, a specific brand, or its core attribute is really not in conflict with another attitude, they may be induced to change their evaluation of the brand (i.e. moving from negative to positive).

Altering components of the multi-attribute model. The overall market for many product categories is often set out so that different consumer segments are offered different brands with different features or benefits. Within a product category, such as deodorants for example, there are brands such as Lynx that stress masculinity and brands such as Dove that stress gentleness. These two brands of deodorants have typically appealed to different segments of the overall deodorant market.

Another strategy for changing attitudes concentrates on changing beliefs or perceptions about the brand itself. This is by far the most common form of advertising appeal. Advertisers are constantly reminding consumers that their product has 'more' or is 'better' or 'best' in terms of some important product attribute. Consumers, however, frequently resist evidence that might challenge a strongly held attitude or belief, while they tend to interpret any ambiguous information in ways that reinforce their pre-existing attitudes. Information suggesting a change in attitude, therefore, needs to be compelling and repeated often enough to overcome natural resistance to letting go of established attitudes.

A further strategy consists of *adding an attribute*. This can be accomplished by adding an attribute that has either previously been ignored or that represents an improvement or technological innovation. Marketers frequently use phrases such as 'new improved version'. Aquafresh, for example, has launched Aquafresh 'white and shine' toothpaste. This new addition to the whitening toothpaste sector not only whitens teeth but also uses micro-buffing particles aimed at polishing away imperfections.

Changing consumer beliefs about competitive brands. Another approach to attitude change involves changing consumer beliefs about the *attributes of competitive* brands or product categories. Comparative advertising is a marketing strategy in which a marketer claims product superiority for its brand over one or more explicitly named competitors, either on an overall basis or on selected product attributes. Tesco, for example, often use this type of strategy to illustrate their lower prices in relation to their competitors Dunnes Stores and SuperValu. Irish telephone directory enquiries provider 11890 also reminds potential consumers that its rates are cheaper than those of its competitor 11850. Generally, this strategy must be used with caution, as comparative advertising gives visibility to competing brands and claims.

Attitudes Towards the Advertisement

Another approach to attitude change is changing consumers' brand attitudes without necessarily changing their beliefs. This approach involves influencing consumer attitudes towards the advertisement. *Attitude towards the advertisement* refers to a consumer's general liking for or dislike of a particular advertising stimulus during a particular advertising exposure. Consumers develop attitudes towards advertisements just as they do towards brands, and these attitudes influence their attitudes towards the brand. If consumers see an advertisement and like it, their liking for the advertisement may rub off on the brand and thereby make their brand attitude more positive. Attitudes towards the advertisement depend on a number of factors, including: the advertisement's content and vividness of imagery; the consumer's mood; the emotions the advertisement evokes in the consumer; and the consumer's liking for or dislike of the television programme in which the advertisement is embedded. These factors influence attitude towards the advertisement under both high- and low-involvement conditions, and whether or not the consumer is familiar with the brand.

Another beneficial impact for marketers of creating strongly positive attitudes towards advertisements in consumers is that it increases the time they will spend watching the commercial. Generally, advertisements that contain high levels of imagery strongly affect consumer attitudes towards those advertisements. *Imagery* refers to the extent that an advertisement causes consumers to envisage their own use of the product and to connect the advertisement to their own feelings and beliefs. Advertisements that employ concrete words, that use vivid verbal or pictorial images, that instruct consumers on how to imagine using the brand, and that are highly plausible have the strongest impact on consumer attitudes towards the advertisement.

WHEN DO ATTITUDES PREDICT BEHAVIOUR?

Marketers are also interested in knowing whether, when and why attitudes will predict consumer behaviour. What consumers intend to do, however, does not always predict what they will actually do. Marketers therefore need to consider which factors affect the attitude–behaviour relationship. Some factors that influence consumer attitudes include:

Level of involvement. Attitudes are more likely to predict behaviour when involvement is high and when consumers think extensively about the information that gives rise to their attitudes (see Chapter 2). Attitudes also tend to be strong and enduring and therefore more predictive of consumer behaviour when affective (or emotive) involvement is high.

Knowledge and experience. Attitudes are more likely to be strongly held and predictive of behaviour when the consumer is knowledgeable about or experienced with the object of the attitude. Thus, a consumer making a decision to update a car is more likely to form an attitude that is based on more detailed and integrated information than a person who has not yet bought their first car. This attitude would then be more strongly held and more strongly related to behaviour.

Analysis of reasons. Asking consumers to analyse their reasons for brand preferences increases the link between attitude and behaviour in situations where behaviour is measured soon after attitudes are measured.

Accessibility of attitudes. Attitudes are more strongly related to consumer behaviour when they can be readily recalled. Alternatively, when an attitude cannot be easily remembered, it will have little effect on consumer behaviour. Direct experience (through product usage) generally increases accessibility of consumer attitudes for attributes that have been experienced (e.g. tasted or touched).

Attitude confidence. Confidence tends to be stronger when the attitude is based on either a greater amount of information or more trustworthy information. Sometimes consumers are more certain about their evaluations than at other times. When consumers are confident, their attitudes are more likely to predict their buying behaviour.

Attitude–behaviour relationship over time. When consumers are exposed to an advertising message but do not try the product, their attitude confidence declines over time. Marketers should therefore plan their advertising schedules to reactivate consumer attitudes and attitude confidence through message repetition.

Personality variables. Certain personality types are more likely to exhibit stronger attitude–behaviour relationships than others. Consumers who really like to think about things will evidence stronger attitude–behaviour relationships because their attitudes will be based on high-elaboration thinking.

HOW AFFECTIVE ATTITUDES ARE INFLUENCED

When consumers apply little intellectual processing effort and instead form attitudes based on feelings, factors which influence affective attitudes will then rely on the communication source, the message and the context.

Communication Source

A large number of advertisements feature attractive models, spokespersons or celebrities, thus suggesting that beauty sells, especially in the beauty business. When consumer motivation to process an advertised message is low, attractive sources will enhance the favourability of consumer brand attitudes regardless of whether the message arguments are strong or weak (Haugtvedt *at al.* 1988). Consumers tend to rate advertisements that use attractive people higher, and these ratings often affect consumer attitudes in a positive way towards the products these models offer.

Celebrities are often used for endorsing products. The likeability of the celebrity can influence affective attitudes. In particular, celebrity sources can be effective when they can be seen to relate to the product or service. The amount of money spent by sponsors on endorsement deals with Irish sports personalities is expected to double to €7 million over the next five years (McCaughren 2007). According to research by Dublin consultants Onside Sponsorship, a handful of top Irish sports people are making up to €500,000 a year through deals with major brands. The current Irish rugby team has generated an unprecedented image and profile and has become the most commercially successful ever in terms of sponsorship and advertising. The Irish rugby captain Brian O'Driscoll has advertising deals with Adidas and Gillette, while Ronan O'Gara is the face of Newbridge silverware for men. Newbridge Silverware's CEO William Doyle believes that Ronan is widely regarded as the epitome of style, both on and off the rugby pitch, calling him an 'ideal ambassador' for the collection (www.independent.ie). O'Gara already has a number of other endorsement deals, including Adidas and Lucozade. His most high-profile endorsement is with the international brand Samsung. This is the television and mobile phone company's first deal with an individual in the Irish market. In 2007, golfer Padraig Harrington signed a landmark deal with Bank of Ireland, worth up to €250,000 a year (McCaughren 2007).

EXAMPLE: CELEBRITY ENDORSED PRODUCTS FUEL MARKET GROWTH IN IRELAND

The continuing obsession among female consumers for celebrity-endorsed beauty products is undoubtedly contributing to the current growth in the colour cosmetics industry in Ireland, according to a study conducted by Mintel (2007). The report shows that the great increase in the number of women in employment in Ireland over recent years has led to greater spending power by many more female consumers for purchases such as colour cosmetics. Edel Gallagher, author of the report, said, 'The trends which have appeared in the Irish markets mirror those of the UK colour cosmetics market. For example the current upsurge in celebrity-endorsed cosmetic brands is a prime driver of this market, as in the UK'. The report confirms that the economic boom encourages female consumers to spend more on colour cosmetic products — with celebrity-endorsed products, foundation, and lipsticks as the prime growth drivers in an overall cosmetics market currently valued at €112.2 million.

Source: adapted from www.cosmeticsdesign-europe.com.

The Message

Just as the source of a message can influence consumer feelings and moods, so too can characteristics associated with the message. Message characteristics include pleasant pictures, music, humour, sex, emotional content and context. Pleasant pictures are often used to influence consumer message processing. Visual stimuli can affect consumer mood or make an advertisement likeable by making it interesting. Internet advertising often uses pleasing pictures and visuals to catch consumers' attention and to generate positive attitudes. Alternatively,

marketers often use fear appeals in an attempt to elicit fear or anxiety by stressing the negative consequences of either engaging or not engaging in a particular behaviour. By arousing this fear, marketers hope consumers will be motivated to think about the message and behave in the desired manner (see Chapter 3). Eircom Phonewatch, for example, in their radio advertising for house alarms, inform listeners that nearly two per cent of Irish homes are burgled each year and that burglary is a real threat to householders in Ireland. Eircom Phonewatch advertisers believe they play a role in helping to appease public fears in this area by offering a potential solution.

Music

Music is frequently used by marketers as a communication tool. The use of music in advertising has been shown to stimulate a variety of positive effects. Music can put the consumer in a positive mood and lead to the development of positive attitudes. Music can also be effective in generating positive feelings such as happiness, serenity, excitement, and sentimentality. Music can also stimulate emotional memories. The Jacob's/Bolands 'Mallows' range, for example, has been immortalised in the timeless advertising jingle 'Kimberly, Mikado and Coconut Cream, someone you love would love some, Mum!'

Humour

Humour is another tool which is frequently used by marketers. An advertisement can use humour in many different ways, including jokes, puns, satire and irony. The use of humour in advertisements seems to be more positive for low-involvement products or services where generating positive feelings about the advertisement is critical. While humour can attract attention to an advertisement, it can also act to distract the consumer from the message. In a world of homogeneous brand messages, humour can often help to get through to consumers. Many of the current examples of humour in Irish advertising are to be found in beer commercials. Promoting the product as a 'bit of craic' alongside the message about enjoying the product sensibly seems to be quite effective. It creates a better feeling towards the product rather than getting any particular message across. Despite humour finding its way into advertisements for cars and even serious subjects such as banking, many companies purposely avoid using comedians. Advertisers do not want to make humour appear forced — consumers respond better to individuals who appear to be typical everyday people, and they also react well if the dialogue seems spontaneous. It is difficult, however, to make an advertisement appear or sound spontaneous.

Sex

Sometimes advertisements have romantic or sexual themes or implications. Sexual suggestiveness involves situations that either portray or imply sexual themes or romance. Another use of sex in advertising is through nudity or partial nudity. Sometimes advertisements contain naked or scantily clad models to generate attention or elicit emotions about a product or service. For some consumers, however, the use of sexual messages in advertising can create negative feelings, such as embarrassment or uneasiness, which would have a negative commercial effect. A consumer's positive or negative reaction to an advertisement using sexual imagery usually depends on whether the sexual content is deemed to be appropriate for the product or service.

EXAMPLE: PROPERTY MARKET GETS SEXED UP

Sex sells, they say, but can it sell apartments? The team behind recent ads for a new estate of houses in Dublin believe so. What made this development different, apart from a high-spec fit-out including garden designs by people such as celebrity designer Diarmuid Gavin, was the decision of the backers of the scheme to take on a creative advertising agency to sex up the imagery and PR around the launch. The result was the raciest imagery ever seen in the normally restrained Irish property advertising market, featuring heavily made-up satin-clad models perched on luxurious furnishings. In one ad, a woman in a red satin dress reclined on a kitchen table, gazing into the camera and eating a strawberry while a dark-shirted man leant over her. Another highly stylised ad featured a group of models lounging around the garden deck in swimsuits and platform shoes. The theme the agency adopted was 'gorgeous living', to appeal to the twenty-somethings, the target buyers of the new scheme, where prices started at a relatively affordable €275,000. The images were styled like an expensive fashion shoot, with elegant furnishings to attract young buyers who now like to move into fully finished homes. Historically, advertisers did little more than put up a 'for sale' sign, but now that has been challenged, so that marketers have to make an even greater effort to get attention.
Source: adapted from C. O'Mahony, Sunday Business Post, *29 April 2007, p.29.*

The Context

The context in which an advertisement appears can affect consumer evaluation of the message. Advertisements shown during a happy television programme may be evaluated more positively than those shown during sad programmes, especially if the advertisements are emotional. If a television programme, however, becomes too emotionally arousing it may distract from the advertisements.

Companies often use *repetition* to help consumers acquire basic knowledge of important features or benefits of their product or service. Generally, consumers do not try to process the information actively, but the constant repetition increases recall through effortless or *incidental* learning (learning that occurs from repetition rather than from conscious processing). Repetition also enhances brand awareness and makes a brand name more familiar, making it easier to recognise in a shop, and it increases the likelihood that consumers will remember it when making a decision. In Ireland, England and Australia, the leader for consumer brand awareness in the wine market is Jacob's Creek. Both Jacob's Creek and Gallo were recognised as the world's best-known wine brands in one of the largest international surveys undertaken about wine drinking in March 2007. Responses were gathered from over 11,000 wine consumers across eleven key wine markets (www.wineintelligence.com).

When familiarity leads to liking an object this is known as the *mere exposure effect*, suggesting that consumers tend to prefer familiar objects to unfamiliar ones. The mere exposure effect may explain why many of the top thirty brands in the 1930s are still in the top thirty today (Hoyer & MacInnis 2004). Marketers may therefore be able to enhance consumers' liking for a new product or service by repeatedly exposing consumers to the offering or messages about it, particularly when consumer involvement is low. Marketers need to devise tactics for increasing exposure to products and messages by using the right medium of communication, optimal shelf placement and sampling.

Repeated exposures, however, build familiarity and liking only up to a point. After this, consumers typically experience *wearout*, which means that they become bored with the stimulus, and brand attitudes can actually become negative. Once a persuasive advertisement has effectively reached the targeted consumer segment, wearout causes a loss of persuasiveness. Wearout is the reason that many advertisers develop an entire campaign of advertisements rather than a single execution.

CASE STUDY: DANONE CHANGING IRISH CONSUMER ATTITUDES TOWARDS THE FRESH DAIRY MARKET

In 1997, Danone brought its worldwide expertise in health and nutrition to the Irish market. At that time, despite our agricultural heritage, Irish consumption of fresh dairy products was remarkably low in comparison to the overall dairy consumption figure for Western Europe. Even today, consumption of fresh dairy produce in Ireland is only 10.2 kilos per capita in comparison to 33.2 kilos per capita in France. Danone realised there was enormous potential to increase the consumption of fresh dairy products among Irish consumers. It set about fulfilling this goal with a market entry strategy involving activities such as:

1. developing an understanding of market segmentation in the fresh dairy market in Ireland
2. identifying gaps in the market by identifying unfulfilled consumer needs
3. introducing Danone's unique range of healthy and tasty products to deliver new benefits to Irish consumers.

Market segmentation in the fresh dairy market
The fresh dairy market has three major product types: yogurts, fromage frais, and chilled desserts. Using this segmentation by product type as a basis, Danone studied the Irish market and segmented its brands according to the different benefits that could be delivered to Irish consumers. It identified where its brands were best targeted in seven key segments in the market:

- *Natural health segment*: consumers in this category are looking for products such as natural yogurt, organic, probiotic yogurts, and yogurt drinks such as Danone Actimel and Danone Activia.
- *Diet segment*: consumers here look for the benefit of very low fat or zero per cent fat from their yogurts and fromage frais products. Typical brands would be Danone Vitalinea and Weight Watchers yogurts.
- *Standard fruit segment*: consumers are moving away from more traditional yogurt in search of products offering additional benefits such as products in the natural health segment.
- *'Full taste' segment*: appealing to consumers who look for the benefit of fuller tasting, more indulgent yogurts, e.g. Müller Corner Pots.
- *Children's segment*: traditionally fromage frais brands in this segment are designed to deliver the unique nutritional benefits required for young children. These include the Danone Gervais range and Petits Filous.

- *Drinks segment*: includes dairy drinks which are mainly targeted at young teenagers and include brands such as Yop and Yazoo.
- *Dessert segment*: designed to appeal to consumers who want to treat themselves to a more indulgent and convenient dessert. They include products such as chocolate mousse and crème caramel.

Danone examined the needs of consumers in these segments and concluded that its range of brands could deliver a range of nutritional and taste benefits not previously available in Ireland. It set about delivering these benefits to three core segments that were under-utilised, namely:

- the natural health segment
- the children's segment
- the diet segment.

The natural health segment is the fastest-growing segment within the fresh dairy product market. Irish consumers are increasingly moving towards products that claim to improve consumers' health. Danone has been instrumental in developing growth within this segment by bringing natural health products to Irish consumers such as Danone Actimel and Danone Activia. In effect Danone's entry into this segment has created an increased market for dairy products. Rather than competing with other companies for a market share Danone was instrumental in increasing the actual size of the market itself.

Danone Actimel was first launched on the Irish market in 1997. It introduced a totally new concept of 'probiotic yogurt drinks', claiming to assist beneficial bacteria. It contains a culture which it calls L. casei immunitas, advertised to improve the body's intestinal balance of beneficial bacteria. As such it is strongly positioned within the natural health segment and appeals to consumers looking for a healthy lifestyle.

Bringing new nutritional benefits to the children's segment. The Danone Gervais range, which includes Danone Gervais Baby and Danone Gervais Toddler, is positioned in the children's segment. Danone Gervais, as a dairy food, is specifically formulated to meet babies' nutritional needs from the age of four months and is available as a fromage frais and yogurt drink.

Delivering important nutrients to the diet segment. Danone Vitalinea is a range of fat-free yogurts enriched with six essential vitamins, fibre, calcium and phosphorous. Because dieting can result in the loss of important nutrients, Danone Vitalinea has been promoted as an agent to replenish important lost nutrients, in a tasty format in both yogurt and adult fromage frais. Danone's entry into Ireland acted as a key driver of growth within the overall fresh dairy market due to its heavy emphasis on probiotic yogurts and yogurt drinks. Not only has Danone driven an increase in focus on the health benefits of yogurt, the activities of Danone have rejuvenated interest in the whole fresh dairy market.

Danone is changing Irish consumer attitudes towards the fresh dairy market. It has injected growth into what was a slowly growing market through the provision of a variety of high-quality, tasty brands with health benefits specifically tailored to consumer needs. This has led the Irish consumer to reappraise yogurt, look for additional health benefits from products, and increase their overall consumption of fresh dairy products in general.

Source: adapted from www.Business2000.ie/cases

CASE STUDY: BORD BIA (IRISH FOOD BOARD) CHANGING GLOBAL CONSUMERS' ATTITUDES TO IRISH FOOD AND DRINK

Bord Bia was established by the Irish government for the strategic market development and promotion of Irish food and drink. It works with the Irish food, drinks and horticultural industries to increase sales and exports by promoting Irish companies abroad and attracting overseas buyers to buy Irish produce. Bord Bia provides invaluable information for marketers while proactively responding to significant market issues affecting the industry. Its objective is to bring the taste of Irish food to more tables worldwide, by positively influencing attitudes towards, and knowledge of, Irish food, drink and horticulture among consumer and trade buyers in target markets.

The face of the food industry in Ireland is changing. Personal health and wellbeing continues to be a dominant driver affecting consumer choice. The belief that 'You are what you eat' has become widely accepted. In the past, food was simply for sustenance or for enjoyment. Consumers now accept that many food items not only maintain good health, but also help reduce the risk, or delay the onset, of certain diseases such as cardiovascular disease and cancer. Today, food is recognised as a key determinant of one's overall physical and emotional wellbeing.

Consumers are demanding more knowledge about the products they consume. *Traceability*, the ability of consumers to trace a product such as meat from the farm on which it was first produced, through the processing, distribution and retail stages, and to the table — can instil confidence so that Irish food and drink products can be enjoyed to the fullest when being consumed. Increasing levels of sophistication in consumer tastes and demands have raised consumer expectations of quality and variety to premium standard and indulgence. Probably the most important factor leading to the growth in premium and indulgent products has been the increase in disposable income and accompanied economic growth since the early 1990s. At the same time, falling average household sizes and changes in work patterns also contributed to growth in premium and indulgent food and drinks markets.

Small speciality food producers have capitalised on this trend by focusing on the more discerning consumer who prioritises quality, authenticity and taste. The food industry continues to explore new markets which will help position Ireland's food and drink industry as innovative, progressive and of high quality in the minds of international buyers and consumers. Another noticeable consumer trend has been the demand for quick options. Consumers have increasingly busy lives with little time to prepare food from scratch. Ready-prepared ingredients and ready-to-eat foods are now in huge demand. Bord Bia market research found snacking is an accepted part of eating habits with almost ninety per cent of Irish consumers agreeing that they regularly treat themselves to snacks. Bord Bia monitors consumer trends, and keeping up to date with the market is crucial in its role of assisting Irish companies to compete in global markets.

As part of Bord Bia's marketing strategy, its marketing plan includes responding to changes in the marketplace and to new consumer trends:

The Food Island — Bord Bia promotes Irish food and drink under the banner 'Ireland: The Food Island'. Europe-wide research has shown that although Ireland is well known for its people and for its landscape there is little association between Ireland and food in the mind of the trade buyer or consumer. 'Ireland: The Food Island' is a strategic marketing concept developed to make this connection.

Development of new markets — China and India are creating new dynamic markets, due to very large populations and rapidly rising incomes. This is resulting in an increased demand for food and drink that cannot be filled by indigenous production. In 2005, Irish food and drink exports to China, including Hong Kong, reached a value of €53.5m, an increase of 84 per cent on 2004 levels. The opportunities in the Chinese market are mainly for dairy, food ingredients, alcoholic beverages and meat. There are numerous challenges, however, facing Irish food and drink exporters. The industry has to face an increasingly competitive trading environment. Exporters must be able to adapt to the challenges to ensure continued growth for the industry and the economy as a whole.

Market research — it is imperative for Irish companies planning to export to carefully analyse the market they hope to break into. The same applies to existing firms that want to introduce new products. Market-gap analysis allows firms to focus on what is not being produced. Careful market research should enable firms to recognise new consumer trends, spot a gap in the market, and tailor products to meet that demand.

Packaging, pricing, etc. — Irish companies must be innovative when presenting their products. A marketing mix that will maximise sales and profits should be created. Packaging in particular provides ample opportunities for creating added-value products. Pricing in the drinks market is extremely competitive. In the water market, Irish companies are introducing innovative pack sizes and packaging formats such as pouch packs. Commercial success depends on reliable information and the right contacts. Bord Bia employs a range of services for exporters. These services help to put Irish companies in touch with potential buyers and also inform them of global market trends.

Market information and research — Bord Bia helps companies by providing market information and original market research. Foresight4FOOD is an initiative to encourage Irish companies to market-test new product concepts and improve their prospects of success once launched in the marketplace.

Trade shows — Bord Bia organises Irish company participation at international trade fairs under the 'Ireland: The Food Island' umbrella branding. Bord Bia is responsible for the stand design, construction, trade receptions and pre-marketing of events to key buyers.

Advertising/marketing — Bord Bia carries out generic advertising campaigns, retail and food service promotions, media relations and other promotional activities to support and raise the profile of Irish food and drink in domestic and overseas markets. The advertising aims to reinforce 'Ireland: The Food Island' as a source of high-quality natural products.

Relationship building and corporate hospitality platforms — Bord Bia has sponsored many prestigious events, including the 2006 Ryder Cup golf classic in County Kildare. This event, one of the top three events in the world sporting calendar, reached an international viewership estimated at one billion. Bord Bia sponsorship raises the profile of 'Ireland: The Food Island', attracting key international buyers while showcasing the best of Irish food, drink, and horticulture.

ICT — the Bord Bia Client portal is a closed user group (extranet) website available to all Irish food and drink manufacturers. It provides 24-hour online access to Bord

Bia material. The Bord Bia producer website provides up-to-date information and statistics on cattle, pig and lamb trades in major markets and is available by subscription.

Mentoring/introductions, etc. — Bord Bia has an extensive in-depth knowledge of the Irish food and drink industry. It can provide companies with details of exports, production, quality standards, health regulations and controls, and new developments in the industry. It acts as a bridge, putting Irish companies in touch with companies appropriate to their areas of interest. For small business and speciality food companies, Bord Bia provides a mentoring programme focusing on the British market.

Brand forum — brands provide an opportunity for companies to differentiate themselves in competitive markets. A brand is a characteristic trademark that helps to identify a particular product. The Bord Bia Brand Forum meets four times a year to help Irish companies develop and promote their brands. These include workshops, publications, study tours and mentoring.

In conclusion, the global food and drinks industry is so dynamic that up-to-date market knowledge and information is crucial. Irish companies hoping to break into global markets can greatly benefit from the services provided by Bord Bia, which can help existing exporters to foster new contacts and expand business.

Source: www.business2000.ie/cases

Questions for Review

1. What are attitudes, and what functions do they serve?
2. Describe how attitudes towards products or services are formed.
3. What are the advantages and disadvantages of featuring celebrities in advertising messages?
4. What roles do source, message, context and repetition play in influencing consumer attitudes?

7

Consumer Decision Processes

CHAPTER OBJECTIVES

After reading this chapter you should be able to:

- Identify levels of consumer decision making.
- Describe the stages in the consumer decision-making process.
- Discuss models of consumer decision making.
- Recognise an impulse purchase situation.
- Explain relationship marketing.

CONSUMER DECISION MAKING

What makes a consumer decide to purchase a packet of Tayto as opposed to Pringles or Walkers? What factors in the decision process cause a consumer to purchase one brand of mobile phone rather than another? These are the kinds of questions pursued by the traditional consumer-behaviour area of study known as *consumer decision making*. Consumer decision making encompasses all the processes consumers go through in recognising problems, searching for solutions and choosing among purchase options. As illustrated in Chapter 2, consumers may have a high or low involvement in their decision processes.

The consumer decision process generally begins when the consumer identifies a consumption problem that needs to be solved, for example, 'I need a new mobile phone' or 'I'd like a new car'. A consumer purchase, therefore, is a response to a problem. *Problem recognition* is the perceived difference between an ideal and an actual state. This is a critical stage in the decision process because it motivates the consumer into action.

The *ideal state* is the way consumers would like a situation to be (e.g. having a top-of-the-range mobile phone or an excellent car). The *actual state* is the real situation as perceived by consumers now. Problem recognition occurs if consumers become aware of a discrepancy between the actual state and the ideal state (e.g., 'My mobile phone is too old', or 'My car looks old-fashioned'). The greater the discrepancy between the actual and ideal state, and the higher the level of motivation, ability and opportunity, the more likely the consumer is to act. When consumers do not perceive a problem their motivation to act will be low.

Once a problem has been recognised, consumers need adequate information to resolve it. *Information search* is the process by which the consumer surveys his or her environment for appropriate data to make a reasonable decision. Typically, the next step is *internal search*. Each consumer has stored in their memory a range of information, feelings and past experiences that can be recalled when making a decision. Because consumers have a limited capacity or ability to process information, and because memory traces can decline over time, consumers are likely to recall only a small subset of stored information when they engage in internal search. Generally, consumers recall four types of information: (a) brands; (b) attributes; (c) evaluations; and (d) experiences.

Recall of Brands

The set of brands that consumers recall from memory whenever problem recognition has been stimulated is an important aspect of internal search that greatly affects decision making. Rather than remembering all available brands in any given situation, consumers tend to recall a subset of two to eight brands known as a *consideration* or *evoked set*. Someone buying bottled water might ordinarily consider Ballygowan or Tipperary rather than any other brand. During 2005, carbonated drinks were the most popular sector in the soft drinks category, with instantly recognisable brands like Coca-Cola and 7Up being particularly prominent with Irish consumers (www.euromonitor.com).

In general, the consideration set consists of brands that you think of 'off the top of your head' or are easy to remember when making a decision. People form preferences for a favourite brand and they may never change their minds in the course of a lifetime. Many people tend to buy the same brand every time they go to the supermarket. This consistent pattern is often due to *inertia*, as a brand is bought out of habit merely because less effort is required (see Chapter 2). Successful organisations also realise that branding is not a once-off project or initiative but rather a way of doing business.

EXAMPLE: XTRA-VISION BUILDS ON ITS STRONG BRAND RECOGNITION

Xtra-vision has been operating in Ireland for more than 20 years. Today, Xtra-vision is owned by Blockbuster Inc. and Viacom, one of the world's largest entertainment and media companies. When Blockbuster acquired Xtra-vision, it retained the Xtra-vision name due to its strong brand recognition in the Irish market place.

When Xtra-vision started business in Ireland it operated in the 'video rental' market, concentrating on VHS videos and a limited product portfolio. If Xtra-vision had continued to perceive its market as the narrow 'video rental' market it would have failed to take advantage of the broader opportunities evolving in the home entertainment industry and thus would have fallen foul of what is termed 'marketing myopia'. Today Xtra-vision has the largest share of the home entertainment market in Ireland due to its successful adaptation to market trends. Xtra-vision has experienced rapid growth and diversification. The home entertainment market in Ireland is changing and developing. Xtra-vision has grown from a movie rental company to a total home entertainment company, providing movies and games to buy, phones, and a broad range of electronics products. The core objective of Xtra-vision's marketing strategy is to make the company 'the one-stop shop for all entertainment needs'. The Irish market is strong, with average rentals per month twice that of the UK.

The continued development of the Xtra-vision brand, signified by its familiar yellow and red logo, is a core component of Xtra-vision's marketing strategy. The Xtra-vision brand has 97 per cent recognition in the Irish marketplace. Regular market research is carried out to measure brand recall, recognition and general attributes attached to the Xtra-vision brand. The Xtra-vision brand is promoted through effective communication by advertising, promotion, and through its website. The overall brand name and image is continuously strengthened by the company's commitment to customer service and guaranteed quality.

Source: adapted from www.business2000.ie/cases

Recall of Attributes

Consumers access only a small portion of the information stored in memory during internal search. Often consumers cannot remember specific facts about a product or service because personal memory of details decreases over time. Nevertheless, consumers can often recall *some* details when they engage in internal search, and the recalled attribute information can strongly influence their brand choices. Some of the variables which influence the recall of attribute information in the information search and decision-making processes include:

Accessibility or Availability

Information that is more accessible or available is the most likely to be recalled and entered into the decision process. Marketers can make information more accessible by repeatedly drawing attention to it in marketing communications or by making the information more relevant. Tesco advertisements repeatedly stress low prices with the slogan 'every little helps', hoping that consumers will remember this attribute when they decide to shop.

Diagnostic information

This helps consumers distinguish objects from one another. If all brands of mobile phones are the same price, then price is not diagnostic, or useful, in making a decision. On the other hand, if prices vary, consumers can distinguish between them, so the information is diagnostic. Interestingly, negative information tends to be more diagnostic than information that is positive or neutral, because the former is usually more distinctive. In other words, because most brands are associated with positive attributes, negative information makes it easier to categorise the brand as different from other brands. In addition, marketers can identify which attributes tend to be more diagnostic for a particular product or service category and try to gain a competitive advantage on one or more of these attributes. Marks and Spencer, for example, created the Per Una range of clothing specifically aimed at younger women and they use this image to send out a more contemporary message to this market segment.

Vividness

Vivid information is presented as concrete words, pictures, or instructions to imagine (e.g. imagine yourself on a tropical beach), or through word-of-mouth communication. Vivid information is easier to recall than less dramatic information but tends to influence judgement and decision making only when consumers have not formed a strong prior evaluation, especially one that is negative.

Recall of Evaluations

Because memory of specific details declines rapidly over time, overall evaluations or attitudes (that is; likes and dislikes) are easier to remember than specific attribute information. In addition, evaluations tend to form strong associative links with the brand; this is why it is important for a company to encourage positive consumer attitudes toward its brands. Barry's Tea, for example, with its series of advertisements aimed at 'turning the moment golden', aim to rekindle happy memories of times past.

EXAMPLE: BUILT TO LAST — THE VALUE OF CONVICTION, CONSISTENCY AND LONG-TERM STRATEGY IN BRAND BUILDING

Brands give businesses a competitive edge, create profit, and must be taken seriously in the boardroom if companies want to succeed. Patrick Rigney, Chairman of the Bord Bia Brand Forum, suggested that, 'In an increasingly competitive environment, brands are wealth generators and critical for success. Branding is a way of doing business that involves mental strength, passion and conviction. In order to succeed, you and your team have to be clear where the company is going and deliver on that work plan.'

Greg Butler, Financial and Marketing Director of Barry's Tea, believes that 'Quality combined with the Irish emotional attachment to tea and tea drinking has kept us successful. We have consistently used "Golden Moments" to communicate in a way that Irish consumers can relate to.' He added that customer loyalty to Irish tea and in particular to Barry's tea was so strong that Lipton, the world's largest tea brand, was unable to penetrate the market here when Lipton was introduced in Ireland in the 1990s. Quality has been at the centre of Barry's Tea since its foundation in 1901. It held 14 per cent of the national tea market before it changed its business model from retail to wholesale. Today, Barry's Tea accounts for 37 per cent of all tea sales in Ireland and has an annual turnover of €31m. The company began advertising only in 1985.

Source: adapted from: www.bordbia.ie

Recall of Experiences

Internal search can involve the recall of experiences in the form of specific images and the effect associated with them. If a consumer, for example, has an experience with a product or service that is either unusually positive or unusually negative, he or she is likely to recall these vivid experiences later. Furthermore, if a consumer repeatedly has a positive experience with a product or service, it will be easier to recall these experiences through that product or service.

EXTERNAL SEARCH: SEARCHING FOR INFORMATION FROM THE ENVIRONMENT

Sometimes a consumer's decision can be based entirely on information recalled from memory. At other times, information is missing or some uncertainty surrounds the recalled information. Then consumers engage in *external search* of outside sources such as dealers, friends or relations, published sources (magazines or books), advertisements, the Internet or the product's package. Consumers use external search to collect additional information about which brands are available, as well as the attributes and benefits associated with brands in the consideration set.

Two types of external search are pre-purchase search and ongoing search. Pre-purchase search occurs in response to the activation of problem recognition. Consumers seeking to buy a new car, for example, can get information by visiting dealers, visiting websites, checking quality rankings, talking to friends and reading consumer reports. *Ongoing search* occurs on a regular and continual basis, even when problem recognition is not activated. A consumer may consistently read car magazines, visit car websites and go to car shows because of a high degree of enduring involvement in cars.

For either pre-purchase or ongoing search, consumers can acquire information from five major categories of external sources:

1. *Retailer search*: visits or calls to shops or dealers, including the examination of package information or pamphlets about brands.
2. *Media search*: information from advertising, online advertisements, manufacturer-sponsored websites, and other types of marketer-produced communications.
3. *Interpersonal search*: advice from friends, relations, neighbours and/or other consumers, including those on chat lines.
4. *Independent search*: contact with independent sources of information, such as books, government pamphlets or magazines.
5. *Experiential search*: the use of product samples, product/service trials (such as a test drive), or experiencing the product online.

Internet Sources

The Internet has dramatically altered the way consumers shop and search for information. Without ever having to leave their homes, consumers can have access to almost any type of information they need to make their purchase decisions. Search engines such as Google and Yahoo allow easy access to information through the use of keywords. Consumers can now use the Internet to access information from all five of the sources mentioned above. Sometimes consumers search for specific information; at other times they simply browse.

The Internet makes it easy for consumers to share information in an *online community*. People with a common interest or condition related to a product or service can converse with each other via electronic message boards, chat lines, and other methods. An increasing number of retailers and manufacturers are tracking consumers' online information-search and purchase patterns to provide additional assistance. Consumers, for example, who examine or buy products from Amazon.com can see related or similar items by clicking on a button that says, 'Customers who bought this product also bought ...'

As more consumers shop on the Internet, search activity may increase because online sources are very convenient. Nevertheless, information search can vary widely from a simple hunt for one or two pieces of information to a very extensive search relying on many sources.

The information that consumers acquire during an external search plays a crucial role in influencing the consumers' judgements and decision making. When searching external sources, consumers usually acquire information about brand name, price and other attributes.

Brand Name

The brand name is the most frequently accessed type of information because it is a central node around which other information can be organised in memory. When consumers know the brand name, they can immediately activate other relevant nodes. If consumers, for example, know the brand name is Jacob's or McVitie's, they can draw on a wealth of prior knowledge and associations.

EXAMPLE: MCVITIE'S MOMENTS

In April 2006, McVitie's set about invigorating the special treats segment of the biscuit market with the launch of a new sub-brand: McVitie's Moments. The launch of McVitie's Moments saw the brand entering the special treats biscuit segment, currently growing by over 16.5 per cent year on year in value terms. As a brand, McVitie's has the scale to unlock the opportunity within the special treats sector, which currently attracts 56 per cent of the Irish population. With Moments, McVitie's leveraged the heritage of the McVitie's brand to accelerate growth in this sector and supported this through investment in-store while a heavyweight marketing campaign including television.

Source: adapted from www.checkout.ie

Price

Consumers search for price information because it can be used to decide about other attributes such as quality and value. The search for price, however, can be less important than marketers believe, due to the low overall extent of the search for some products. In 2006, German discounter rivals Lidl and Aldi, however, increased their market share to the highest level since entering the Irish market. The discounters had a combined market share of 6.7 per cent, with Lidl ahead at 4.2 per cent and Aldi at 2.5 per cent (www.retailnews.ie).

Other Attributes

After searching for brand name and price, consumers will search for additional information depending on which attributes are important to them. Consumers are more likely to access information that is relevant to their goals. If, for example, an action holiday was a major goal when choosing a two-week holiday, a consumer would typically collect information about a location's available activities, nightlife and local events.

THE CONSUMER DECISION-MAKING PROCESS

Consumer decision making consists of a series of five stages:

1. problem recognition
2. information search
3. evaluation of alternatives
4. purchase decision
5. post-purchase behaviour.

In the problem-recognition stage, consumers recognise that they have a need for something. One goal of advertising, of course, is to cause consumers to recognise a problem. An organisation's marketing activities are a direct attempt to reach, inform and persuade consumers to buy and use its products. These inputs into the consumer's decision-making process take the form of specific marketing-mix strategies that consist of the product itself (including its package, size and guarantees), pricing policy, all promotional efforts, and the selection of distribution channels to move the product from the manufacturer to the consumer.

If the need is sufficiently strong, it may motivate the person to enter the second stage of the consumer decision-making process: the search for information. The search for information can be either extensive or limited, depending on the involvement level of the consumer (high or low involvement). The degree of perceived risk can influence this stage of the decision process. In high-risk situations, consumers are likely to engage in complex and extensive information search and evaluation. In low-risk situations, consumers are likely to use very simple or limited search and evaluation tactics. A number of factors are likely to increase the search for information. These include: *product factors* (price, much variation in features, frequent changes in product styling); *situational factors* (first-time purchase, no past experience because the product is new); *demographic characteristics of the consumer* (well-educated, high income); *social acceptability* (the purchase is for a gift, the product is socially visible); and *value-related considerations* (purchase is discretionary rather than necessary, other options have both desirable and undesirable consequences, the purchase involves ecological considerations).

In the third stage, consumers evaluate the alternatives they have identified for solving their problem. The evaluation of alternatives includes the formation of attitudes regarding the alternatives (see Chapter 6). The criteria consumers use to evaluate alternative products are usually expressed in terms of important product attributes. When a company knows that consumers will be evaluating alternatives, it sometimes advertises in a way that recommends the criteria that consumers should use in assessing product or service options. When consumers compare or evaluate different brands or models of a product they reach a decision on the one that just feels, looks, or performs 'right'. Research shows that when consumers discuss such 'right products', there is little or no mention of price or brand names. The product often reflects personality characteristics or childhood experiences and it is often 'love at first sight'.

Choice is the fourth stage of the process. At this stage, consumers decide which action to select (e.g. which brand to choose, whether to spend or save, or from which store to purchase the product). Consumers make three types of purchase: *trial purchases, repeat purchases* and *long-term commitment purchases*. When a consumer purchases a product for the first time and buys a smaller quantity than usual, this purchase would be considered a trial. A trial, therefore, is the exploratory phase of purchase behaviour in which consumers attempt to evaluate a product through direct use. Consumers can also be encouraged to try a new product through such promotional tactics as free samples, coupons or sale prices.

When a new brand in an established product category (e.g. biscuits, cakes or chocolate) is found by trial to be more satisfactory or better than other brands, consumers are likely to repeat the purchase. Repeat purchase behaviour is closely related to the concept of *brand loyalty*, which most organisations try to encourage because it contributes to greater stability in the marketplace. Gateaux, for example, is the number one selling cake brand in Ireland. Old favourites such as Gateaux Swiss roll and Gateaux logs are constant big sellers, as are Gateaux sponge cakes, trifle sponges, queen cakes and Battenbergs. This brand loyalty has allowed Gateaux to successfully introduce a premium range of luxury Swiss rolls to complement their existing Swiss roll collection; these are available in two flavours: chocolate and raspberry (www.checkout.ie).

Unlike trial, in which the consumer uses the product on a small scale and without any commitment, a repeat purchase usually signifies that the product meets with the consumer's approval and that he or she is willing to use it again and in larger quantities.

Finally, in the post-purchase stage consumers consume and use the product or service they have acquired. They also evaluate the outcomes of the consequences of their behaviour and engage in the ultimate disposal of the waste resulting from the purchase. As consumers use a product, particularly during a trial purchase, they evaluate its performance in light of their own expectations. There are three possible outcomes of these evaluations:

1. actual performance matches expectations, leading to a neutral feeling
2. performance exceeds expectations, leading to satisfaction
3. performance is below expectations, leading to dissatisfaction.

An important component of post-purchase evaluation is the reduction of any uncertainty or doubt the consumer might have about the selection. As part of their post-purchase analysis, consumers try to reassure themselves that their choice was a wise one. Consumers attempt to reduce *post-purchase dissonance* or *post-purchase conflict*. They may do this by rationalising the decision as being wise; they may seek advertisements that support their choice and may avoid those of competing brands; they may attempt to persuade friends or family to buy the same brand; or they may turn to other satisfied owners for reassurance.

The degree of post-purchase analysis that consumers undertake depends on the importance of the product decision and the experience acquired in using the product. When the product lives up to expectations, consumers will probably buy it again. The consumer's post-purchase evaluation acts as *experience* and serves to influence future related decisions. When the product's performance is disappointing or does not meet expectations, however, consumers will search for a more suitable option.

MODELS OF CONSUMER DECISION MAKING

From the late eighteenth century through to much of the 1970s, researchers viewed the consumer decision-making process as a linear procedure, as described above. In the late 1970s, however, researchers began to question the concept that all consumer purchases result from a careful analytical process. Some suggested that in many instances consumers do not engage in any deliberate decision making at all prior to making a purchase (Mowen & Minor 1997). It was also recognised that many consumer behaviours do not involve only the purchase of goods, such as cars and cereals. Consumers also buy experiences in the form of services such as holidays, concerts, cinema tickets, books and art. Given the limitations of the traditional consumer decision process, researchers have proposed alternative decision-making models that place different emphases on each of the stages identified above. The term *models of consumer decision making* refers to a wider view or perspective on how and why individuals behave as they do. Four well-known models of consumers may be examined as follows.

Economic Model

This model, called the *economic man theory,* portrays the consumer as making rational decisions. The model has been criticised by consumer researchers for a number of reasons. To behave rationally in the economic sense, a consumer would have to: (a) be aware of all available product options; (b) be capable of correctly ranking each option in terms of its advantages and disadvantages; and (c) be able to identify the *one* best option. Realistically, however, consumers rarely have all of the information or sufficiently accurate information or even an adequate degree of involvement or motivation to make the so-called 'perfect' decision.

It has also been argued that the economic model of an all-rational consumer is unrealistic on the grounds that consumers are limited by (a) their existing skills, habits and reflexes; (b) their existing values and goals; and (c) the extent of their knowledge (Simon 1965). Consumers operate in an imperfect world in which they do not maximise their decisions in terms of economic considerations, such as price–quantity relationships. A consumer is generally unwilling to engage in extensive decision-making activities and will settle instead for a 'satisfactory' decision, one that is 'good enough'. For this reason the economic model is often rejected as too idealistic and simplistic.

Passive Model

Quite opposite to the rational economic model of consumers is the passive model, which depicts the consumer as basically submissive to the interests and promotional efforts of marketers. In the passive model, consumers are perceived as impulsive and irrational purchasers. The main limitation of the passive model is that it fails to recognise that the consumer plays an equal, if not dominant, role in many buying situations — sometimes by seeking information about product alternatives and selecting the product that appears to offer the greatest satisfaction, and at other times by impulsively selecting a product that satisfies the mood or emotion of the moment. Research on consumer motivation, attitudes, communication and selective perception, however, support the proposition that consumers are rarely objects of manipulation. The passive model, therefore, regarding the simple and single-minded view that consumers are ready to yield to the aims of marketers, should also be rejected as unrealistic.

Cognitive Model

The third model portrays the consumer as a *thinking problem solver.* Within this model, consumers are frequently pictured as either receptive to or actively searching for products and services that fulfil their needs and enrich their lives. The cognitive model focuses on the processes by which consumers seek and evaluate information about selected brands and retail outlets.

In the context of the cognitive model, consumers are viewed as information processors. Information processing leads to the formation of preferences, before purchase intentions are formed. The cognitive model also recognises that the consumer is unlikely even to attempt to obtain all available information about every choice. Instead, consumers are likely to cease their information-seeking efforts when they perceive that they have sufficient information about some of the alternatives to make a 'satisfactory' decision.

The cognitive model describes a consumer who falls somewhere between the extremes of the economic and passive models, who does not (or cannot) have total knowledge about available product choices, and therefore cannot make *perfect* decisions, but who nonetheless actively seeks information and attempts to make *satisfactory* decisions.

Emotional Model

Consumers are likely to associate deep feelings or emotions, such as joy, fear, love, hope, fantasy, and even a little magic, with certain purchases or possessions. Rather than carefully searching, deliberating and evaluating alternatives before buying, consumers are likely to make many purchases on impulse, on a whim, or because they are emotionally driven.

When a consumer makes what is basically an emotional purchase decision, less emphasis is placed on the search for pre-purchase information. Instead, more emphasis is placed on current mood and feelings. This is not to say that emotional decisions are irrational. Buying products, for example, that afford emotional satisfaction is a perfectly rational consumer decision. Some emotional decisions are conveyed in expressions such as 'you deserve it' or 'treat yourself'. Research by Bord Bia illustrates that Irish consumers are 'always on for a quick treat that allows them to shoehorn some more "me-time" into their hectic day'. Current Irish treats include Baileys Minis, Lily O'Brien's chocolate, Butler's cafés and Wild Orchard Smoothies (www.bordbia.ie).

Consumers' *moods* are also important to decision making. A mood can be defined as a 'feeling state' or state of mind (Gardner 1985).

Unlike an emotion, which is a response to a particular environment, a mood is more typically an unfocused, pre-existing state — already present at the time a consumer 'experiences' an advertisement, a retail environment, a brand or a product. In comparison with emotions, moods are generally lower in intensity and longer lasting and are not as directly coupled as emotions with action tendencies and explicit actions.

Moods appear to be important to consumer decision making, because they impact on *when* consumers shop, *where* they shop, and *whether* they shop alone or with others. Some retailers attempt to create a mood for consumers, even though consumers enter the store with a pre-existing mood. Research suggests that a store's image or atmosphere can affect shoppers' moods; in turn, shoppers' moods can influence how long they stay in the store, as well as other behaviour that retailers wish to encourage (Smith & Sherman 1993). In general, consumers in a positive mood recall more information about a product than consumers in a negative mood.

Impulse Purchases

An *impulse purchase* is defined as a 'buying action undertaken without a problem previously having been consciously recognised or a buying intention formed prior to entering the store' (Rook 1987). Impulse buying, therefore, is a sudden, powerful, persistent and unplanned urge to buy something immediately, without much regard for the consequences. An impulse purchase may be described as a choice made on the spur of the moment based on the development of a strong positive feeling regarding an object. Such purchases happen when the consumer encounters a product, processes the information about it, and reacts with an extremely strong positive affect. These positive feelings lead to a desire to experience the product or service, which results in a purchase. Impulse purchases are often instigated by the consumer's exposure to an external stimulus, such as an in-store display, catalogue or a television advertisement with a phone number.

To cater to such urges, so-called *impulse items* such as chocolate, sweets and chewing gum are conveniently placed near checkouts. Similarly, many supermarkets have installed wider aisles to encourage browsing, and the widest tend to contain products with the highest profit margins. Low mark-up items that are purchased regularly tend to be stacked high in narrower aisles to allow shopping trolleys to speed through. Eye-level and eye-catching displays, including end-of-aisle displays, electronic bulletin boards and blinking lights, can increase sales dramatically — mostly from impulse purchasers. Irish consumers spend €590 million each year on chocolate and sugar confectionery. Nine out of ten people in Ireland enjoy confectionery, with average consumption standing at 14.5kg per person, including 8.8kg of chocolate and 5.7kg of sugar confectionery. The market breaks down into single bars — 50 per cent; take-home — 29 per cent; and gifts — 21 per cent. The key drivers for confectionery sales are location — where it is located in-store; space — how much space is allocated; variety — the choice on offer; and tempting displays — because many confectionery purchases are made on impulse (www.retailernews.ie).

EXAMPLE: SUBTLETY IS THE KEY TO UNLOCKING BRAND POWER

Have you ever had the experience of returning from a day of shopping with something that you hadn't planned to buy? If you didn't really want or need it, have you ever wondered why you decided to purchase it? This illustrates brand power — otherwise referred to as 'impulse purchasing'. Marketing teams all over the world develop and exploit this capability of a brand regularly to ensure they reach their sales targets. Marketing teams are generally so sure that we will fall prey to our impulses that entire marketing strategies are often devised around building brand power to ensure impulse purchasing behaviour. Marketing teams develop a brand that people want to own and be associated with and, as a result, they happily purchase these brands because they believe the product being purchased will improve their lives.

Typically, a person sees an average of 4,000 marketing messages every day, all promoting products and brand images. We are also constantly bombarded with subliminal branding messages, through a variety of means, which aim to reinforce the image we have of these products. But what is it that makes a particular brand appeal to us? A brand utilises a variety of means to relate to potential customers on a personal level, and brand managers will endeavour to portray a desirable image that people will aspire to. Whether it is sex appeal, health, luxury or indulgence, a powerful brand can subconsciously trigger an emotional reaction in the potential purchaser. This is often enough to tempt a customer.

Shopping as a branding experience in Ireland has changed dramatically over the past twenty years. In the 1980s, individuals had less disposable cash and were more price-sensitive than brand-aware. In those days, the hard sales approach, including bright neon signs and pushy sales people, was used to encourage consumers to buy. Today, however, people are more cash-rich and they want a more subtle approach when it comes to shopping. They prefer the soft sell and a 'less is more' approach from brands. Subtlety is favoured. For example, a Raymond Weil watch speaks volumes but is not brash or ostentatious. In an increasingly image-conscious Ireland, customers have also become captivated with designer brands, reflecting how we feel about ourselves and the lifestyle we want to project to our friends, family and environment. Male consumers think nothing of splashing out on a suit from Louis Copeland or Burberry cufflinks, while women purchase Jimmy Choo shoes and Hermès handbags as if they were a necessity.

It is also important to point out, however, that customers do not, sheeplike, blindly follow crowd trends. Consumers are now increasingly aware of but more resilient to brands, so brand managers have, in turn, responded to this and developed newer, more creative and, more important, less obvious ways to capture our interest.

Source: adapted from P. Kinsley, Sunday Business Post, *28 May 2006, p. 22.*

RELATIONSHIP MARKETING

Many organisations have established *relationship marketing* programmes (sometimes called *loyalty programmes*) to foster usage loyalty and commitment to their products and services. The aim of relationship marketing is to create strong, lasting relationships with a core group of consumers. The emphasis is on developing *long-term bonds* with consumers by making them feel good about how the company interacts (or does business) with them and by giving them some kind of personal connection to the business. A true relationship marketing programme is more than simply the use of database marketing tactics to improve targeting of consumers: instead, the consumer must believe that he or she has received something for being a participant in the relationship. Relationship marketing offers loyal consumers special services, discounts and increased communications. Although directing marketing, sales promotion and general advertising may be used as part of a relationship marketing strategy, relationship marketing stresses long-term commitment to the individual consumer. Advances in technology (such as scanning equipment and relational databases) have provided techniques that make tracking consumers simpler, thus influencing the trend toward relationship marketing. *Database marketing* involves tracking consumers' buying habits very closely and crafting products and messages tailored precisely to people's wants and needs based on this information. In a positive vein, organisations have been finding that the Internet is an inexpensive, efficient and more productive way to extend customer services. This has resulted in a new phrase 'permission marketing'. This is the art of asking consumers if they would like to receive a targeted email advertisement, promotion, or message *before* it appears in their inbox.

Relationship marketing programmes have been used in a wide variety of product and service categories. Many organisations call their relationship programme a club, and some even charge a fee to join. Membership of a club may serve as a means of conveying to consumers the notions of permanence and exclusivity in a committed relationship. Airlines and major hotel chains, in particular, use relationship marketing techniques by awarding points to frequent consumers that can be used to obtain additional goods or services from the company. Ultimately, it is to an organisation's advantage to develop long-term relationships with existing consumers because it is easier and less expensive to make an additional sale to an existing consumer than to make a new sale to a new consumer.

Loyalty cards have been in operation in Ireland since 1993, when Superquinn introduced its SuperClub loyalty card scheme. This is regarded as having been the prototype for such schemes in Europe. Loyalty cards, however, did not expand until 1997, when Tesco Ireland introduced its Clubcard scheme. This was essentially a simple expansion of the same card used by Tesco in Britain. Dunnes Stores responded with the introduction of their own ValueClub scheme.

Why is relationship marketing so important? Research indicates that consumers today are less loyal than in the past, due to six main forces:

- abundance of choice
- availability of information
- entitlement: consumers repeatedly ask 'what have you done for me lately?'
- commoditisation: many products/services appear to be similar; nothing stands out
- insecurity: consumer financial problems reduce loyalty
- time scarcity: not enough time to be loyal.

These six forces result in consumer defections, complaints, cynicism, reduced affiliation, and greater price sensitivity (Schriver 1997). Consequently, successful relationship programmes that can retain consumers are a central part of a company's marketing programme.

CASE STUDY: AIB CUSTOMER RELATIONSHIP MANAGEMENT

The environment in which financial institutions operate has changed in recent years. It is now one of:

- increased competition
- growing product commoditisation
- diminishing margins.

Banking customers have also changed in recent years. Customers are more knowledgeable, sophisticated and assertive. They demand higher levels of customer service, are less loyal, and more inclined to switch to a competitor. Modern customers require flexibility in hours of operation, greater convenience, customisation, transparency, accessibility and control. Competition to attract new customers is very strong. Customer defection rates are higher than ever because of increased market competition. With so many different financial institutions to choose from, consumers can now demand better-quality services and more customised products from their banks. In this consumer economy, attracting and — crucially — keeping customers for the long term is a key challenge for all businesses.

In AIB, this has led to a shift in business focus from *transactional marketing* to *relationship marketing*. AIB Group employs approximately 25,000 people worldwide in more than 800 offices. AIB has approximately 1.5 million active customers. Maintaining an existing customer base, which has already chosen a particular business over its competitors, is an invaluable asset and an investment in the future of the business. Research shows that it costs far less to retain existing customers than to win new ones. AIB has access to information about its customers' financial history and their dealings with the bank, as well as demographic information. This information is updated regularly. Analysing this data can help the bank identify the customers' present and future financial needs. This deeper understanding of customers helps the bank provide solutions to meet individual customer needs.

What is customer relationship management?
Customer relationship management (CRM) is the term for a company-wide system used by businesses to seek, obtain and maintain customers. CRM helps businesses manage customer relationships in a more organised way. A successful CRM system involves all people, processes and information technology associated with marketing, sales and customer service. According to CRM consultants, 'The idea is to have the same information available to everyone in the company so that

every product or service need of the customer is met. CRM implies that everyone in the enterprise is focused on the customer.' AIB recognises that customers are the lifeblood of the business and that the way to protect and grow its customer base — and ultimately its profitability — is to build strong customer relationships through delivery of superior quality service and to meet customer needs better than the competition. The CRM approach adopted by AIB focuses on maximising value for the customer and the bank. Research has shown that the key drivers of customer loyalty are:

- positive staff attitude
- honesty, integrity and reliability
- proactive advice and delivery of promise
- consistent delivery of superior quality service
- simplicity and ease of doing business
- good after-sales service
- a fair and efficient complaints resolution policy.

AIB has approximately 1,500 relationship managers, each designated as the prime contact for an assigned group of customers. Relationship managers proactively contact customers and offer customised products and services in a timely manner. Understanding the customers' growing needs for choice, convenience, and an anytime/anywhere banking service, AIB provides access for customers to products and services through a number of other delivery channels such as the 24-hour call centre, Internet, and ATM network. The relationship managers, branch service staff, and call-centre staff have participated in CRM training and have developed their relationship and service skills to enhance their customer interactions. Accurate customer information is crucial to providing effective customer service. It is just as important to update customer information regularly as it is to collect the information in the first place. Quality customer information provides a better understanding of what each customer wants so that businesses can offer customers the right products and services, at the right time, through the right marketing channel. With poor-quality customer information, a business may miss out on the potential to add value both for customers and its own business.

As part of the CRM framework, AIB has set up a Business Intelligence Centre. A team of highly skilled analysts interpret customer information and distribute it to the appropriate relationship manager or business area for action. Their analysis of reported information focuses on key customer relationship management strategies, including:

- dynamic customer segmentation
- customer needs analysis
- customer retention
- customer value management
- customer contact programmes
- development of tailored propositions, encompassing the appropriate marketing mix.

Ongoing support and information for CRM is provided by weekly, monthly, and quarterly performance reports. Reports can help with day-to-day customer contact planning, encourage sharing of best practices and strengthen business performance. The success of AIB's CRM strategy is also measured by annual customer service research, market share research and annual results. Customers can now visit any branch and AIB customer service representatives can access customer information efficiently and securely. Customer service representatives can avoid double selling and offering unrelated products and services to customers. By listening and reacting to customers, businesses can develop customer-centric products and services based on customer wants, tailored to their needs. Through its relationship management programme, AIB maintains and builds on existing customer relationships, adds value by retaining clients and cross-sells products and services.

In conclusion, by developing and utilising an effective CRM system, AIB has positioned itself as a leading provider of quality financial products and services. AIB observed the changing financial services industry and changing customer attitudes, and adapted accordingly. It has been successful because AIB was flexible enough to change its overall business strategy. Staying abreast of current industry and market trends while focusing on customers, the most valuable asset of a company, is proving a smart way to stay ahead in business.

Source: adapted from www.business2000.ie/html/case_studies

CASE STUDY: CADBURY: A WHITE OPPORTUNITY, ADULT WHITE CHOCOLATE

Strong brands are very important in the chocolate confectionery market. Almost 80 per cent of chocolate purchases are made on impulse. Buyers generally decide quickly which confectionery product to buy, with almost half of purchase decisions made within ten seconds of arriving at the confectionery fixture in the retail outlet.

Strong branding of confectionery is therefore important, since consumers use brands and packaging to recognise familiar products quickly and to reduce possible risks in purchasing a newly launched brand. Chocolate confectioners recognise the importance of strong brands and spend more on advertising than any other food category. Such widespread marketing and advertising gives rise to numerous strong brands in the chocolate confectionery category. Its universal appeal encourages Irish consumers to purchase and eat more confectionery.

Chocolate confectionery is very much a part of everyday life in Ireland. We have the third highest per capita consumption of chocolate in the world at approximately 10kg of chocolate per annum and spend over €100 per person. Market estimates value the total Irish chocolate market at about €375 million, of which the white chocolate market segment is currently valued at €12 million, almost three per cent of the total chocolate market. This clearly represented an area for future growth. With proven levels of confectionery consumption, and growth opportunity in white chocolate, Cadbury identified a gap in the Irish market for a new white chocolate brand. Previously, white chocolate was targeted only at the children's market. The success of the previous launch in 2000 of Cadbury's Snowflake, a white chocolate bar covered in milk chocolate, encouraged the subsequent successful introduction of a mainstream white chocolate brand. Cadbury saw a further opportunity to create a very strong brand, the Cadbury Dream bar, with an adult market, thus capitalising on the growing appeal of white chocolate and the development of a new product category.

Market research also shows that women purchase almost two-thirds of all confectionery but eat just over half of what they buy themselves, as they are the gatekeepers when making purchasing decisions for the rest of the family. By targeting the gatekeeper with a new product the chances of a successful launch is increased. Within the female market, research shows an increasing preference for white chocolate. The white chocolate market is considered to offer significant potential for growth, especially within the impulse segment.

The technical development of Cadbury's Dream took place over four years and involved extensive use of consumer feedback. Market research carried out among chocolate consumers found that consumers associated a unique intimacy with white chocolate. The popularity of the product in market testing was attributed to several key features including flavour, sweetness, a creamy aftertaste and a melt-in-your-mouth texture. These identified features would later be incorporated into the product's brand image and advertising. The name for the new product was chosen following extensive market research in New Zealand. Research found that the name 'Dream' represented the characteristics that Cadbury wanted to reflect in the brand's personality so that it would appeal to the target market of women in the 25–34 age category.

A product's brand personality is a description of its characteristics in relation to the target market for the product. It assists marketers in developing suitable advertising and promotional campaigns for the product. In the case of Cadbury's Dream, the key elements of its brand personality were designed so that they would appeal to female consumers seeking style, confidence, sophistication and self-assuredness in their lifestyles.

The packaging for Cadbury's Dream was also determined by consumer research and influenced by the Cadbury's Dream brand personality. It was designed to fit with the product's image of being soft and indulgent and had a particular appeal among the female target market. Indeed the selected colours on the packaging of a combination of blue and white were used for their attractiveness, as reflecting indulgence to the female purchaser. Feedback described Dream as having a better chocolate taste, creamy, not as sweet, a better texture and more natural taste than other white chocolate. The research also found that white-chocolate buyers were more likely to spend more on chocolate and likely to buy blocks of chocolate more frequently. By acquiring an understanding of consumer intentions and attitudes toward a product, the Cadbury's marketing team gained a better understanding of Irish consumers' decision-making processes. This information would be used by Cadbury to convert a consumer who has an awareness of the brand to move to actual purchase.

For Cadbury it is important that its traditional image is retained, as there are benefits for the new products to be associated with traditional Cadbury's brand values that were developed over years (Cadbury's brand has been in existence since 1824). Research shows that colour recognition of purple is strongly associated with Cadbury and that the Cadbury logo has the highest recognition of any logo among popular consumer brands. This is part of a 'Choose Cadbury's' marketing strategy using the established 'glass and a half' corporate purple with flowing script that has become synonymous with Cadbury.

Cadbury's Dream was launched in the Irish market in February 2002. The advertising theme for the Cadbury's Dream product launch was 'All in a Cadbury's Dream'. The advertising strategy was developed around the brand personality of the product and it sought to appeal to female chocolate consumers in particular, to their tastes and desired lifestyles. This theme incorporated the characteristics of indulgence and luxury associated with the product. TV advertising ran across all the main channels. This was supported by a widespread outdoor campaign on billboards in prominent places and at train stations. Product trial and sampling programmes were run both before and after the launch. An extensive sampling programme was used before and during the launch to generate awareness and trial.

For Cadbury, innovation remains one of the key elements in the company's success, with new brands catering for changing tastes and lifestyles. Identifying these changes in taste and lifestyle and matching them with quality products with strong brand values will mean that new product development will continue to be an integral part of the Cadbury business strategy. There will also be further development of the Cadbury's Dream range.

Source: adapted from www.business2000.ie/cases

Questions for Review

1. Discuss the *internal* and *external* search processes a consumer may engage with when seeking information about a product or service.
2. Apply the stages of the consumer decision-making process to a product of your choice.
3. Compare and contrast the economic, passive, cognitive and emotional models of consumer decision making.
4. Discuss the implications of impulse purchases for marketers.
5. Relationship marketing is all about building trust between an organisation and its customers. Discuss.

8

Consumer Behaviour and Communication

CHAPTER OBJECTIVES

After reading this chapter you should be able to:

- Understand the components of communication.
- Explain barriers to communication.
- Trace the move from mass marketing communications.
- Discuss ethics and social responsibility in marketing communications.
- Describe the public relations function in an organisation.
- Explain the advertising function in the communication process.
- Describe how persuasive communications work.

COMPONENTS OF COMMUNICATION

Communication has been defined as *the transmission of a message from a sender to a receiver via a medium (or channel) of transmission* (Schiffman & Kanuk 2007). In relation to consumer behaviour, therefore, communications from marketers try to influence or persuade potential consumers by conveying a message. The components of communication consist of:

- sender (source)
- message
- channel (medium)
- receiver (consumer)
- feedback.

These five components are known as a *communication model*. Communication begins with a source of information that encodes and delivers a *message*. The message is delivered through some *medium* of transmission. This medium may be face-to-face, newspapers, journals, television, radio, cinema, billboards, telephone or the Internet. The characteristics of the medium influence the interpretation of the message as well as how its information is processed. Additionally, various characteristics of the audience such as age, personality, gender, intelligence and culture will influence how the message is received. Finally, consumers provide feedback to marketers on the message they have received by either buying or not buying the product or service.

Sender (Source)

The source of information can be a company, a salesperson, a celebrity or any person(s) transmitting a message. The characteristics of the source play an important role in influencing consumers' beliefs, particularly when they have a low involvement with the product or service. The term *source credibility* refers to the extent that a source is perceived to have expertise and trustworthiness. Source *expertise* refers to the extent of knowledge the source is perceived to have about the subject on which he or she is communicating. Source *trustworthiness* refers to the extent that the source is perceived to provide information in an unbiased and honest manner.

EXAMPLE: DUNNES STORES SIGNS UP CELEBRITY TV CHEF

Neven Maguire, the owner of the MacNean Restaurant in Blacklion, Co Cavan, has appeared in press and TV commercials for the Dunnes Stores food division since late 2006. Maguire, a winner of many cookery awards and a well-known face after many appearances on RTÉ, was approached to take on the role by Michael Heffernan, son of Dunnes director Margaret Heffernan. Maguire has a commercial arrangement with Dunnes which excludes him from working with other supermarkets. Maguire's agent John Masterson said, 'The key things we've focused on are Neven's interest in fresh food, quality cooking and quality Irish ingredients. By a happy coincidence, a week after the deal had been arranged, Neven's MacNean Restaurant was named Georgina Campbell's Restaurant of the Year.'

Prior to the arrangement, Dunnes food advertising had been more price-driven than brand-related. The move to sign up Maguire reflects the shift in Dunnes' strategy for its homeware division, which saw it signing up designer Paul Costelloe and former model Olivia Treacy, among others.

Source: adapted from C. O'Mahony, Sunday Business Post, *10 December 2006, p.31.*

The *physical attractiveness* of the communication source is also important to marketers. Physically attractive communicators are generally more successful than unattractive ones in changing beliefs. A physically attractive source is often used for sexually suggestive messages. The *likeability* of the source can also influence affective behaviour. Likeable sources can create a positive mood that affects consumer evaluations of the advertisement or brand and can make consumers feel more positive about the endorsed product or service.

The source of information also provides *meanings*. Meanings become attached to the celebrity and these meanings are transferred from the celebrity to the product. In turn, the meaning of the product is transferred to the consumer. In other words, a celebrity can bring together producers and consumers by means of the products with which he or she is associated.

The Irish charity Goal was founded in 1977 by John O'Shea. In the past thirty years Goal has spent over €450 million implementing relief and development programmes in fifty countries. Goal and John O'Shea have become synonymous with each other.

Overall, an important decision for marketers when developing advertising communications is what kind of source to use, as this is a vital component in delivering a message to an audience.

Message

Just as the source can influence consumer buying behaviour, so too can the characteristics associated with the message. The *message* can be *verbal* (spoken or written), *non-verbal* (a photograph, an illustration, a symbol), or a combination of the two. A verbal message, whether it is spoken or written, can usually contain more specific product/service information than a non-verbal message. Non-verbal information often takes the form of symbolic communication. Marketers often develop logos or symbols that are associated exclusively with their products and that achieve high recognition. In May 2005, Ireland's first ever Internet-only bank RaboDirect.ie was launched. RaboDirect used a straight-talking online approach to empathise with consumers, in a pioneering way. The slogan 'Life's more interesting when you're direct' was devised to bring this brand character to the fore. Campaign tracking showed that after just eight weeks the advertisements had spontaneous recall of 29 per cent and prompted recall of 55 per cent. In all cases, consumers correctly attributed all communications to RaboDirect (www.marketing.ie/nov05).

Message content refers to the strategies that are used to communicate an idea to consumers. Marketers have to make decisions regarding the use of emotional rather than factual advertisements and whether to use simple or complex messages.

Message construction refers to the physical makeup of a message. Marketers need to decide on what information should be included in the message, where the information should be placed and how often the message should be repeated.

From an information-processing perspective, for a message to have impact, the receiver must go through the exposure, attention and comprehension stages. *Message complexity* strongly influences comprehension. If too much information is given, consumers may be overwhelmed and react negatively. Thus another consideration for marketers to be wary of is advertising overload. By lunchtime each day, Irish consumers are typically exposed to over 2,000 advertisements and that figure is rising all the time (www.marketingmagazine.ie).

Moral appeals in a message are directed to the consumers' sense of what is right or proper. They are often used to urge consumers to support social causes such as a cleaner environment or workforce diversity, or to donate money to worthy causes. The advertisements also use an emotional appeal, such as concern and sympathy for sufferers, in order more successfully to convey the cause to the target audience.

Marketers need to be aware that their message should contain a brand-differentiating message. The communication, therefore, will aim to stress a unique attribute or benefit of the product.

Channel (Medium)

The channel or medium of communication can be impersonal (e.g. a mass medium) or *interpersonal* (a conversation between a salesperson and a consumer, in person, by mail or online). Mass media are generally classified as print (newspapers, magazines, billboards), broadcast (television and radio), or electronic (the Internet). *Direct marketers* or *database marketers* use broadcasts, print and online advertising as well as *direct mail*. Home shopping networks are expanding dramatically as consumers demonstrate their enthusiasm for television and online shopping. Direct marketers use data on the recent buying behaviour of their consumers to generate purchases from new consumers.

The increase in online advertising in Ireland has rapidly expanded. The Irish Institute of Advertising Practitioners calculates that the amount spent on website display advertisements, banners, buttons, etc. was up ninety per cent in the first half of 2007 over the previous year. By the end of 2007, the total online spend in Ireland was estimated at €75 million, up 50 per cent on 2006, with more growth expected in future years. Driving the growth is the adoption of broadband by most Internet users. Broadband subscriptions in the first quarter of 2007 showed the highest quarterly growth levels since broadband was launched in Ireland five years before. Broadband subscription levels practically doubled between early 2006 and early 2007. Marketers keep a close eye on which sites draw the most visitors. Recently, for example, the most popular Irish websites (with number of unique users) were:

- rte.ie — 1.56 million
- ireland.com — 1.18 million
- eircom.net — 1.03 million
- independent.ie — 956,000
- daft.ie — 760,000
- carzone.ie — 470,000
- irishjobs.ie — 414,000
- buyandsell.ie — 349,000
- myhome.ie — 339,000 (O'Connell 2007).

EXAMPLE: STATE OF THE NET

There are signs that online shopping is almost like a new religion in Ireland, according to Aileen O'Toole, Managing Director, AMAS (Irish consultancy online services). Devotees praise the convenience, the choice and price competitiveness. A quarter of online users say they shop online and one in two said they plan to spend more at Christmastime. The most popular purchases for Irish online shoppers at Christmas are DVDs/CDs/videos, books, video games, computer software and clothes. If international trends are any guide, traditional shopping choices in Ireland are also being influenced by online content. Irish shoppers are carrying out research online and may be more easily swayed by blogs and consumer reviews than by marketing messages from particular brands.

What is behind the increased adoption levels of online shopping? First and most obviously, more people are online. The number of households with Internet access has grown from twenty per cent in 2000 to 50 per cent in 2007, according to the CSO, and broadband penetration is accelerating. Second, more time spent online translates into changed behaviour. Men, for instance, aren't as wedded to the social nature of conventional shopping as women and see online shopping as liberating. Third, early impediments to online shopping, concerns about consumer rights and security are no longer as contentious. Interestingly, EU law now gives greater rights to online shoppers than to conventional shoppers. There is also the eBay factor; the world's best-known online commerce site has acted not only as a hi-tech garage sale but it is educating thousands of Irish consumers about online buying and selling. eBay has close to a quarter of a million Irish registered users.

Online consumers are now more confident and more empowered. They have a myriad of shopping choices only a search engine query away. Businesses, even those who don't sell online, cannot ignore this. Customers, both business and professional, are using the Web to buy and to research their buying decisions. Positioning a product or service, defining its unique selling proposition and communicating its value will become far more challenging in this digital age.

Source: adapted from www.amas.ie

Interestingly, research conducted with Irish consumers during 2006 illustrated that newspapers, the oldest advertising medium, are also increasing in popularity. Some three-quarters of a million people buy a newspaper every day in Ireland and a total of two million adults read a paper every day, suggesting that the older media are correctly addressing consumer needs for their millions of readers (www.amarach.com).

Some interpersonal communication channels are controlled directly by the communicator, as in the case of a company salesperson who contacts consumers in the target market. Other interpersonal communications about the product or service may reach consumers through channels not directly controlled by the company. These might include neighbours, family or friends talking to target consumers. This channel is known as *word-of-mouth influence* and has considerable effect in many product areas. Personal influence carries great weight for products that are expensive, risky, or highly visible. Buyers of cars and appliances, for example, often go beyond mass-media sources to seek the opinions of people they trust.

EXAMPLE: THINKING OUTSIDE THE BOX

The world of advertising is changing. As consumers increasingly take control of how they engage with providers of products and services, the trend is moving towards more interactive experiences, using emerging platforms such as social networks, blogs and other content-sharing forums. Whether positive or negative, these developments can and will influence business strategies of companies and how they engage with their target markets. While predictions about the early demise of the print media, radio and television have proved groundless, emerging platforms now present positive opportunities for advertisers to establish more one-to-one relationships between consumers and marketers.

Research carried out by PricewaterhouseCoopers suggests that consumers in the 18–24 age bracket expect advertising in the wireless, online and gaming environments to be much more sophisticated and relevant to their lives. Instead of the traditional one-way broadcasting to generic consumers, marketers are now interacting with newer digital and more dynamic two-way systems of conversation with engaged consumers. This is also referred to as lifestyle advertising, as it is connecting with the lifestyle and interests of the individual consumer. This aims to attract and engage potential customers with what is relevant to them. By making the connection and building a two-way relationship with them, the loyalty and brand association is strengthened and this encourages further interaction and thus more revenues. Technology and Internet developments are creating not merely an opportunity but, increasingly, a consumer expectation of more sophisticated interactions among consumers, advertisers and content providers. This more elaborate engagement offers the potential for greater reward for marketers who listen to consumers and employs new opportunities presented by emerging platforms. Major advertisers are beginning to shift larger percentages of their media investment to experiential, digital and social media to capture the benefits and gain new insights from them.

Source: adapted from B. O'Connor, Irish Times *Business Magazine, 11 June 2007, pp 58–9.*

Receiver (Consumer)

The receiver of formal marketing communications is likely to be a potential consumer and may also be a member of the marketer's target audience. *Unintended* audiences are also likely to receive marketers' communications. Unintended audiences include everyone who is exposed to the message who is not specifically targeted by the sender. Unintended receivers of marketing communications include members of the public such as shareholders, creditors, suppliers, employees, bankers and the local community. It is important for marketers to realise that the audience — no matter how large or how diverse — is composed of *individual receivers*, each of whom interprets the message according to his or her own personal perceptions and experiences.

Feedback

Feedback is an essential component of both interpersonal and impersonal communications. Since marketing communications are usually designed to persuade a target audience to act in a desired way (e.g. to purchase a particular brand or service), the ultimate test of marketing communications is the receiver's response. For this reason, it is essential for the sender to obtain feedback as promptly and as accurately as possible. Prompt feedback allows the sender to reinforce, to change, or to modify the message to ensure that it is understood in the intended way. Generally, it is easier to obtain feedback (both verbal and non-verbal) from interpersonal communications than impersonal communications. A good salesperson, for example, is usually alert to non-verbal feedback provided by the prospective consumer. Such feedback may take the form of facial expressions (a smile, a frown, an expression of disbelief).

EXAMPLE: ONE IN TWO CONSUMERS DO NOT COMPLAIN ABOUT POOR FOOD HYGIENE

An awareness campaign by Safefood, the Food Safety Promotion Board (a North/South body set up across Ireland as a result of the Good Friday Agreement), informs consumers about their rights in terms of food hygiene standards when eating out and encourages consumers to report it if not satisfied. Its 'Speak Out' campaign was established after a study found that one in two consumers are reluctant to speak out if they are unhappy with food hygiene standards when dining out or buying food from shops. The campaign began in October 2007 and includes radio commercials and an outdoor advertising campaign at bus stops and other central locations across the island of Ireland. The study, conducted by Amárach Consulting for Safefood, also found that 62 per cent of consumers will not return to a food business if they experience poor food hygiene standards and will most certainly tell others of their bad experience.

Safefood's Chief Executive, Martin Higgins, says: 'Our research revealed that 53 per cent of people feel reluctant to speak out if they are unhappy with food hygiene standards.' He added, 'Whether it's grabbing a lunchtime sandwich, having a takeaway or visiting a restaurant, eating out has increasingly become part of our daily lives. As consumers, we can play our part too in ensuring the highest standards of food hygiene are met and this campaign will focus on educating and enabling consumers to trust their own instincts and make informed choices.'

Safefood uses Safetrack consumer-tracking research which works in tandem with Safefood's communications programme. Using this research, the organisation is provided with useful feedback regarding consumers' attitudes and behaviour towards food safety, hygiene and nutrition.

Source: adapted from www.safefood.eu/ and www.consumerconnect.ie

Obtaining feedback is as important in *impersonal* (mass) communications as it is in *interpersonal* communications. Unlike interpersonal communications feedback, mass communications feedback is rarely direct: it is usually inferred. Senders infer how persuasive their messages are from the resulting action or inaction of the targeted audience. Receivers either buy or do not buy the advertised product or service. Because of the high costs of advertising space and time in mass media, many marketers consider impersonal communications feedback to be even more essential than feedback from interpersonal communications. The company that initiates a message must develop some method for determining whether its mass communications are received by the intended audience, understood in the intended way and effective in achieving the intended objectives. Sometimes companies seek feedback from mass audiences by identifying the degree of customer satisfaction or dissatisfaction with a product purchase. They try to discover and correct as quickly as possible any problems with the product or service in order to retain their brand's image of reliability. Many companies now have 24-hour hotlines to encourage comments and questions from their consumers and they also solicit consumer feedback through online contact.

One of the most difficult decisions facing a company is how much to spend on communications. The company must divide its budget among the main communication tools available — advertising, personal selling, sales promotion, direct marketing and public relations.

BARRIERS TO COMMUNICATION

Various barriers to communication may affect the accuracy with which consumers interpret messages. These include *selective perception* and *psychological noise*.

Selective Perception

Selective perception means that consumers carefully read advertisements for products or services they are interested in and tend to ignore advertisements that have no special interest or relevance to them. Technology provides consumers with increasingly sophisticated means to control their exposure to various forms of media. Consumers with the use of a remote control may decide to switch television channels during commercial breaks, or to fast-forward through commercials when watching a programme they recorded. The growth of satellite radio also allows consumers to avoid hearing radio advertisements. Caller ID and phone answering machines allow consumers to screen out telemarketing and other unsolicited contacts from marketers.

Psychological Noise

'Noise' covers any factors that interfere with any aspect of the communication process between the sender and the receiver. Psychological noise means that consumers may not receive and retain a message due to competing advertising messages or distracting thoughts. If there are too many advertisements, for example during a commercial break, the consumer may actually receive and retain almost nothing of what he or she has seen. The impact of a message may also be reduced if the consumer is surrounded by messages that are all equally stimulating and exciting and there is the risk of messages becoming confused with each other in the receiver's mind. Similarly, if a motorist is too absorbed in his or her thoughts while driving, he or she may not observe the content of radio advertisements. Noise can cause the message to be distorted in the receiver's mind or to fail to reach the receiver's attention at all (Mallen 1977). Marketers need to be aware of these communication barriers and must develop methods of overcoming them, for example they may repeat an advertisement several times to help consumers recall the message. Marketers also need to ensure that they are targeting the correct audience through effective positioning and highlighting a unique selling proposition.

THE CHANGING FACE OF MARKETING COMMUNICATIONS

Two major factors are changing the face of marketing communications. First, as mass markets have fragmented, marketers are shifting away from mass marketing. They are developing focused marketing programmes designed to build closer relationships with consumers in more narrowly defined micromarkets. Second, improvements in computer and information technology are speeding the movement towards segmented marketing. New technology helps marketers keep closer track of consumer needs as more information is available about the consumer at the individual and household levels. This shift from mass marketing towards one-to-one marketing is creating the generation of more specialised and highly targeted communications efforts.

Given this new communications environment, marketers must rethink the roles of various media. Mass media communications has long dominated the promotion mixes of consumer-product companies. Although television, magazines and other mass media remain important, their dominance is declining. Market fragmentation has resulted in media fragmentation with an emphasis on more focused media that better match the target audience of a company. In recent years, for example, there has been a proliferation of special interest magazines reaching more focused readerships.

This shift from mass marketing to targeted marketing poses additional problems for marketers, since consumers are exposed to a greater variety of marketing communications from a broader array of sources. Consumers, however, do not distinguish between message sources in the way marketers do. In the consumer's mind, receiving messages from different media such as television, magazine or online sources blur into one. Messages delivered through different promotional approaches such as advertising, personal selling, sales promotion, public relations or direct marketing all become part of a single overall message about the company. Conflicting messages from these different sources can result in company images and brand positions.

If companies fail to integrate their various communications policies the consumer can become confused. If, for example, mass media communications advertise one aspect, a product label may send a different message, a price promotion may give a different signal and the company website may give different, even contradictory, information. To overcome such anomalies or difficulties, more companies are now adopting the concept of *integrated marketing communications*. Under this concept, the company carefully integrates and co-ordinates messages across its many communications channels — mass media, advertising, personal selling, sales promotion, public relations, direct marketing and packaging — to deliver a clear, consistent message about the organisation and it products and services. Companies aim to build strong brand identity by tying together and reinforcing all company positioning, images and messages across all its marketing communications venues.

Today, both marketers and consumers use blogs as a means of communication. In a *blog* (which is an abbreviation of 'weblog'), entries are written in chronological order and commonly displayed in reverse chronological order. Many blogs provide commentary or news on a particular subject; others function as more personal online diaries. A typical blog combines text, images and links to other blogs, web pages and other media related to its topic. The option for readers to leave comments in an interactive format is an important part of many blogs. Blogs provide marketers with useful feedback from consumers.

EXAMPLE: BLOGGING

Blogging can generate value-added content in an environment which builds brands and increases sales. It is a simple concept and involves a business sharing knowledge and expertise on a particular topic which people find relevant and of interest. Specialist food stores and wine merchants are creating blogs to share knowledge and advice and consumers interact with brands through blogs. Creating a successful blog enables companies to optimise their rankings on search engines like Google. Murphy's ice cream in Dingle, for example, created a blog that ranks ahead of the HB brand when a person searches online for 'ice cream'. Murphy's developed the pull strategy by becoming a conduit for information in their given field. The initiative has resulted in potential consumers coming to them when people want to know more about ice cream, chocolate and coffee. Anyone can start a blog through www.blogs.ie.

Source: adapted from www.marketing.ie/oct07

ETHICS AND SOCIALLY RESPONSIBLE MARKETING COMMUNICATION

The consumer's loss of privacy is an increasingly problematic ethical issue as marketers manage to identify and reach out to increasingly smaller audiences through innovative media. As discussed above, the old mass media model of broadcasting where large audiences are reached with the same print messages is in decline. Marketers are increasingly adopting *narrowcasting*, a technique that allows them to send many directed messages to very small audiences on an ongoing basis. Narrowcasting is made possible by sophisticated data providers who compile individual profiles from credit card companies, banks, direct mail responses, surveys and product warranty cards completed by consumers. Sophisticated analysis of such data enables the compilation of extremely specialised lists of consumers.

Marketers can learn not only *who* consumers are (e.g. their personal characteristics) and *what* specific purchases consumers make, but also *where* consumers are at any given moment through their mobile phones, mobile email devices or satellite navigation.

While most marketers work hard to communicate openly and honestly with consumers, some abuses can occur. By law, companies must avoid false or deceptive communications. Marketers must not make false claims, such as suggesting that a product cures some illness when it does not. Marketers must also avoid deceptive sales promotions that attract buyers under false pretences.

The Advertising Standards Authority for Ireland is an independent self-regulatory body set up and financed by the advertising industry and committed, in the public interest, to promoting the highest standards of marketing communications in advertising, promotional marketing and direct marketing. The objective is to ensure that all commercial marketing communications are 'legal, decent, honest and truthful'. It is a self-regulatory body and its members include advertisers, advertising agencies, media specialists, direct marketing companies, sales promotion consultants and the various media — print, radio, television, cinema and outdoor interests. As well as ethical communications, companies can also invest in communications to encourage and promote socially responsible programmes and actions. Many large organisations set up charitable foundations or donate cash directly to community or charitable causes.

Sponsorship

Companies also send out messages through their involvement in sponsorship. Sponsorship can emphasise the company's positive sense of social responsibility and good corporate citizenship. It can also increase product awareness and enhance product and corporate image. Marketers see sponsorship as an investment that makes good marketing sense. Sponsorship, however, should not be used as a substitute for advertising. An important consideration for a company in relation to sponsorship is *relevance*. The selected sponsorship must be appropriate for the particular audience targeted, which the company is seeking to influence. Marketers must also ensure that the sponsored activity is *compatible* with the sponsor's overall promotional objectives. Betting group Paddy Power invested at least €100,000 in hosting the 2008 Bingham Cup, an international gay rugby tournament. This investment represents the biggest single sponsorship deal ever secured for an Irish gay event. Paddy Power's proposed the deal to the organisers in order to expand their image beyond its traditional remit which was largely men betting on sporting events. Paddy Power's see betting as 'an entertainment' and realise that the gay and lesbian market also represents a significant consumer force. It is estimated that the Irish gay and lesbian population has a combined annual income of €8.75 billion (O'Mahony 2007).

EXAMPLE: FORD IRELAND SPONSORS FOOTBALL AND FASHION

The Professional Footballers' Association of Ireland (PFAI) announced that Ford has become the official sponsor of its highly successful annual players' awards. As part of the sponsorship, Ford will provide the Premier Division and First Division Players of the Year with the exclusive use of a new Ford Focus for the following year. The agreement between Ford and the PFAI further demonstrates Ford's commitment to Irish football. Late in 2006, Ford announced its official car sponsorship deal with the FAI and subsequently the company also agreed to be the main sponsors of the FAI Senior Cup, which is now the FAI Ford Cup. Mr Eddie Murphy, Chief Executive of Henry Ford and Son, Ireland, said that the extension of the sponsorship of football to embrace the players was particularly appropriate: 'We are delighted to extend our sponsorship of Irish football and particularly to provide direct rewards for the players, who are the lifeblood of the game. Without them we would have none of the passion and the skills that light up the FAI Ford Cup. The PFAI sponsorship builds on Ford's association with football throughout the world, which includes its longstanding involvement with Europe's foremost football competition, the Champions League.' Mr Murphy added, 'Both the Premier Division and the First Division Players of the Year will each receive the use of a car for a year. I believe this will add an extra edge to an individual award that is already recognised as the ultimate accolade a professional player can win.'

Henry Ford and Son, Ireland was also the sponsor of the RTÉ *Off the Rails* live fashion event at the RDS held during November 2007. RTÉ fashionistas Caroline Morahan and Pamela Flood announced the sponsorship. The full range of Ford models were on display at the RDS, and the Focus Coupé Cabriolet was among the stars of the catwalk at the non-stop fashion shows. 'The Ford blue oval represents much more than just cars. In addition, Ford's association with female fashion nicely balances the brand's involvement with the more male pursuits of soccer and rugby,' said Denis McSweeney, Marketing Director, Ford Ireland.

Source: adapted from A. English, Sunday Independent, 28 October 2007, p.33.

PUBLIC RELATIONS

Another important mass promotion communication technique is *public relations* (PR). This concerns building good relations with the company's various publics by obtaining favourable publicity, building up a good 'corporate image' and handling or heading off unfavourable rumours, stories and events. Public relations includes publicity, press relations, product publicity, corporate communications, lobbying and counselling. Public relations can have a strong impact on public awareness at a much lower cost than advertising. The company does not pay for space or time in the media. Instead, it pays for its staff to develop and circulate information and to manage events.

There are a number of public relations tools. First, there must be some favourable *news* about the company and its products or people. Sometimes news stories occur naturally, at other times the public relations person can suggest events or activities that would create news. The types of news story to be communicated and the communication objectives of the story must be defined, for example awareness creation or knowledge dissemination, and the specific target audiences must be carefully chosen.

Speeches also create product and company publicity. Company managers must answer questions from the media or give talks at trade associations or sales meetings. These events can either build or harm the company image. Another public relations tool is *special events,* ranging from news conferences, press tours and grand openings to multimedia presentations.

Public relations also includes *written materials* such as annual reports, brochures, articles and company newsletters and magazines. *Corporate identity materials* also help create an identity that the public immediately recognises. Logos, stationery, brochures, signs, business cards, buildings, uniforms, company cars and trucks make effective marketing communications when they are attractive, distinctive and memorable. Public relations results are difficult to measure because public relations is used with other promotion tools and its impact is often indirect.

EXAMPLE: CORK INSTITUTE OF TECHNOLOGY (CIT) CHANGES ITS VISUAL IDENTITY

Cork Institute of Technology is one of Ireland's major higher education institutions, with almost 17,000 students. Courses span five main fields 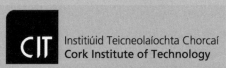 — science, business, engineering, art and music — leading to qualifications ranging from doctorates to degrees to higher certificates. Internationally recognised trade craft courses are offered, and research and development and services to industry are also a significant part of CIT's work.

The mission statement of CIT is:

To provide student-centred education with a career focus for the benefit of the personal, intellectual and professional development of the student and for the benefit of the whole of society.

CIT's previous visual identity had reached the end of its useful life. It no longer reflected CIT's present situation or ambitions. As CIT is a national institution, it has a broad target audience. Stakeholders in CIT's identity include: academic staff, administration, students and their families, the Department of Education and Science, HETAC (qualifications awarding authority) and the wider community. The general characteristics of the new visual identity include: 'distinctive, timeless but reflecting innovative character of CIT, impactful, simple, clean, unbusy, serious, based around the letters CIT.'

The tone of the new visual identity had to be 'focused on learning, innovative, creative, practical, exciting, institutionally strong, grounded and dependable'. The new identity also complies with statutory requirements regarding the Irish language.

ADVERTISING

Advertising can be defined as any paid form of non-personal promotion transmitted through a mass medium (Brassington & Pettitt 2000). The advertisement may relate to an organisation, a product or a service. A product-orientated advertisement focuses on the product or service being offered, whether for profit or not. Its prime task is to support the product in achieving its marketing goals. Product-orientated advertising can use *pioneering* or *competitive* or *reminder and reinforcement* advertising.

Pioneering advertising is used to communicate with consumers in the early stages of the life-cycle of the product when it is necessary to explain what the product will do and the benefits it can offer. *Competitive advertising* is concerned with emphasising the special features of the product or brand as a means of outselling the competition. A company seeks to distinguish the product from its competitors and to communicate its unique benefits in order to give it a competitive edge. *Reminder and reinforcement advertising* tends to operate after purchase. This type of advertising reminds consumers that the product still exists and that it has certain positive properties and benefits. This should increase the chances of repurchase and sometimes may even persuade consumers to buy larger quantities. The main aim of this form of advertising is not to create new knowledge or behaviour but to reinforce previous purchasing behaviour and reassure consumers that they made the correct choice in the first place.

In contrast, *institutional advertising* is not product-specific. It aims to build a sound reputation and image for the whole organisation and to achieve a wide range of objectives with different target audiences. Institutional advertising may be undertaken for various reasons such as image building, presenting new developments in the organisation, or presenting the organisation's point of view on an issue.

Advertising media are called on to perform the task of delivering the message to the consumer. The advertiser needs to select the media most appropriate to their target audience and within the budget available. The main steps in media selection are: deciding on *reach, frequency* and *impact*; choosing between chief *media types*; selecting specific *media vehicles*; and deciding on *media timing*.

Reach is a measure of the *percentage* of people in the target market who are exposed to the advertising campaign during a given period of time. *Frequency* is a measure of *how many times* the average person in the target market is exposed to the message. The advertiser must also decide on the desired *media impact*; that is, the qualitative value of a message exposure through a given media. Products, for example, that need to be demonstrated visually are more suited to television than to radio.

The advertiser needs to choose between media types and media vehicles. The media habits of target consumers will affect media choice, and the message type will also require different media. For radio and television in most countries there are numerous stations and channels to choose from, together with thousands of programmes from which the advertiser must choose to place the particular advertisement. The advertiser needs to be aware of circulation figures and the costs of different advertisements, colour options and advertising submission deadlines.

Another decision that must be made concerns timing, for example, scheduling the advertisement over the course of the advertising campaign. *Continuity* means scheduling advertisements evenly within a given period. *Pulsing* means scheduling advertisements unevenly over a given time period: the idea is to advertise heavily for a short period to build awareness that carries over to the next advertising period.

Given the complexity and expense involved in advertising, many organisations employ an *advertising agency* to handle the development and implementation of advertising programmes. Advertising agencies provide a full range of services such as research, creative artwork and media buying. It is almost impossible that one free-standing advertisement in the press or on television would be sufficient to achieve the results expected, in terms of impact on the target audience. Normally, advertising agencies think about a *campaign*, which is communicated through a series of messages placed in selected media chosen for their expected cumulative impact on the specified target audience. Advertising campaigns can run for varying lengths of time — a few weeks, a season, even many years. The key difference between advertising and other forms of promotional communication is that it is impersonal and communicates with large numbers of people through paid media channels.

DESIGNING PERSUASIVE COMMUNICATIONS

In order to create persuasive communications, the sender must first establish the objectives of the communication. These objectives might consist of creating awareness of a product or service, encouraging or discouraging certain practices, creating a favourable image, increasing sales, or any combination of these and other communications objectives. The appropriate audiences for the message and the appropriate media through which to reach them must then be selected. The message must be carefully designed in a manner that is appropriate to each medium and to each audience. Finally, the communication should include a means by which consumers can provide feedback in order for the sender to modify or adjust the media or the message.

There are a number of models that depict how persuasive communications work. The *cognitive models* of communication depict a process in which exposure to a message leads to interest and desire for a product or service and, ultimately, to buying behaviour.

Variations in a consumer's level of involvement, as presented in Chapter 2, will result in different cognitive processes. The level of involvement will determine which aspects of a communication are processed. The *elaboration likelihood model* assumes that once a consumer receives a message he or she begins to process it. Depending on the personal relevance of this information, the receiver will follow one of two routes to persuasion. Under conditions of high involvement, the consumer takes the *central route* to persuasion. Under conditions of low involvement, a *peripheral route* is chosen.

The Central Route to Persuasion

When a consumer finds the information in a persuasive message relevant or interesting, he or she will attend to the message content. The consumer is likely to actively think about the message presented and generate cognitive responses to the data presented. Beliefs are carefully formed and evaluated, and the strong attitudes and beliefs that result will be likely to guide behaviour. Consumers are more likely to devote active cognitive effort to evaluating the pros and cons of a product in a high-involvement purchase situation. The elaboration likelihood model proposes that for high-involvement products marketers should present advertisements with strong, well-documented, issue-relevant arguments that encourage cognitive processing.

The Peripheral Route to Persuasion

The peripheral route to persuasion is taken when consumers are not motivated to really think about the arguments presented. The consumer is likely to use other cues in deciding on the suitability of the message. These cues might include the context in which the message is presented, or the use of celebrities or music or a spokesperson. When consumer involvement is low, marketers should follow this route in order to provide consumers with pleasant associations with the product or service, which in turn should result in positive buying behaviour.

CASE STUDY: LUCOZADE SPORT FOCUSES ON COMMUNICATION STRATEGY

Building on the reputation of the internationally successful Lucozade brand, Lucozade Sport was launched in 1990 to meet the particular energy needs of athletes competing at the highest level. Since then, Lucozade Sport has become Ireland's and Britain's favourite sports drink, catering for athletes' needs during sport and training. In addition, the brand has been extended to include a wider range of products, such as sports carbohydrate gels, recovery drinks and energy snack bars, which address more serious or professional athletes' needs before and after training.

The Lucozade brand is now an *umbrella brand* for the following sports products: Lucozade Sport (to replenish lost energy and rehydrate during sport); Lucozade Hydro Active (a fitness water which contains essential salts, selected vitamins and has a light fruit flavour to encourage consumption during exercise); Lucozade Sport Nutrition (the Lucozade sports bar and carbo energy gel products, which have been formulated to deliver an optimum diet for athletes in a convenient, portable format).

When developing an extended product range like Lucozade Sport, a company must build on a well-defined market segmentation strategy. The philosophy behind the Lucozade Sport brand is to provide a complete product range to address the nutritional needs of athletes of all abilities for preparation, performance and recovery in sporting activities. The ultimate benefit of Lucozade Sport is to improve sporting performance. The success of Lucozade Sport can be largely attributed to strong market growth rates, particularly over the last three years.

Communicating the Message: 360° Marketing

The marketing mix for Lucozade Sport is complex; however, it is largely centred on its marketing communications strategy. This focuses on two major areas:

- *Rational communication*: getting the brand benefit across to the consumer.
- *Emotional communication*: involves sponsoring popular, well-known sporting heroes like Ronan O'Gara and Damien Duff to endorse the brand.

The marketing strategy for Lucozade Sport is built on identifying 'brand touchpoints' with the consumer. These are occasions and opportunities to connect directly with target consumers. Brand touchpoints emerge from market segmentation and enable marketers to identify suitable target markets for their products. In competitive consumer markets, marketing managers must deliver a message to consumers to draw attention to their products and to remind buyers of the benefit their products provide. The marketing communications mix provides marketers with the tools to achieve this. The main methods or channels of communication include television, radio and print advertising; outdoor advertising, including on-pitch signage and bottles on the pitch; sales promotions in shops or on the packaging; and public relations. The 360° marketing approach is also known as integrated marketing communications. This concept means that marketers use as many channels as possible to communicate with consumers and, most important, that the marketing message is always the same. By doing this, marketing managers ensure that consumers get one clear message about a product and understand the benefit they will get from that product.

In the case of Lucozade Sport, the message has been consistent: 'Lucozade Sport keeps top athletes going 33 per cent longer.' This message is communicated by sponsoring top athletes to endorse the product. Damien Duff, Ronan O'Gara and GAA stars, including Oisín McConville, among a host of other Irish sports stars, were filmed training together for a television campaign which carried the powerful strapline 'Hunger has a Thirst'. This demonstrates that the highest sporting ambitions can be supported and performance improved by drinking Lucozade Sport before a match to prevent dehydration.

TV Campaign: Hunger has a Thirst

In a series of television spots, a variety of sports stars trained together on a rainy day to demonstrate their skills and to have fun. Damien Duff is seen 'walloping' balls in the rain and also trying his hand at hurling, without much success. Ronan O'Gara, hero of the triumphant Munster team of 2006, tries out Gaelic football, only to be told by the amused Gaelic players that rugby is definitely his game! While entertaining and amusing, this advertisement also succeeds in communicating that top performance takes great commitment, preparation and teamwork.

The integrated nature of the marketing campaign for Lucozade Sport is carried through with billboards (and print advertisements) again featuring key stars highlighting the 'Hunger has a Thirst' message. In conclusion, the success of the Lucozade Sport brand in Ireland and in Britain is based on two main foundations: ongoing scientific development and effective and consistent marketing communications. These in turn build on a solid market segmentation strategy to identify the major target markets for this product.

Source: adapted from www.business2000.ie/cases

CASE STUDY: UNICEF IRELAND AND DEEP RIVERROCK — A CORPORATE PARTNERSHIP

UNICEF Ireland was established in 1962 and focuses exclusively on providing support for the world's poorest children. UNICEF Ireland has a driving passion to build a better world for children, in which every child's right to dignity, security and self-fulfilment is achieved. Every day, across the world, funds raised in Ireland are helping forge a better future for children whose lives have been torn apart by poverty, war and natural disasters. UNICEF Ireland provides funding for UNICEF work worldwide as well as directly funding a growing number of country-specific programmes in the areas of health, water and sanitation, education, child protection and emergency relief.

UNICEF Ireland and Deep RiverRock recently announced the re-signing of their corporate partnership through to 2009. Since 2005, Deep RiverRock has been one of UNICEF Ireland's corporate champions, and by 2009 the four-year partnership will have raised €100,000 for UNICEF safe water programmes globally.

Cause-related marketing campaigns that form partnerships like Deep RiverRock and UNICEF Ireland allow a company to offer their consumers the opportunity to support work for child survival worldwide, simply with their product purchases. Deep RiverRock's commitment to UNICEF Ireland helps provide safe water and sanitation facilities for children throughout the world.

Thousands of children die every day from diarrhoea and other water-, sanitation- and hygiene-related diseases, making the lack of safe water the second largest killer of children under the age of five. In 2007, UNICEF Ireland and Deep

RiverRock organised a campaign entitled 'Buy in July', which was conducted in 150 Campbell's catering outlets for the month. For every 750ml bottle of Deep RiverRock water sold during this time, a donation went directly through UNICEF Ireland to help the children of Darfur, a previously independent area in the west of Sudan. Safe water for children was recognised as absolutely essential, particularly in the crowded camps throughout the Darfur region. Today, millions of war-affected people in Darfur have supplies of safe water from operations run by UNICEF and its partners, but funding is urgently needed to sustain long-term delivery of safe water and sanitation facilities.

Every ten cents raised, for example, will supply a sachet of oral rehydration salts, which, when mixed with safe water, can treat a child suffering from dehydration and diarrhoea. Two decades ago, diarrhoea was responsible for around five million deaths annually. Through major public health efforts to prevent and treat dehydration, this has decreased to around two million. The use of oral rehydration salts has proven very effective in the prevention of childhood deaths from diarrhoea. Support from the corporate sector through selective partnerships, as with Deep RiverRock, helps UNICEF raise urgently needed funds as well as raise the profile of humanitarian disasters such as the crisis in Darfur. These elements are critical in helping UNICEF Ireland continue their life-saving work.

Source: www.unicef.ie

Questions for Review

1. Explain the components of communication. Illustrate your answer with an example of a communication process which could be used for a new product.
2. Discuss the main barriers to communication and suggest methods for overcoming such barriers.
3. Distinguish between the main methods of advertising available to marketers, giving the advantages and disadvantages of each method.
4. What is meant by persuasive communication?

9

The Influence of Culture, Subculture and Social Class on Consumer Behaviour

CHAPTER OBJECTIVES

After reading this chapter you should be able to:

- Define culture.
- Identify cultural influences on consumer behaviour.
- Explain the role of consumer goods in a culture.
- Describe subculture.
- Recognise popular culture.
- Understand social class.
- Describe materialism and symbolism.
- Recognise the impact of ethnic influences on consumer behaviour.

CULTURE AND THE COMPONENTS OF CULTURE

Culture has been defined in a variety of ways. Culture requires an examination of the character of a whole society, including factors such as language, knowledge, laws, religions, food customs, music, art, technology, work patterns and other dimensions that give a society its distinctive flavour. Culture may be described as a way of life which is made up of ideas and values and may also include the material objects of a society. In relation to culture and consumer behaviour, Schiffman and Kanuk (2007) define culture as the 'sum total of learned beliefs, values and customs that serve to direct the consumer behaviour of members of a particular society'. The *belief* and *value* components of the definition refer to the accumulated feelings and priorities that individuals have about 'things' and possessions.

A culture, therefore, is *learned*; it is not present in our genes. Culture is transmitted from generation to generation, influencing future members of the society. The process of learning one's own culture is called *enculturation*. Culture is transferred from the older to the younger generation by parents, schools, churches, clubs and other agents. This is called *socialisation*. The difficult task of learning a new culture is called *acculturation*; it is the transfer of culture to adults who have grown up in different cultures. Ethnic minorities frequently form their own cultures, including their own habits and consumer behaviour (subculture), within the culture of a country. Acculturation is an important concept for marketers who plan to sell their products in foreign or multinational markets. A culture is also *adaptive* because it changes as a society faces new problems and opportunities.

Culture must be supported by groups of people. A private belief is not a culture. Minority beliefs, such as the subcultures of ethnic minorities in any country, may form a *subculture*. Norms and values are part of the non-material culture. *Norms* are beliefs regarding how to behave or not to behave and are more specific than values. People differ in the extent to which they accept and comply with norms. Norms and values create expectations and criteria regarding the conduct of others. *Values* are core beliefs or standards used to judge one's own behaviour and that of others. Values often have a religious, ideological or humanistic background. *Goals* may be derived from values. *Mores* are customs that emphasise the moral aspects of behaviour. Frequently, mores apply to forbidden behaviours.

Another element of culture is the mythology of its people. *Myths* are stories that express the key values and ideals of a society. The story often features some kind of conflict between two opposing forces and its outcome serves as a moral guide for people. In this way, a myth reduces anxiety because it provides consumers with guidelines about their world. Every society possesses a set of myths that define that culture. *Conventions* describe how to act in everyday life and these frequently apply to consumer behaviours. Each culture has its own set of symbols, rituals and values to which marketers promote their products and services. To acquire a common culture, members of a society must be able to communicate with each other through a common language. To communicate effectively with their target audiences, marketers must use appropriate *symbols* to convey desired product images or characteristics. These symbols can be verbal or non-verbal.

In Ireland today, in the context of a rapidly changing economic and social environment, many quintessentially Irish cultural traditions and customs have changed or disappeared. The traditional Irish custom of socialising in pubs underwent a change in recent years as newer eating and drinking habits prevailed. Increasing numbers of consumers, for example, now purchase from off-licences and choose to drink and entertain at home. The smoking ban, high drink prices and lifestyle changes were important factors contributing to this change. The smoking ban may have encouraged Irish consumers away from the pub in favour of drinking at home; however, it has provided an opportunity for pubs and restaurants to promote their food menus and attract consumers who previously avoided the smoky atmosphere of these establishments.

EXAMPLE: BRINGING DRINK BACK HOME

The pub may still be the safest place to drink in a responsible manner, but at-home drinking is growing faster than drinking in pubs, cafés, clubs and restaurants. Ireland's drinking habits are changing; alcohol is now bought for consumption at home instead of making a trip to the local. This change in drinking, which began in Ireland in 2006, is commonly described as 'cocooning', or the desire among consumers to do most of their socialising in the comfort of their own homes. Longer working hours and busier lifestyles have left Irish people with less time for socialising in bars. At home there is no waiting for service and no snooty barman to glare at you if you laugh too loudly. And if you're a smoker, you can smoke. The low cost of alcohol sold in supermarkets and off-licences has also led to a culture of drinking in the home. Off-licences have gained a boost from the more frugal attitude to drink and they now sell €1.35bn worth of the total alcohol consumed in Ireland.

Richard Barry is spokesperson for the National Off-Licence Association, which represents in excess of 330 independent specialists off-licences around Ireland. He said, 'I think there has been a natural move over the last ten years from drinking in pubs to drinking at home. Certainly, watching sporting events at home has become very popular over the last decade. This is due probably to a number of different reasons, such as the distance of satellite towns or suburbs to city centres, the cost of houses, the vast improvements in home entertaining, such as home cinemas and the popularity of barbecues. I think the decision to drink at home or in a pub are two very different thought processes, of which the cost is just one of the deciding factors.'

Source: adapted from A. O'Riordan, Sunday Independent, 23 September 2007, p.30.

Another noticeable effect of the changing culture in Ireland today is the continuing growth of chains of specialist coffee shops. Ireland has traditionally been a tea-drinking nation. However, the rapid transformation of the Irish economy over the last few years, increased globalisation and an expanding convenience culture has led to a fundamental and growing change in consumer tastes. Tea, with its genteel, unhurried and reactionary image, is increasingly losing consumers to coffee. Image and lifestyle choices in Ireland are more important than ever, with the accent firmly on youth, sophistication and fast-paced living. Coffee, with its energy-providing properties as well as its refined continental image, fits better with the rising professional class in Ireland (www.foodandbeveragesreport.com).

This boom in Irish coffee drinking has, in part, been fuelled by the exponential growth in the on-trade retail chained coffee shops. Starbucks and Costa Coffee entered Ireland in 2005 to take on the leading domestic chain, Insomnia Coffee Co. Rather than take share away from the incumbent, all three chains have experienced impressive growth over the past few years. This clearly demonstrates Ireland's emerging new food and drink culture.

Another noticeable change in Irish consumer tastes has been the increased consumption of smoothies.

EXAMPLE: IRISH CONSUMERS ARE REAL 'SMOOTH OPERATORS'

Irish consumers have demonstrated that they are real smooth operators as the smoothie market growth in Ireland was reported to be twice that of the chilled juice category for the period of September 2005 to March 2006. Research reports that over the last few years the soft drink market in Ireland has noted a marked change in consumer behaviour as Irish shoppers have become increasingly attentive to product ingredients, which has changed their purchase behaviour accordingly. Specifically, functional drinks, bottled water and fruit/vegetable juice have all increased in popularity at the expense of carbonates and concentrates. One of the new rising stars that is forging its own market sector is the smoothie, which since the launch of the Innocent brand in Ireland in 2005 has seen dramatic growth and an increase in the demand for quality branded natural products.

Source: adapted from www.foodprocessing-technology.com

CULTURAL INFLUENCES ON CONSUMER BEHAVIOUR

A culture is influenced by the dominant values of the society. An important task for marketers is to ascertain what role consumer goods play in a culture. *Cultural meanings* refer to the values, norms and shared beliefs that are symbolically communicated. They are transferred from the culturally constituted world to consumer goods and from consumer goods to individuals. People interpret the world around them through their culturally constituted world, which is made up of the values, mores and norms that make up a particular society. According to Mowen (1995), the transfer of meaning from culture to object may take place through advertising and fashion systems. The transfer of meaning from consumer goods to individuals may take place through various rituals, including possession, exchange, grooming and divestment rituals.

Consumption choices cannot be understood without considering the cultural context in which they are made. A consumer's culture determines the overall priorities that they attach to different activities and products, and it also determines the success or failure of specific products and services. A product or service that provides benefits consistent with benefits desired by members of a culture has a much better chance of attaining acceptance in the marketplace. McWilliams (2005:6) suggests that 'Drinking is an Irish badge of honour', and we drink more than any other nation. Four out of five young Irish men are regular drinkers in comparison with the EU average of 34 per cent. Young Irish women drink ten times more than their Italian counterparts. As a nation, the population of Ireland drink more pure alcohol than anyone else in the world at 25.3 pints on average per person per year. Every year €1,584 per head is spent on drink, leading McWilliams to summarise that as we have got wealthier, we have got drunker.

Culture, however, is not static. It is continually evolving, synthesising old ideas with new ones. According to Geertz (1973), a cultural system consists of three functional areas:

Ecology: the way in which a system is adapted to its habitat. Industrialised cultures versus Third World cultures, for example, and the means used for obtaining and distributing resources in these different cultures.

Social structure: the method by which orderly social life is maintained. This includes political and domestic groups that are dominant within the culture.

Ideology: the mental characteristics of a people and the way in which they relate to their environment and social groups. This concerns the notion that members of a culture possess a common *world view*. They share certain ideas about principles of order and fairness. They also share an ethos, or a set of moral and aesthetic principles.

THE ROLE OF CONSUMER GOODS IN A CULTURE

Marketers need to be aware of the role consumer goods play in a culture. Marketers must therefore carefully monitor the socio-cultural environment in order to market an existing product more effectively or to develop promising new products. This is not an easy task as the culture of a society is continually evolving and many factors are likely to produce cultural changes within a society (e.g. new technology, population shifts, changing values and customs borrowed from other cultures). The changing nature of culture means that marketers have to reconsider *why* consumers are now doing what they do, *who* the purchasers and the users of their products and services are, *when* they do their shopping, *how* and *where* they can be reached by the media and *what* new product and service needs are emerging.

Economic–cultural changes have important consequences for consumer behaviour. Consumer confidence partly determines expenditure and savings. In the case of an economic boom, consumers spend more on durables and luxury goods and services than in the case of an economic downturn. During an economic boom period, relatively little is saved and more credit is taken. Consumers dare to invest in the future. On the other hand, during a recessionary period, there is a low level of consumer confidence; therefore, expenditure tends to decrease, especially on discretionary goods and services, such as cars, holidays, restaurants and luxury clothing. Pessimistic consumers have to have a buffer as a precaution against an uncertain future.

The recent years of the 'Celtic Tiger' economy in Ireland has meant that all kinds of goods have become available to the masses. Purchasing power has increased and so has the general standard of living. This has also been associated with a growth in welfare and with social progress. New social problems have arisen: individuals had to learn how to cope with their increased consumption of goods; leisure time has to be filled; the role of the worker has to be combined with that of consumer; and lots of goods have to be sold. The timing of consumption is another concern for marketers. Previously, products were only replaced when they were worn out. Nowadays, replacement frequently occurs earlier and the timing of replacement is primarily determined by the consumer. Because of this, the dependency relationship between supplier and consumer has been reversed; now the supplier is dependent on the whims of the consumer. The transition from scarcity to affluence has induced a 'consumption culture' in society which is characterised by the following elements:

- The level of consumption is considerably above subsistence level.
- Goods and services are obtained more by acquisition than by household production.
- Consumption is considered to be an acceptable and appropriate activity.
- People are inclined to judge others, and possibly also themselves, on the basis of their consumption level and style. (Rassuli & Hollander 1986)

Additionally, increased production capacity and improved technology contribute considerably to a society of mass consumption. Because of this, goods can be produced more cheaply and in greater quantities, resulting in lower prices and greater affordability for the lower social classes. The rise in income and the lowering of prices also contribute to the increase in consumption. The abundance of goods also stimulates demand and increases a materialistic mentality of acquiring and possessing substantial amounts of desirable goods and services. In a consumer society, advertising not only stimulates the sales of certain products, but also promotes the entire idea of consumption. It influences not only the pattern of consumption but also its level. Advertising also stimulates imitation of influential others, such as those from a higher social class, leading-edge or trendy consumers. In this way, the consumer hopes to take on, to some extent, the status of the people imitated by wearing clothing indicative of a particular status. Because of this phenomenon, consumer behaviour trickles down from the higher social class to the masses, thus diminishing the distinctions between social layers of the population.

Two examples of the role of consumer goods and services in Ireland are the purchase of cars, and eating out. During the first three months of 2006, more super cars (Porsches, Ferraris, Aston Martins, etc.) were sold than in all of 2005.

As Ireland has become more affluent, our eating habits have changed to reflect cultural influences arising from increased travel abroad, changing work patterns and increased discretionary spend. For the first time in our history, we spend more on eating food outside the home than in the home (www.aramark.ie). This illustrates that if eating out was once the preserve of the better-off in Ireland, this is no longer the case. Interestingly, 17 per cent of all food is now eaten at the dashboard of cars, which increases the need for new cars to feature pull-out dining trays (www.checkout.ie). Another significant change in Irish eating habits is that the potato, which was once the core of our diets, is now in second place to pasta and rice.

SUBCULTURE

Consumers' lifestyles are affected by group membership *within* society at large. These groups are known as *subcultures*, whose members share beliefs and common experiences that set them apart from others. Every consumer belongs to many subcultures. These memberships can be based on similarities in age, race or ethnic background, or place of residence. For many people, *nationality* is an important subcultural reference that guides what they value and what they buy. These groups tend to be bound together by cultural ties that can, in turn, strongly influence their consumer behaviour.

Ethnic Subculture

Ethnicity is another major factor influencing consumer behaviour. An *ethnic subculture* is a self-perpetuating group of consumers who are held together by common cultural or genetic ties and is identified both by its members and by others as a distinguishable category. Members of these ethnic groups share a common heritage, set of beliefs, religion and experiences that set them apart from others in society. These groups tend to be bound together by cultural ties that can in turn strongly influence their consumer behaviour.

Two important influences on consumption patterns are the consumer's level of acculturation and the intensity of ethnic identification (how strongly people identify with their ethnic group). Consumers who identify strongly with their ethnic group and who are less acculturated into the mainstream culture are more likely to exhibit the consumption patterns of their ethnic group. Ethnic and religious identity is a significant component of a consumer's self-concept.

Over recent years, Ireland has undergone a dramatic transformation from being a country of net emigration to a country of substantial net immigration. *Immigration* refers to a process by which someone leaves their native land and arrives in a country as a permanent resident (as distinct from a holidaymaker). Many different cultures are represented in Ireland today, and consumers may expend great effort to keep their subcultural identification from being submerged into the mainstream of the dominant society surrounding them.

The 2006 census shows that the culture and composition of the consumer market in Ireland has changed radically, far more than in previous decades: for example, there is far greater diversity. It is estimated that out of a population of almost 4.3 million people in Ireland, there are 160 different nationalities with almost 400,000 foreign-born people registered in the state (CSO 2005). Non-Irish nationals now account for ten per cent of the population. The majority are from Britain (112,548), followed by Poland (63,276), Lithuania (24,638), Nigeria (16,000) and Latvia (13,319). According to Fás figures, 300,000 PPS (Personal Public Service) numbers have been issued to workers since the ten new member states joined the EU on 1 May 2004 (Fás 2006).

To encourage assimilation, the government recently appointed a minister of state with special responsibility for integration policy. Immigrant communities have been established across the country, not just in urban areas but also in smaller towns. Gort, in County Galway, is one such town. Home to the biggest Brazilian community in the country, a third of its population of 3,500 now come from Brazil. In the area of ethnicity, 95 per cent of the Irish population is white, followed by Asians (1.3 per cent) and a black population of 1.1 per cent (CSO 2006).

EXAMPLE: NEW IMMIGRANTS TO IRELAND BUYING HOMES

Irish nationals prefer to own their own homes rather than to rent them. New arrivals to Ireland appear to have the same preference, with one estate agent reporting that foreign buyers represent up to thirty per cent of buyers of new homes. The level of immigration to Ireland has created new purchasers and tenants looking to get on the property ladder. Polish, Czech, Filipino, Indian, Chinese, Russian, Spanish and Lithuanian people working in Ireland are no longer content to pay rent and are acquiring their own properties. Estate agents have noticed that certain nationalities are interested in specific schemes or areas. Filipino and Indian nurses and doctors are looking for homes around the bigger hospitals and word of mouth in close-knit communities means that certain nationalities often buy in the same areas.

The foreign-national market is a 'really significant target group', according to Ronan O'Driscoll from Hamilton Osborne King. That firm reported that during 2005 almost thirty per cent of sales of new homes were made to foreigners, up from less than five per cent only two years previously. From levels of very low percentages in previous years, this group of buyers has expanded dramatically. Eastern Europeans are among the bigger group of new buyers, while Chinese purchasers have always been a fairly significant group, according to O'Driscoll.

Source: adapted from www.workpermit.com

On the other hand, many countries in the world have sizeable Irish ethnic minorities, including the United States, Canada, England, Australia and Argentina. While many of these people are descendants of mid- to late- nineteenth-century emigrants, many others are descendants of more recent Irish emigrants, and others were born in Ireland. These ethnic communities identify to varying degrees with Irish culture and they are distinguished by their religion, dance, music, dress, food and secular and religious celebrations (the most famous of which are the St Patrick's Day parades that are held annually in Irish communities around the world on 17 March).

Marketers need to be aware of targeting advertisements at ethnic minorities. In practice, however, this usually entails only translating an existing advertisement into a particular language, for example Polish or Mandarin, and running the new version in a publication or on a radio station that addresses that ethnic group. This, however, misses the point, as foreign-born residents of this country are more than just an adjunct to our society: they are a real and important part of it. Their presence among us has fundamentally changed who we are as a nation and that means that companies need to look at their marketing differently.

Advertisers need to communicate with everyone, Irish- and foreign-born, as collective members of a multicultural society. A current example of acknowledging the Polish and Chinese communities is the new television licence advertisement. In this commercial, Irish-born people are trying to pass themselves off as Polish and Chinese in an effort to avoid paying their television license by pretending they cannot speak English. Needless to say their plot does not work, but why would it? What does work, however, is the completely seamless way in which these two nationalities are presented as being part of this new Irish society. Not only is the result humorous, it is smart, timely and illustrates that in marketing, integration can be more powerful than segmentation (Noonan 2007).

At the same time, a large number of ethnic shops have opened in Ireland, providing the 'new Irish' with brands they are familiar with from their own countries. This creates a challenge as Irish brands must compete with the immigrant's affinity to their domestic brands. Banks and telecommunications companies have been the early adopters of targeted advertising to the immigrant community in Ireland. AIB's Polish subsidiary, Bank Zachodni WBK (BZ WBK) has a network of more than 400 branches in Poland. The bank ran a campaign in Ireland, in June and July 2007, targeted at Poles who live and work in Ireland. The campaign was designed to inform people they could use their Bank Zachodni WBK account in Ireland. The campaign included advertising in the Polish press in Dublin and an outdoor campaign, including messages on eighteen buses.

The fast-moving consumer goods sector has also begun to pay particular attention to the 'new Irish' as a specific target market. There are, for example, many Polish shops, pubs, bakeries, newspapers and magazines and barbers throughout Ireland. *Polski* is a new creative lifestyle magazine which is published fortnightly and is free of charge. It is written in Polish and is designed for the members of the Polish community in Ireland. There are also many Polish priests and translation services to help people access services like banks and social welfare.

EXAMPLE: DUBLIN HERALDS A NEW ERA IN PUBLISHING FOR IMMIGRANTS

If it's Wednesday, it must be *Polski Herald* night. Dublin's *Evening Herald* found a way of increasing its sales every week by publishing a twelve-page Polish language pull-out every Wednesday. Stephen Rae, editor of the *Evening Herald*, says their pioneering experiment, as a news organisation in democratic Europe, of printing a foreign language supplement for new immigrants has been a commercial and social success. According to Rae, 'When we publish *Polski Herald* every week, we put on an extra 3,000 sales. In addition, there are extra advertisements in Polish for things like cars and jobs as well as flights back to Poland.' The *Evening Herald* now employs a full-time *Polski* news editor and two sub-editors. One of their reporters, Iwona Krauze, said, 'Poles in Dublin really want hard information. They like to know about jobs available here; they like to find out about their rights as EU citizens in Ireland; one of their favourite pages is 'Pomoc', which advises them on things like how to become a full Irish citizen and of course they are keen on learning about how to sort out their taxes. They are very practical in their tastes.' Stephen Rae added that the *Herald* is considering adding pull-out supplements for the sizeable new Chinese community in Dublin and maybe another supplement for the many Latvians now in the city.

Source: adapted from H. McDonald, the Observer, *12 March 2006, p.11*

In an attempt to integrate immigrants in Irish society, Sport Against Racism Ireland (SARI) was set up in 1997. SARI is a not-for-profit organisation with charitable status which supports and promotes cultural integration and social inclusion through sport. It was set up as a direct response to the growth of racist attacks from a small but vocal section of people in Ireland. The organisation presents sporting and cultural events that bring together people from different cultures and backgrounds. It aims to promote a positive attitude towards people from different ethnic and cultural backgrounds. SARI also works with local sports clubs encouraging them to provide a 'level playing field' for all people, regardless of colour, religion or any other form of difference (www.sari.ie).

Religious Subculture

Another type of subculture is based on religious beliefs. Religion provides individuals with a structured set of beliefs and values that serve as a code of conduct or guide to behaviour. It provides ties that bind people together and make one group different from another. The so-called Protestant work ethic, for example, is understood to mean that members of the Protestant subculture generally tend to be more hardworking than those of many other subcultures.

Religious beliefs can affect consumer behaviour as some belief systems forbid the consumption of particular products or services. Jews do not eat pork or shellfish and all mammal meat and poultry must be certified as kosher. Muslims may not eat pork or drink alcohol. In Ireland today, Muslims now represent the third largest religious grouping, behind Catholics and members of the Church of Ireland. The 2006 census shows that the number of Muslims rose by 13,400 to more than 32,500 since the previous census four years before. Catholics now number 3.6 million (an increase of 218,800 since 2002), while there are 125,600 members of the Church of Ireland (an increase of 10,000). The religious grouping with the highest proportion of Irish foreign nationals was Orthodox Christian, with its members mainly from Eastern Europe.

Marketers sometimes use religious themes to sell products. A common example would include special products or packages produced during times of religious holidays, for example Christmas and Easter. To appeal to a broad array of consumers while not alienating certain groups, marketers may avoid images with overt religious meaning. This is why snowmen, Santa Claus and Christmas trees are widely replacing traditional religious figures at Christmas time. Commenting on such trends regarding religion, a senior Irish Catholic cleric, Dr Donal Murray, Bishop of Limerick, noted that 'modern Irish society is a religion-free zone'. He suggested that, 'Our affluent society has certainly forgotten something. Nobody talks about God and, since the departure of *Glenroe*, nobody goes to church. Soap operas, for instance, are largely religion-free. A great deal of modern life proceeds as if the question of faith did not matter. We have passed from a society where faith and public manifestations of faith were the norm, to a society which is, at best, embarrassed by any public visibility of faith' (in Hogan & Deegan 2007).

Age Subcultures

Each age sub-grouping of the population can be thought of as a separate subculture. Important shifts occur in an individual's demand for specific types of products and services as he or she develops from childhood to old age. The percentage of elderly people in Ireland is increasing relative to the overall population. The average age of the population in Ireland has increased by five months since the previous census in 2002, rising from 35.1 years to 35.6 years in 2006. Over the next twenty years, the number of citizens aged over sixty-five will more than double to nearly nine hundred thousand. Today, one in ten of the population is over 65; in two decades this figure will be close to one in five. By 2031, two hundred thousand people will be aged over 85.

Marketers need to be aware of the needs of this subculture and of the way they will want to spend their money. Advertisers also need to address the needs of this subculture as, generally, a large proportion of advertising portrays the image of young, healthy consumers who are typically in their twenties. The most disposable money, however, is held by people in their forties and fifties and these people should not be overlooked. The Central Statistics Office reported that Irish people spent nearly €1.5 billion on international trips in the last three months of 2006, twenty-five per cent more than the amount spent during the same period of the previous year. Interestingly, these trips are increasingly being made by people aged between 60 and 69, which reflects the importance of this age group for marketers.

According to McWilliams (2006), in addition to being wealthy, this older subculture will be well-travelled and educated. Over the coming two decades, most of the Irish population — the baby-boomers of the late 1960s and 1970s — will move into what was traditionally termed middle age. But they will not class themselves as middle-aged; they will be something else. This is the Bob Geldof Generation. Like fifty-something Bob, they are not middle-aged, they are middle youth. They wear combats, parkas and trainers. They receive iPods for Christmas. Their CD (or downloaded) collection is remarkably similar to that of their children. Geldof Generation mothers often weigh less than their daughters. They are healthy, fit and plugged in. They are also rich.

Another notable recent cultural change in Ireland that is driven by this subculture is the boom in the 'wellness industry'. The wellness industry includes health spas, yoga, organic food, vitamin supplements and adult education. These consumers are also changing shopping patterns by moving from the supermarket to organic or wholefood shops and farmers' markets. They are also socially and environmentally aware and purchase Fairtrade coffee and locally grown produce in order to reduce air miles. This new subculture contrasts with that of their parents who at fifty-something were slowing down, putting their feet up and thinking about retirement (www.davidmcwilliams.ie).

POPULAR CULTURE

According to Bell (1982), *popular culture* is the culture of mass appeal. Popular culture has the following characteristics:

- It taps into the experiences and values of a significant portion of the population.
- You do not require any special knowledge to understand it.
- It is produced in such a way that large numbers of people have easy access to it.

The spread of popular culture can be fast or slow. It has a life cycle that can vary from short (i.e. a fad) to very long, but its impact cannot be underestimated. Fads are usually adopted by relatively few people. Adopters of fads may belong to a common subculture but rarely break out of that specific group. At the same time, however, popular culture may influence millions of people in their everyday lives because of its ability to appeal to mass trends.

> **EXAMPLE: ROLLER SHOES FOR KIDS**
>
> Roller Shoes are one of the fads currently grabbing the attention of school-aged children and young adults in Ireland. These are athletic shoes with a wheel insert known as Heelys or roller shoes. Heelys is the brand name, but they are also referred to as Wheelies or Roller Shoes. Roller Shoes provide the wearer with an immediate transition from walking and running to rolling, simply by altering their stance. These are high-quality street shoes that have a single removable wheel in the heel of each shoe.

Because popular culture includes anything that has mass appeal and is used in non-work activities, the range of subject matter encompassed by the term is extremely large. Advertising, for example, becomes popular culture when its images, themes and icons are embraced by a large proportion of the public. Television also creates popular culture. According to Alley (1989), television has become pre-eminently *the* popular culture and is a primary purveyor of values and ideas. Music can also shape popular culture. McWilliams (2005) suggests that the 'new Ireland' is a pop-nation and a *You're a Star* generation. On the last night of *You're a Star* in 2005, the national phone system crashed momentarily. Over 1.6 million texts were sent. The *Podge and Rodge Show* (RTÉ2) is another example of popular culture. These puppets, known as the gruesome twosome, purvey a style of humour that is tailor-made for adults. The show was nominated as best Irish entertainment show in 2006.

Fashion is also part of popular culture. Fashion is dynamic as it constantly changes over time. The longevity of a particular style of fashion can range from a month to a century. A broad definition of fashion includes any use of products to express self-image or role position. *Fashion* is a set of behaviours temporarily adopted by people because the behaviours are perceived to be socially appropriate for the time and situation. From this perspective, fashion involves the adoption of symbols to provide an identity. The symbols may include clothing, jewellery, cars, houses, artwork, or any other socially visible object that communicates meaning within the popular culture. Fashion can be thought of as a *code* or a *language* that helps consumers decipher these meanings.

Fashion is a very complex process that operates on many levels. At one extreme, it is a societal phenomenon affecting many people simultaneously. At the other, it exerts a very personal effect on individual behaviour. A fashion (or style) refers to a particular combination of attributes. To be *in fashion* means that this combination is currently positively evaluated by some reference group. A consumer's purchase decisions are therefore often motivated by his or her desire to be in fashion. Many psychological factors help to explain why people are motivated to be in fashion. These include conformity, variety seeking, personal creativity and sexual attraction.

The meaning that is imparted to products reflects underlying *cultural categories* that correspond to the basic ways in which consumers characterise the world. Cultures make distinctions between different times, between work and leisure and between  genders. Irish designer for a|wear, Peter O'Brien, has a challenge to design a collection of fashionable clothes that both a 16-year-old and a 60-year old would like to buy. He believes that style can be individual and ageless. He also believes in using women he admires or knows personally rather than professional models to show his clothes because they appear more real and to have more integrity (McQuillan 2007).

Another example of popular culture is the popularity of the Bebo website. According to Amárach Consulting (2006), a quarter of a million Irish adults have visited the Bebo website. Indeed, one in every four people visiting the website has created their own Bebo page, which accounts for approximately 60,000 Irish consumers. 'Bebo-ers' in the survey tended to be fairly evenly distributed throughout the country, with slightly more males than females (58 per cent as against 42 per cent), with four in ten over 25 years of age (www.amarach.ie).

SOCIAL CLASS

Social class is defined as 'the division of members of a society into a hierarchy of distinct status classes, so that members of each class have relatively the same status and members of all other classes have either more or less status' (Schiffman & Kanuk 2007). It is determined by a complex set of variables, including income, family background and occupation. The place one occupies in the social structure is an important determinant not only of *how much* money is spent but also *how* it is spent. People try to move up the perceived social order whenever possible. This desire to improve one's personal standing, often to let others know that one has done so, is at the core of many marketing strategies.

Social classes, however, are considered more or less permanent and homogenous categories in society. In the past, social class was determined by birth. A working-class child could never belong to the middle classes. In modern times, however, social mobility has increased due to equal rights and equal opportunity of education. Children frequently attain higher educational and professional levels than their parents. For this reason, they frequently belong to higher social classes than their parents and are often upwardly mobile. Additionally, differences in income and consumption between social classes have become less profound. In modern society, the concept of social class has become less used and is frequently replaced by other concepts such as lifestyle (see Chapter 4).

The term 'social class' is now used more generally to describe the overall rank of people in a society. People who are grouped in the same social class are viewed as approximately equal in terms of their social standing in the community. They work in roughly similar occupations and they tend to have similar lifestyles by virtue of their income levels and common tastes. These people tend to socialise with one another and share many ideas and values regarding the way life should be lived (Coleman 1983). Although people may not like accepting that some members of society are better off than or 'different' from others, most consumers acknowledge the existence of different classes and the effect of class membership on consumption. As a result of democratisation, class differences have become less important.

Social class categories are usually ranked in a hierarchy, ranging from low to high status. Thus, members of a specific social class perceive members of other social classes as having either more or less status than they do. To many people, therefore, social class categories suggest that others are either equal to them (about the same social class), superior to them (higher social class), or inferior to them (lower social class). In this context, membership of a social class serves consumers as a frame of reference (or a reference group) for the development of their attitudes and behaviour.

In the *subjective* approach to measuring social class, individuals are asked to estimate their own social class positions. The resulting classification of social class membership is based on the participants' self-perceptions or self-images. Social class is treated as a personal phenomenon, one that reflects an individual's sense of belonging or identification with others. This feeling of social group membership is often referred to as *class consciousness*. Subjective measures of social class membership, however, tend to produce an overabundance of people who classify themselves as middle class (thus understating the number of people who would perhaps be more correctly classified as either lower or upper class). In 2005, Amárach consultants carried out a survey among Irish people to investigate what class they believed they were in. Just over fifty per cent of those who responded believed that they belonged to the broad middle class, while fewer than thirty per cent believed that they were working class, ten per cent believed they had no particular class and a small two per cent claimed to be upper class.

In contrast to the subjective method, which requires people to envision their own class standing or that of other community members, *objective* measures consist of selected demographic or socioeconomic variables concerning the individual under study. These variables are measured through questionnaires asking respondents several factual questions about themselves, their families, their place of residence, occupation, amount of income and education.

The hierarchical aspect of social class is important to marketers. Consumers may purchase certain products because these products are favoured by members of either their own or a higher social class and consumers may avoid other products because they perceive the products to be lower-class products (e.g. a 'no name' brand of denims). Thus, the various social class divisions provide a natural basis for market segmentation for many products and services as several aspects of consumption are associated with social class. A positive correlation exists between social class and income and wealth, due to higher salaries paid within professions requiring higher education. Higher social classes frequently own more goods and these goods are usually of higher quality. Social class is sometimes associated with the prestige associated with membership of various charity boards or membership of the Rotary or Lions Clubs.

In Ireland, the concept of luxury needs to be redefined, due to economic growth and accompanying high levels of confidence which have given rise to a new habit of acquiring more assets, including cars and holiday homes. It has also led people to see shopping as a leisure activity, to take three or more holidays a year and to increasingly use credit cards. Stockbrokers NCB have predicted soaring demand for cars, homes and luxury items, but it is also important for marketers to note that the new rich and super-rich (who include around 30,000 Irish millionaires) will continue to seek new ways to set themselves apart from others.

MATERIALISM AND SYMBOLISM

Consumers show different attitudes towards symbolism in their behaviour. *Symbolism* indicates the extent to which individuals invest mental energy in their possessions. Where a product is not particularly symbolic, then the consumer attaches considerable importance to its functional characteristics, for example, the use of a car to travel long distances. This can also be viewed as materialist, not in the sense of possessiveness but in the sense of concern with instrumentality and control. In a situation of high symbolism, the consumer transcends the material world by building relationships with goods or by associating them with family, friends or special events. The types of goods viewed in this way include art, antiques, family heirlooms and holiday souvenirs. Fashionable clothing and other products that have a symbolic or psychosocial meaning appeal strongly to consumers' egos. Consumers frequently like well-known brands because of the status they provide. Often these products are not qualitatively better than others but they are positioned as status objects by means of advertising. The symbolic meaning of brands develops mainly by learning and by advertising. For a product to have symbolic value, it must have a shared reality among consumers. Thus large numbers of consumers must have a common conception of the symbolic meaning of the product. For a car to have a symbolic prestige value, others in the relevant social group must view it in the same manner as the buyer.

The symbolic meaning of goods can manifest themselves in society by *rituals* and by *social exchange*. *Rituals* are often associated with primitive behaviour or with public events. A ritual has been defined as an expressive, symbolic activity, comprising a number of behaviours occurring in a fixed order, frequently repeated (Antonides & van Raaij 1998). Ritualistic behaviour occurs in relation to ordinary behaviours such as eating, going on holidays, personal care, sports and giving gifts. Rituals can be short and simple, such as a greeting, or lengthy, such as a wedding; they are an essential part of Christmas, birthdays, graduations and organised public events. Rituals are important for marketers as certain products become associated with the ritual and are seen to enhance its performance.

Social Exchange

Gifts not only have functional attributes, they also convey symbolic meaning. In the *gift-giving ritual*, consumers purchase the perfect gift, remove the price tag and carefully wrap the item (symbolically changing it from a commodity to a unique good) and deliver it to the recipient. Every culture has certain occasions and ceremonies for giving gifts, whether for personal or professional reasons. In terms of money spent each year and how gifts make givers and receivers feel, gifts are a particularly interesting part of consumer behaviour. Products and services chosen as gifts represent more than ordinary or everyday purchases. Because of the symbolic meaning of gifts, they are associated with events such as births, birthdays, engagements, weddings, graduations and many other occasions. Gifts generally include a giver and a receiver, but they can also be gifts to oneself, or *self-gifts*. Consumers may treat themselves to self-gifts that are products (clothes, jewellery), services (spa membership, restaurant meals), or experiences (socialising with friends).

EXAMPLE: BROWNIEPOINTS.IE HELPS MEN CHOOSE THE PERFECT GIFT

Browniepoints.ie was founded in October 2006 and focuses on helping men to buy superior gifts for women. The site helps time-pressed, idea-starved men buy the ideal gift — often earning them a few brownie points in the process. Packed with designer handbags, jewellery, sleepwear and accessories, guys can pick their own gift or choose to get a present recommendation from the 'Help me Shop' service. Fiddly wrapping paper is a thing of the past as the gifts come in a specially designed Browniepoints gift box. Delivery in Ireland is free and a selection of handmade Irish gift cards is available. Managing Director Maureen O'Rourke says, 'We heard a lot of stories about terrible presents — one girl received a camping kit, another a jar of chillies and one poor girl an electric blanket! At Browniepoints we've spent a lot of time on our gift selection to make sure all our presents are beautiful and desirable. We do everything possible to make sure she's one hundred per cent happy with the gift.'

Many of the designers on www.browniepoints.ie are Irish-based. Handbags are provided by Holden Leather goods in Kerry and a number of its jewellery designers are based in Dublin — Eve Ella, Mo Muse, Saba and LuLa. International representation comes from high-end designers Botkier in New York, worn by Heidi Klum and Angelina Jolie. Neesh, an up-and-coming brand from London, is available in Ireland exclusively through Browniepoints, as is Philippa Holland jewellery — loved by Sienna Miller and also worn by Cameron Diaz and Kylie Minogue.

Source: adapted from: www.pressreleaseireland.com 2007

Many marketers promote their products for gift-giving occasions. Often, gift-giving occasions are the primary focus of their business — for example, the greeting-card industry. A different trend in gift-giving has been the rise of alternatives to traditional gifts. Knowing that some consumers are becoming weary of commercialism and materialism surrounding gift-giving occasions like Christmas, some charities adopt the practice of asking consumers to give gifts to people around the world who are truly in need. The Irish charity organisation Bóthar, for example, works in thirty-two developing countries around the world. Bóthar is part of a community of non-governmental organisations using livestock in development aid. Bóthar establishes micro-farming units by giving families the gift of a farm animal. Bóthar recognises that a farm animal not only benefits families' immediate needs, such as a balanced diet and income, it can also provide a family with hope for the future (www.bothar.ie).

CASE STUDY: KERRYGOLD DEEPLY EMBEDDED IN IRISH TRADITION AND CULTURE

Ireland has traditionally been known as the 'emerald' or 'green' island. A land of one hundred thousand welcomes where the air is fresh and clean, the grass lush and the rain soft and unpolluted. Ireland's dairy herds graze freely outdoors on green pastures for most of the year. Irish dairy farmers continue the traditional farming practices of their ancestors and produce plenty of pure, creamy fresh milk, the raw material for Kerrygold premium dairy products.

Objectives of the Kerrygold brand included: the brand name should evoke a sense of the product's origin; it had to have strong connotations of farming, naturalness, goodness and, above all, quality milk; it had to be an exclusively Irish name that was strong but easy to pronounce. Out of a list of sixty names only six were chosen for consideration by the board of the Irish Dairy Board. These were: Buttercup, Shannon Gold, Kerrygold, Leprechaun, Tub-o-gold and Golden Farm. Common to each was the designation 'Irish creamery butter'. In the end a consensus was reached and the Kerrygold brand was born. Kerrygold was successfully launched in England in October 1962.

The first advertisement delivered its origin: 'Ireland is the emerald isle with the greenest of pastures on which the finest dairy herds graze. Their milk is taken each morning to the local village creamery where it is churned that same day into butter, Irish creamery butter, and it's called Kerrygold, the butter that's pure village-churned.'

The Kerrygold brand today can be found on supermarket shelves in over sixty countries worldwide, from China to Chile, Sweden to South Africa, Australia to the USA, as well as in markets closer to home such as Greece, Belgium and Spain. Over four million packs of Kerrygold butter are bought every week, making Kerrygold one of Ireland's truly internationally known food brands.

Kerrygold is produced to exacting requirements and standards; it enjoys worldwide recognition as a quality food item. Its natural content is highlighted by its attractive golden colour and controlled taste. Made from fresh milk, Kerrygold butter from grass-fed cows is high in omega 3, beta carotene and vitamins. As well as making butter, Kerrygold also manufactures cheese and milk powder. Its cheeses include: Blarney Castle, mild vintage cheddar, Dubliner, Emmenthal, mozzarella, Ivernia and Regato. Kerrygold full cream milk powder is a premium powder produced from fresh, high-quality full-fat milk. Reconstituted instantly, Kerrygold full cream milk powder provides convenience and nutrition while preserving the natural wholesome flavour of Irish milk.

Over the years, the Kerrygold brand has firmly established itself among Irish consumers as well as among its worldwide consumer base. Rural Ireland, romance and the positive connection between Ireland and France are ongoing themes that run through Kerrygold's television advertising. Although France is a relatively small market for the brand, it has used the French theme in its advertising because of France's association with excellence in food. Kerrygold has now adopted a new modern, bold and direct style of advertising to communicate how Kerrygold softer butter is different from most competitor spreadables. This new communication included a redesign of the Kerrygold brand in 2006. A new campaign aims to highlight that it is naturally spreadable, unlike other butters which depend on up to one third vegetable oil as an ingredient to make them spreadable. Kerrygold also uses a road show, which facilitates direct interaction with consumers. The company sums up its advertising campaign as: 'Kerrygold. It's all pure butter. One of life's pure pleasures.'

Source: adapted from www.kerrygold.ie

CASE STUDY: MI-WADI REINSTATES THE STRONG CONNECTION THE BRAND TRADITIONALLY HAD WITH IRISH FAMILIES

Mi-Wadi is viewed as a traditional and trusted Irish brand, loved by children since its launch in 1927. However, by the mid-nineties, Mi-Wadi had been under attack for some time. British brands like Robinson's and Kia-Ora had invested heavily in this market and had pushed Mi-Wadi into third place among cordial drinks. By 1995, it was a brand under threat of survival. It was a rapidly declining line in a gradually declining category. Under-investment in marketing and tough market competition left Mi-Wadi the weakest in cordial drinks sales. The multinational competitors had the advantage of high-quality advertising and the market did not seem big enough for three major cordials. There was significant internal debate on whether the required investment levels were warranted. A review to assess the viability of the Mi-Wadi brand was undertaken. Following this review, C&C made a strategic decision that Mi-Wadi was a viable brand, so they put in place a strong marketing programme. This represented a significant risk at the time.

Mi-Wadi needed heavy investment in marketing in order to maintain relevance to the big trade buyers and consumers. It was agreed that it needed to be at least a number two player in the category. Advertising was identified as a key lever in the effort to reinstate the strong connection the brand once had with Irish families. The marketing strategy focused on simple objectives:

- To rescue the Mi-Wadi brand. This meant re-connecting with consumers by rejuvenating the image while retaining its existing consumers.

- To secure a strong number two position. To bring the fight to the multinational competitors and increase sales.
- To build a long-term future for Mi-Wadi. Because the investment required was significant, continuing success would be required to repay the investment and allow for future endeavours.

The key to the success of the brand would lie, as always, with the consumer. But who was the target audience? Mums, kids, mums and kids? Focusing on the correct audience became a critical decision. Extensive qualitative and quantitative research was conducted to identify the most relevant potential consumer base and to gauge the influence of mothers (still the traditional gatekeeper) over their children's decision-making process and of the children's influence on their mothers as shoppers.

Research demonstrated that, although pester power was a factor, the mother was still the key decision maker when it came to cordial purchase. Not surprisingly, it was also discovered that mothers' primary motivation was for a quality product, one they could trust to be good for their children. It also had to deliver on taste and ingredients. However, it was also essential that the brand would be one that children would accept (or, even better, one they would seek out). This conclusion was the most important single decision in the success of the communication programme. It gave a focus for both the creative and media strategy, allowing the investment to work harder.

An advertising strategy was developed between 1996 and 1999 to establish a quality platform that would allow Mi-Wadi to demonstrate its product credentials to mothers. From there it had to move on to engage both mothers and children, with more emotional connections to the desirability of Mi-Wadi for all generations. The creative platform used the line 'Mi-Wadi, Mi-goodness' to deliver on the motivating consumer promise of 'you can trust this brand', an essential ingredient for success with mothers.

From 1999 to 2004, it was decided to deepen the emotional connection as the decline had been reversed and the brand was now growing. The challenge became one to ensure long-term viability by strengthening Mi-Wadi's emotional bond with both sets of consumer groups. Accepted wisdom was that real success came from focusing on either the mums or the kids. By speaking in the real, train-of-thought style of a kid, Mi-Wadi was able to connect with them and with the mothers who recognised the all-too-familiar logic of the average seven-year-old's thinking. Much like successful children's programming, the language of the commercials operated on two levels. This convention-breaking approach allowed a push strategy to mothers with a greater degree of acceptance from kids. The tone of the language used has been consistent for nine years, i.e. childlike and fun. The commercials developed were set in a children's world, universal enough to be recognised by children of most ages, yet strongly evocative for parents everywhere. 'It's not your Wadi — it's Mi-Wadi' became the rallying call of disaffected pre-teens around Ireland. After nine years of consistent advertising investment, Mi-Wadi became the market leader in cordials in Ireland.

Source: adapted from www.iapi.ie

Questions for Review

1. Explain different components of culture.
2. Discuss the cultural influences on consumer behaviour in Ireland today, using a product or service you are familiar with to illustrate your answer.
3. Identify the impact that subculture has on Irish consumer behaviour.
4. Highlight the importance of ethnic influences on consumer behaviour for marketers, citing Ireland as an example in your answer.

10

Organisational, Reference-Group and Family Influences on Consumer Behaviour

---

CHAPTER OBJECTIVES

After reading this chapter you should be able to:

- Distinguish between organisational consumers and individual consumers.
- Recognise various reference groups and their influence on consumer behaviour.
- Explain the influence of gender and sexual orientation on consumer behaviour.
- Discuss family influence on consumer behaviour.
- Identify changing trends in household structures and their impact for marketers.

ORGANISATIONAL CONSUMERS VS INDIVIDUAL CONSUMERS

Just as individual consumers and families make purchases, so do organisations. Overall, there are three main classes of organisational consumer: *commercial enterprises*, *government bodies* and *institutions*, each of which has strong buying power. Businesses or commercial enterprises comprise profit-making organisations which produce and/or re-sell goods and services for a profit. Government bodies (local and national) are very large and important purchasers of goods and services. Their range of purchasing is wide, from office supplies to public buildings, from motorways to management consultancy. Because of traditional bureaucracy and the requirements of public accountability, government-sector purchasing is regulated by specialised purchasing procedures which are often more explicit and formal than those found in many commercial organisations. Such a procedure would include *tendering for the right to supply*. Some jobs are open to tender only from organisations already on an approved list, while others are open to anyone. The submitted tenders are assessed and the winning one is chosen. Tendering is a very competitive process which requires prospective suppliers to become very familiar, at the early stages, when tenders are on offer. The final group of organisational consumers includes non-profit-making organisations, such as local authorities, schools and hospitals.

Table 10.1

Organisational consumers usually:	Individual consumers usually:
Purchase goods and services that meet specific business needs	Purchase goods and services that meet individual or family needs
Need emphasis on economic benefits	Need emphasis on psychological benefits
Use formalised, lengthy purchasing policies and processes	Buy on impulse or with minimal processes
Involve large groups in purchasing decisions	Purchase as individuals or as a family unit
Buy large quantities and buy infrequently	Buy small quantities and buy frequently
Want a customised product package	Are content with a standardised product
Experience major problems if supply fails	Experience minor irritation if supply fails
Find switching to another supplier difficult	Find switching to another supplier easy
Negotiate on price	Accept the stated price
Purchase directly from suppliers	Purchase from intermediaries
Justify an emphasis on personal selling communication	Justify an emphasis on mass media

Source: adapted from Brassington and Pettitt (2000)

An *organisational buying centre* is defined as those in an organisation who participate in the buying decisions and who share the risks and goals of the decision (Hutt & Speh 1992). Because buying centres are composed of people, the same behavioural factors (psychological, sociological) that impact on consumers will also impact on the individuals within an organisation. Like individual consumers, when making decisions, organisational buyers move through a decision process that closely resembles the decision-making process described in Chapter 7. Thus, organisational buyers will recognise problems, search for information, evaluate choices, select a choice and then engage in post-acquisition processes. There are several differences between organisational and consumer buying behaviour, but the main differences are be summarised in Table 10.1.

REFERENCE GROUPS

A *reference group* is a set of people with whom individuals compare themselves as a guide when developing their own attitudes, knowledge and behaviours. Reference groups may be further broken down into:

- aspirational reference groups
- associative reference groups
- dissociative reference groups
- virtual groups.

Aspirational reference groups are groups individuals admire and wish to emulate, but of which they are not currently a member. Sports stars and music stars, for example, can be aspirational reference groups for their followers. Marketers often associate their products with aspirational reference groups, for example by explicitly using celebrities to endorse their products. Johnny Logan, for example, is the new face of McDonald's eurosaver meals in Ireland. The campaign, which features three different television advertisements, is for a low-price menu mainly aimed at teenagers and students. The choice of Johnny Logan, now aged in his fifties, might not seem ideal, but this was decided after he re-released his two Eurovision Song Contest-winning songs, 'Hold Me Now' and 'What's Another Year?', with Belgian rapper Kaye Styles. Research conducted by Lansdowne Market Research with Irish 18- to 24-year-olds illustrated that celebrities such as Roy Keane, Sinéad O'Connor and Robbie Williams are heroes, not because of specific accomplishments or activity, but because they are seen as staying true to their own convictions. Young people were also enthusiastic in their praise of humanitarians such as Mary Robinson, Bob Geldof, Bono and Ali Hewson. Reflecting their commercial edge, they also admire business achievers like Michael O'Leary and Denis O'Brien. Most of those interviewed credited these entrepreneurs with creating the Irish boom (www.marketing.ie).

Associative reference groups are groups to which individuals actually belong, such as extended family, friends, a work group or a club. The gender, ethnic and age groups to which consumers belong are also associative reference groups with whom consumers identify. Associative reference groups, such as family and friends, play an important role for marketers. Parents, for example, influence what type of products, television programmes and advertisements their children are exposed to. Friends or peers are also important associative reference groups. They contribute to the expressive element in which a consumer buys for materialistic or social reasons (e.g. buying to 'keep up with the Joneses'). In terms of influence, after an individual's family, friends are most likely to influence his or her purchasing decisions. Opinions and preference of friends are an important influence in determining the products or brands a consumer ultimately selects. Marketers of products such as brand-name clothing, jewellery, snack foods and alcoholic beverages recognise the power of peer group influence and frequently depict friendship situations in their advertisements.

EXAMPLE: BINGE DRINKING IS THE NORM FOR IRISH CONSUMER LIFESTYLES

Irish people drink far more than their European counterparts, which translates to more problems per drinker, according to the 'Consumer Lifestyles in Ireland' report from Euromonitor International. While Euromonitor International's research shows that the alcoholic drinks industry in Ireland was worth €6.6 billion in 2004, alcohol-related problems are estimated to cost Irish society around €2.4 billion per year. One of the fastest growing causes of death in Ireland is chronic liver disease and cirrhosis, in which alcohol is the major contributory factor. Deaths from chronic liver disease and cirrhosis have grown by 108 per cent between 1990 and 2003 and in 2003 it was reported that chronic liver disease and cirrhosis was the cause of death of half a million Irish people.

A drinking occasion in Ireland involves binge drinking more often than in any of the other countries surveyed, to the extent that binge drinking is now regarded as 'the norm' for Irish men and occurs in about one-third of drinking occasions for women. Many Irish people exceed their recommended weekly intake on a Friday or Saturday night alone. On the Continent, alcohol is generally drunk slowly and often accompanied by food. In Ireland and Britain, however, pub culture now promotes over-indulgence on a typical weekend night's drinking. As a result of this high alcohol consumption, there are a significant number of people with alcohol dependency problems such as alcoholism, depression and other alcohol-related illness, according to the report. A survey of ten GP surgeries throughout the country involving 2,290 patients found that 68 per cent of patients were low risk, while 13 per cent were teetotal or in recovery from alcohol addiction. However, 16 per cent were in the hazardous category, while a further three per cent were in the harmful/dependent category. This means that around one in five patients surveyed had a problem with alcohol.

Source: adapted from www.euromonitor.com/alcohol

Dissociative reference groups are groups whose attitudes, values and behaviours most individuals disapprove of and do not wish to emulate. Gangland crime groups, for example, are dissociative reference groups for the majority of Irish people.

Virtual groups. Advances in computer and Internet technologies have facilitated the emergence of a new type of group — virtual groups or communities. Adults and children now frequently log onto the web and visit special-interest websites, often with chat rooms. These are known as 'Internet communities' or 'virtual communities' and include web-based consumer groups. These virtual groups provide their members with access to extensive amounts of information and social interaction covering an extremely wide range of topics and issues. Virtual groups provide opportunities for a marketer to address consumers with a particular common interest. Consumers are also able to enhance their consumption experience via discussion with others.

Reference groups are important for marketers as they serve as frames of reference for individuals in their purchase or consumption decisions. The degree of influence a reference group exerts on an individual's behaviour usually depends on the nature of the individual and the product and on the specific social factors. When consumers perceive a reference group as credible, attractive or powerful it can affect consumer attitude and induce behaviour change. When consumers are concerned with obtaining accurate information about the performance or quality of a product or service, they are likely to be persuaded by those whom they consider trustworthy and knowledgeable. That is, they are more likely to be persuaded by sources with *high credibility*. When consumers are primarily concerned with the acceptance or approval of others whom they like or with whom they identify, or with those who offer them status or other benefits, they are likely to adopt their product, brand or other behavioural characteristics.

Groups can also influence consumers by providing them with information and encouraging them to express particular types of values. Reference-group influence varies according to the type of product purchased: for example, reference-group influence is higher for 'public' products such as cars than for 'private' purchases such as cookers. In part, this is because high-visibility luxury products typically communicate status — something that may be valued by group members. As a result, reference groups have more influence on the purchases of luxury products than necessities.

A further way reference groups influence consumer behaviour is through *socialisation*, the process by which individuals acquire the skills, knowledge, values and attitudes that are relevant for functioning in given circumstances. *Consumer socialisation* is the process by which individuals learn to become consumers and come to know the value of money; the appropriateness of saving versus spending; and how, when and where products should be bought and used (Ward 1974). Through socialisation, consumers learn motives and values as well as the knowledge and skills for consumption.

GENDER AND SEXUAL ORIENTATION INFLUENCES ON CONSUMER BEHAVIOUR

Gender refers to a biological state (male or female), whereas *sexual orientation* refers to a person's preference for certain behaviours. *Masculine* individuals (whether male or female) tend to display male-oriented traits and *feminine* individuals tend to exhibit female characteristics. In addition, some individuals can be *androgynous*, having both male and female traits.

These sexual orientations are important for marketers because they can influence an individual's preferences and behaviours. Women who are more masculine, for example, tend to prefer advertisements that depict non-traditional women. Sexual identity is a very important component of a consumer's self-concept. People often conform to their culture's expectations about how people of their gender should act, dress, speak and otherwise behave. It is unclear to what extent gender differences are innate or culturally shaped, but they are certainly evident in many consumption decisions.

The year 2005 represented a significant year for the Diet Coke brand in Ireland. The Diet Coke tradition of specifically targeting female consumers ended and the first unisex advertisement was launched. This shift in strategy was an acknowledgement of the growing male appetite for diet drinks and the reality that approximately fifty per cent of Diet Coke's consumers are now men. The new campaign also focuses on the 'sugar-free' message of Diet Coke, in response to the health and wellness agenda increasing for this target consumer (www.checkout.ie).

Another noticeable change in Irish male consumer behaviour has been the growth of men's grooming products. These products proved to be one of the major driving forces in the Irish cosmetics and toiletries market in 2005 with constant growth levels being maintained. Irish males in the 18- to 24-year-old demographic who enjoy high disposable income were responsible for a sustained boom in sales of men's grooming products. Men's razors and blades — particularly the premium brands — and post-shave and deodorants accounted for most sales in this sector. Older Irish men are also beginning to explore new options, no longer content with the cheapest brands. As product standards rise, so do male consumer attitudes towards them, which in turn means a boost for men's grooming products (www.euromonitor.com).

A behaviour considered masculine in one culture may not be viewed as such in another country. The norm in Ireland, for example, is that males should be seen to be strong and to repress tender feelings ('real men don't eat quiche') and male friends avoid touching each other (except in 'safe' situations such as on a sports field). In some Latin and European cultures, however, it is common for men to hug and kiss one another. Each society determines what 'real' men and women should do or should not do.

Many products are also *sex-typed*. They take on masculine or feminine attributes and consumers often associate them with one gender or another. The sex-typing of products is often created or perpetuated by marketers and begins with targeting very young children. Children pick up on the concept of gender identity at an earlier age than was previously believed, perhaps as young as age one or two. By the age of three, for example, most children categorise driving a truck as masculine and cooking and cleaning as feminine (Collins 1984). Toy companies perpetuate these stereotypes by promoting gender-linked toys with commercials that reinforce sex-role expectations through their casting, emotional tone and copy. Even cartoon characters that are portrayed as helpless are more likely to wear frilly or ruffled dresses.

Recognising the powerful role toys play in consumer socialisation, doll manufacturers are creating characters they hope will teach little girls about the real world, not the fantasy 'bimbo' world that many dolls represent. Barbie's rebirth as a career woman illustrates how concerns about socialisation can be taken seriously by a firm. Although the Barbie doll was introduced as an astronaut in 1965 and as an airline pilot in 1999, there was never much detail about the careers themselves — girls bought the uniform and accessories but they never learned about the professions represented. Now a working-woman Barbie is on the market as the result of a partnership between the manufacturers and *Working Woman* magazine.

Barbie now comes with a miniature computer and mobile phone as well as a CD-ROM with information about understanding finance (Hays 2000).

FAMILY/HOUSEHOLD INFLUENCES ON CONSUMER BEHAVIOUR

A *family* is usually defined as a group of individuals living together who are related by marriage, blood or adoption. The most typical unit is the *nuclear family*, consisting of a father, mother and children. The *extended family* consists of the nuclear family plus relations such as grandparents, aunts, uncles and cousins.

Household is a broader term that includes a single person living alone or a group of individuals who live together in a common dwelling, regardless of whether they are related. This term includes cohabiting couples (an unmarried male and female living together), gay couples, and singles. The traditional stereotype of the Irish family consisted of a husband as the primary wage earner; a wife, who was a non-wage earner, at home; and children. Households are important to marketers because their needs vary greatly. Households can also differ in terms of the *family life cycle*. Families can be characterised in terms of the age of the parents and how many children are living at home. Thus, families progress from the bachelor stage (young and single), through marriage and having children, to being an older couple/person without children at home. Households may also consist of unmarried singles, couples without children (younger and older) and older couples who delay having children. Various changes such as death or divorce can alter household structure by creating single-parent households. In general, consumer spending increases as households shift from young singles to young married and then remains high until spending falls at the older married/single stages. This pattern, however, depends on what is purchased. New parents tend to spend more on health care, clothing and housing. Older single households and couples increase spending on home-based products, health care and travel. The gay market is more likely to spend on travel, clothing and the arts. These stages do not capture all types of household as there are others, such as never-married single mothers, which also constitute important market segments.

EXAMPLE: 'KIDULTS' ARE FINDING VALUE FOR MONEY BY LIVING WITH THEIR PARENTS

There is a growing trend among young men in Ireland to remain at home and live with their parents; sixty-five per cent of men aged 20–25 still live at home. This is partly due to rising affluence among parents, which means that fewer of these 'kidults' are pushed out of the family home. In addition, pull factors such as personal freedom and new relationships are hampered and marriage is often delayed until later in life, particularly as house prices and the cost of living increase beyond affordability. Significantly, the rising cost of living together because of exorbitant house prices means that it is difficult for many young people to acquire their first property, until they are in a long-term relationship and able to combine their income with that of a partner. Kidults are therefore finding value for money by living with their parents.

Source: adapted from Men's Lifestyles Report 2006,
www.mintel.com/ireland/press07

Additionally, many households also consider their pets to be valued family members. Pet owners are an important market segment as they spend vast amounts of money on pet-related goods and services. In Ireland during 2007 more human food trends crossed over to pet food. Products were marketed using language designed to appeal to pet owners. Buzz words like 'natural ingredients', 'low-fat' and 'improved dental hygiene', coupled with products tailored to suit different life stages of pets, struck chords with consumers who looked for products to cater for their pets' various dietary requirements. Many of these ranges carry veterinary endorsements and guidance, which is adding to their popularity. Growth in disposable income for Irish consumers impacted greatly on treats, with owners now more inclined than ever to spoil their pets. Competition is strong, particularly in dog treats, and there is an abundance of new products coming on the market from niche companies.

Another trend which has an impact on pet owners is the increased urbanisation of the Irish population, which leads to space shortages in cities and means that providing space for larger animals is difficult. The small pet population is rising in Ireland due to a trend towards more apartment living and because the smaller pet is perceived to be easier to maintain. Combined with busy consumer lifestyles, high-maintenance pets are increasingly being eschewed for cats, small mammals and fish. These pets are perceived to be reasonably self-sufficient and do not need as much attention as dogs. As a result the cat population is now rising faster than the dog population (www.euromonitor.com).

Changing Trends in Household Structure

Many factors have altered the basic structure and characteristics of households. These include:

- delayed marriage
- cohabitation
- dual careers
- divorce
- smaller families.

Delayed Marriage

In Ireland, an increasing number of individuals are either delaying or avoiding marriage. For many, a career has become more important than marriage. Because it is now more socially acceptable for a man and a woman to live together before marriage, many do not see an immediate need to enter into a long-term marital commitment. The average age of Irish grooms in 2005 was 33.1 years, compared with 30.2 years in 1996. The pattern for Irish brides is similar, with the average age increasing from 28.4 years in 1996 to 31 years in 2005. The average age of Irish mothers in 2006 was 32.9 years within marriage and 27.1 outside marriage (www.cso.ie).

The trend towards delayed marriage is important for marketers because single-person households exhibit different consumption patterns. Single men, for example, tend to spend more than married men on alcohol, new cars, restaurant meals, clothes and education. This group essentially consists of college students and older men (divorced or never married). According to Hoyer and MacInnis (2004), single men are more likely than married men to give gifts of jewellery, watches and clothes.

By delaying marriage by a few years, couples typically find themselves in a better financial position. In addition, when couples delay marriage, they typically delay having children, which has led to greater spending on designer baby clothes, housekeeping services and high-quality furniture.

EXAMPLE: RELATIONSHIPS AND COMMITMENT

The Men's Lifestyles Report (2006) examined attitudes towards marriage and commitment. Although men and women are delaying their commitment to both marriage and mortgages and enjoy spending their disposable income on themselves and their own leisure activities, men do have a positive attitude to marriage. Men aged over 25 are in favour of marriage and commitment to a single partner (eventually) but believe that the pressure for marriage comes from women, viewing weddings as 'the girl's day', adding that 'There is no magazine called Irish Groom.' For many men, marriage is seen as an extra cost on top of the mortgage and this partly suggests why many men will delay getting married until they are much older and in a position to afford commitment to marriage.

Seventy-two per cent of men interviewed, however, believe it is important to have a lasting relationship with one partner; in many cases marrying their long-term partner is seen to have financial advantages, including the sharing of mortgage and other costs.

Source: Adapted from Men's Lifestyles Report 2006,
www.mintel.com/ireland/press07

Cohabitation

As a result of changing social norms in Ireland, more and more individuals are deciding to live together outside marriage. The number of cohabiting couples in Ireland grew by more than fifty per cent from 77,600 in 2002 to 121,800 in 2006. Sociologists point out, however, that Ireland's proportion of cohabiting couples (which now account for 11.6 per cent of all family units) is still low compared with Scandinavian countries. The number of same-sex couples recorded in the Irish 2006 census was 2,090, an increase from 1,300 in 2002. Two-thirds of these were male couples. It is estimated that there are 200,000 lesbians and gay men living in Ireland.

According to Hoyer and MacInnis (2004), a defining aspect of unmarried couples (in comparison with married couples) is the tendency of the partners to be more self-oriented. They tend to view possessions as personal rather than jointly owned items and leave open the possibility that the relationship may break down. Identifying possessions as belonging to one or the other protects each person if the relationship ends. It is more likely when individuals are cohabitating that both individuals work outside the home; therefore, they often have higher discretionary income than married couples of a similar age (with a non-working spouse). Unmarried couples are therefore of interest to marketers because they are more frequent consumers of entertainment and holidays than are married couples.

Dual Careers

The increasing number of dual-career households (in which both partners work) has had a big impact on household consumer behaviour. Women's employment rates in the global workforce, including Ireland, have increased dramatically since the 1970s. More women work in paid employment today than ever before. In 1971, Irish women's labour force participation rate was very low, at just 28 per cent. Today, the proportion of women employed in all sectors of the economy has reached almost 59 per cent (CSO 2006).

Having two incomes increases discretionary spending. Dual careers also means that the female partner is bringing additional financial resources to the family, thereby giving her greater influence over family decisions for important or expensive products and services such as holidays, cars and housing. Additionally, the increased burden of having both a career and a family leaves less time for many activities, including cooking, housekeeping and shopping. This is why dual-career families value products and services that save time, such as microwaveable dinners, housekeeping services, childcare, fast food and food delivery services. Women who are part of a dual-career couple are an important target market because they have limited shopping time, they are more likely to buy the same brands, be brand loyal and to buy impulsively. Males who are part of a dual-career couple are taking on more household responsibilities, including grocery shopping (Thompson & Walker 1989). One consequence of dual careers for marketers is that women are not as readily accessible through traditional media as they once were. Because working women do not have much time to watch television or to listen to radio, many advertisers now use direct marketing or Internet sites as ways of shopping for many household and family needs. This trend of dual careers is also reflected in advertisements which are targeted to men who are, for example, sharing the responsibility for household shopping and cooking.

Another change in consumer behaviour for convenience foods has occurred because of negative press reviews of dried processed food and frozen food. This has led to affluent Irish consumers spending more money 'trading up' to premium, fresher options such as chilled processed food and meal kits. In Ireland, sales of premium chilled ready meals, often purchased on impulse with the intention of being consumed within one to two days, increased by 11 per cent to €52 million in 2006. Packaged food that is not only convenient but also healthy is the fastest growing segment of convenience food and is diverting more consumer expenditure away from unhealthy fast food (www.euromonitor.com).

EXAMPLE: BUSY DUBLINERS THINK THERE AREN'T ENOUGH HOURS IN THE DAY

According to a nationwide survey commissioned by O'Briens Sandwich Bars during 2007 on the lunchtime eating habits of Irish people, 50 per cent of people skip lunch at least once a week, with 38 per cent of Dubliners admitting to missing lunch twice a week. According to the survey, it would appear that some of us are just too busy for lunch, with 29 per cent of those surveyed admitting to eating their lunch at their desks. Dubliners came out the busiest, with 39 per cent of those surveyed owning up to eating their lunch at their desks. However, some of us do find the time to relax and enjoy a substantial lunch, with a further 29 per cent choosing their favourite sandwich bar as their preferred lunchtime destination. The humble sandwich and trusty roll are the two most popular lunchtime food choices (28 per cent and 27 per cent respectively). Sixteen per cent of Dubliners surveyed went for the more cosmopolitan option of a wrap, with a very low percentage from Cork and Galway selecting this lighter option.

Source: adapted from www.obriensonline.com

Divorce

A decade after divorce was introduced in Ireland, the number of people availing of it grew significantly: in 2005 59,500 people said they were divorced, compared with 35,000 in 2002, a seventy per cent rise in just four years. Separation is more common still, with 107,000 people describing themselves as separated or divorced (CSO 2006).

Divorce can lead to a major change in lifestyle, and acquiring products and service can be part of forming a new identity during this period. A recently divorced consumer, for example, might buy a new house, apartment, car, clothes, or go on a holiday in order to assume a new image or to feel better. If the couple was childless, the newly divorced are typically older and may therefore have greater discretionary income for transportation and housing if they are working. Divorce also creates single-parent families when children are involved. These families are generally time-pressured because the single parent must both earn an income and raise children, which means that more convenience products and services, such as packaged or fast food, are purchased. Divorced individuals with children are now remarrying with greater frequency, creating more stepfamilies. Stepfamilies can also have unique consumption needs, for example children who travel between families require duplicate supplies of clothes and toys. Greeting card companies, for example, are also recognising non-traditional families and have developed cards that deal with step-family and cohabitation relationships.

Smaller Families

The average household size is getting smaller in many countries. Couples are now having fewer children because of dual careers, financial burdens and concerns about overpopulation. The 2006 Irish census shows that falling fertility is having a significant impact on family size, with the average number of children per family declining from 2.2 in 1986 to 1.4 in 2005. In Ireland, from 2002 to 2005, lone-parent families also increased by about 23 per cent to almost 190,000.

In terms of consumer behaviour, smaller family size means consumers have greater discretionary income to spend on holidays, recreational items, toys and entertainment. Smaller families can also spend more on each child. Childless married couples are also of interest to marketers. These households have more discretionary income than other households. In comparison to couples who have children, childless couples spend more on food, restaurant meals, entertainment, alcohol, clothing and pets (Paul 2001).

Smaller household sizes have contributed to some restructuring of family meals; consumers living alone or in two-person households are more likely to buy convenience foods such as ready meals or individual-portion products. Recent growth in income, a healthy economy and higher consumer confidence has helped to underpin demand for value-added convenience foods such as ready meals. This is particularly the case for frozen and chilled ready meals.

CHILDREN AS CONSUMERS

Children play an important role in household decisions by attempting to influence their parents' consumer behaviour. Children are also of interest to marketers because of the desire to create brand loyalty as early as possible in consumers' lives. Many pre-adolescent children acquire their *consumer behaviour norms* through observing their parents and older siblings, who function as role models and sources of cues for basic consumption learning. In contrast, adolescents and teenagers are likely to look to their friends for models of acceptable consumption behaviour (Roedder John 1999).

In recent decades, there has been a trend towards children playing a more active role in what the family buys, as well as in the family decision-making process. This shift in influence has occurred as a result of families having fewer children (which increases the influence of each child), more dual-income couples who can afford to permit their children to make a greater number of the choices, and the encouragement by the media to allow children to express themselves. Additionally, single-parent households often push their children towards household participation and self-reliance.

Food, sweets and toys are the most important product categories of interest to children. Advertising directed at children usually stresses the immediate pleasure provided by the product. Children at a young age hardly distinguish between television programmes and commercials. The most common stereotype is that children pester their parents until the adults finally give in. Children are more likely to influence parents for child-related products such as cereals, biscuits, sweets, snacks and ice cream. Ballygowan responded to the needs of younger customers with the launch of a 250ml sports pack-style bottle, designed specifically for children. Available since August 2006, the 250ml bottle is being sold individually and also in multiple packs of ten; this new size is designed for school lunchboxes. Ballygowan believes that, with sports and dust cap, it is comfortable for small hands to hold and is also ideal for picnics, car journeys and children on the move. Additionally, most parents are aware of the health benefits of drinking water and are keen for their children to take the healthier option more often. With the ever-growing reports on childhood obesity in Ireland, Ballygowan is adding extra choice for parents and their children as an alternative to sugary drinks (www.checkout.ie). It is estimated that over 300,000 children in Ireland now have a weight problem (Sheehan 2007).

The government health campaigns focusing on childhood obesity and heart disease also have an effect on Irish society. The National Taskforce on Obesity reported in 2005 that 39 per cent of Irish adults are overweight, including 18 per cent who are obese. Annually, approximately 2,000 premature deaths are attributed to obesity. In response to the information from the government health campaigns, sales of health and wellness packaged food products have increased. Manufacturers have responded to this trend by introducing new products that are presented, through labelling and advertising, as healthy and fresh. Both retailers and manufacturers realise that product innovations which are both convenient and healthy will continue to be the fastest growing segment of packaged food, which consumers are also willing to pay more for (www.euromonitor.com).

In relation to children as consumers, children's advertising can be a contentious issue among adults. Some critics believe children need special protection from advertising. Others argue that young children are more likely to believe claims made in advertisements and are easily persuaded to want to buy, or have their parents buy, something they do not need or that may even be bad for them. Yet others maintain that children today are media-aware and capable of making their own decisions in relation to advertising. The Broadcasting Commission of Ireland is an independent government-appointed body which is responsible for licensing, regulating and developing independent radio and television services in Ireland. It draws up codes of standards which apply to many areas of general advertising, including children's advertising. Its children's advertising code applies to all broadcasts since 2005. The code's main points include:

- advertising breaks must be clearly distinguished from programmes
- advertisements aimed at those under fifteen years of age cannot be inserted into children's programmes that are less than thirty minutes long

- Christmas-themed advertising cannot be shown before 1 November (www.business2000.ie/cases).

EXAMPLE: MARS STOP ADVERTISING TO CHILDREN

Advertisements for chocolate such as Mars, Snickers, Maltesers and M&Ms are not targeted at the under-12s, since Masterfoods, which manufactures the confectionery products, discontinued advertising on children's programmes or in magazines aimed at younger readers. The Irish Heart Foundation has welcomed the step, but would like food companies to ban television advertising for unhealthy snacks before 9pm. A spokeswoman for Masterfoods Ireland said its products were aimed primarily at 16- to 24-year-olds. 'There may be some children watching programmes such as *ER* or football that carry our advertising, but we're not aiming at them.'

Source: adapted from www.consumerconnect.ie

Irish children as young as eight are now going online for the first time, according to a new report on Irish Internet usage. Young people are embracing the online medium, with a typical teenager spending an average of two hours a day on the Internet. The web is now becoming the 'channel of choice' for those in the communications business in a bid to reach younger consumers. Irish children are 'web savvy' and want to be allowed make their own choices about how they use the Internet, according to new research by the European Commission. The Commission conducted a survey of children from all over Europe to see how they use new media. According to the report, children generally know the risks of using the Internet and mobile phones; however, when faced with trouble online, minors will generally ask an adult only as a last resort (http://test.enn.ie).

CASE STUDY: UNCLE BEN'S MEETING IRISH LIFESTYLE CHANGES WITH NUTRITIONAL FOOD

The position of Uncle Ben's as worldwide rice leader is based upon providing a quality meal, which performs to the highest standards in terms of taste, texture and nutrition. The brand's unique manufacturing process includes 215 separate quality checks and ten separate cleaning stages. Every grain is individually scanned by an electronic eye for consistency, colour, length and thickness. The technology is such that 330,000 grains are checked every second. The cooked quality is also continually checked for appearance, colour, smell, taste and cooking time.

Today Uncle Ben's is the leader in the Irish rice market, with over forty-five per cent market share. The rice market is growing at approximately thirteen per cent per annum and is valued at around €13 million. This trend is a clear indication of the acceptance of rice as a central part of the Irish person's diet. This success, however, did not happen without a clear marketing strategy to overcome obstacles to growth. For centuries the potato was the main ingredient of the staple diet in Ireland and eighty per cent of our meals included the potato as part of the ingredients. It would require a lot of work to persuade households to introduce Uncle Ben's rice products into the weekly shopping basket.

In order to make rice one of the staple goods for the Irish food market, Uncle Ben's undertook intensive market research. A staple good is one that is bought on a regular basis, such as milk, toothpaste or bread. By studying the lifestyles of the Irish consumer, Masterfoods found a way of establishing a foothold in the Irish consumer market and ensuring that Uncle Ben's could be positioned as an alternative to the potato. Uncle Ben's rice has been available in Ireland since 1983. The brand has been successfully marketed primarily on the basis of its quality and consistency. These key benefits are illustrated by the brand taglines: 'It Never Sticks' and 'Perfect Every Time'. Traditionally, the preparation of rice was seen as a skilled task, which required a degree of expertise to avoid the cook being left with a sticky burnt mess on the bottom of the saucepan! Uncle Ben's rice, with its unique parboiling preparation process, changed all this. Suddenly there was a foolproof method of preparing rice. The key task then was to let the consumer know about the product's ease of use and to lower the barrier to purchase by allowing them to sample it.

A strong marketing programme was undertaken, including an advertising campaign, a sampling campaign and in-store promotions. Rice as a meal component has grown in popularity over the recent decades. Today, over seventy per cent of Irish households purchase rice on a regular basis, reflecting a stark shift in emphasis from using the potato as the basis of the Irish diet. Another reason, however, for an increased use of rice was the change in people's lifestyles. As people travelled more, their tastes became more exotic, while at the same time Chinese and Indian takeaways have grown in popularity in Ireland. The average shopper, for example, was not content to just purchase long-grain rice, but preferred to broaden their tastes by exploring other options such as basmati and pilau rice. This reflected changing consumer values, as the Irish consumer was willing to try new and differentiated meal options. Basmati rice is now the fastest growing rice product in the Irish rice market.

Ireland has expanded economically since the 1990s and the phrase 'time is money' has become familiar in people's lives. Many people commute to work from satellite towns, which can be eighty kilometres or more from their place of work. While average household income has increased, time constraints on these householders have also grown. Longer working hours mean that more demands are made on free time. This factor has been described as 'cash rich, time poor'. The convenience sector of the food market is the fastest growing sector, with a recognition that consumers have less time than ever before to prepare traditional dinners. The average length of time spent preparing the main meal of the day has decreased from forty minutes in the 1970s to about twenty minutes today. In response to the changing lifestyles of consumers, Uncle Ben's launched a range of frozen ready meals, microwaveable in just eight minutes. Uncle Ben's rice bowls come in six varieties, each providing a complete meal and containing less than five per cent fat. Research has shown, however, that despite the lack of free time available to the consumer, we still try to maintain a balanced diet. Masterfoods also realised that Uncle Ben's could continue to reflect the pace of today's lifestyle. Uncle Ben's was the first to introduce the unique parboiled process to rice, reducing cooking time to just ten minutes, which revolutionised the use of rice in the Irish household.

More recently, Masterfoods continued to reduce cooking times for nutritional and tasty meals by introducing six varieties of microwaveable express rice. These products can be cooked in their packaging in a microwave oven in just two minutes. Along with this, a number of pasta options were also launched. These meals are also single portions for ease of cooking, again reducing the preparation time.

Source: adapted from www.business.2000.ie/cases

CASE STUDY: BONO LAUNCHES RED CAMPAIGN TO FIGHT AIDS IN AFRICA

Is red the new black? If Bono has his way, it will be soon. During 2006, the U2 singer partnered with Bobby Shriver, nephew of the late President John F. Kennedy, to launch the Red campaign, his latest effort to fight AIDS in Africa. The programme encourages shoppers to buy Red-branded goods, with manufacturers channelling up to 50 per cent of the profits to AIDS programs financed by the UN-backed Global Fund.

Brands that license the Red mark make a five-year commitment to create unique products and contribute a significant percentage of sales or portion of profits from the sales of those products into Global Fund-financed AIDS programmes, with a special emphasis on women and children affected by AIDS in Africa. Since the inception of the Global Fund in 2002, the private sector has contributed $5 billion, greater than the $4.9 billion from governments around the world. The Red campaign will create a new income stream into the Fund. Bono said, 'The idea is simple, the products are sexy and people live instead of die,' and 'When you buy a Red product, the company gives money to buy pills that will keep someone in Africa alive.'

US companies that have signed up to the initiative include Gap (which is offering Red-branded T-shirts and jeans), Motorola (a red mobile phone), Converse (a series of limited edition shoes), Apple (a red iPod Nano) and Giorgio Armani (a collection of clothes and accessories). These companies have committed to the brand for five years and have pledged to give an average of forty per cent of profits from the products to the global fund. Bono wants companies selling Red products to make a profit by helping the poor — doing well by doing good. 'Many of the world's greatest minds are in commerce,' he says. And if there is something in it for them, he thinks, companies will spend far more money promoting Red than Bono could ever hope to mobilise through charity. Bono's main pitch to companies is that Red will bring them more customers and make their existing customers more loyal.

The Red campaign works alongside the One Campaign to Make Poverty History — a longer-term project launched in 2005 by Bono and eleven US aid and non-profit groups, a campaign that has more than two million members. 'This generation can be the generation that says "no" to extreme poverty in Africa,' Bono said while promoting the campaign on American television.

Source: adapted from www.U2online.org

Questions for Review

1. What are the main differences between organisational consumers and individual consumers?
2. List four main types of reference groups and highlight their impact on consumer behaviour.
3. What impact does gender have on consumer behaviour? Illustrate your answer with a product or service you are familiar with.
4. Discuss the impact of changing household structures in Ireland for marketers.

References

Aaker, J. L. (1997). 'Dimensions of brand personality', *Journal of Marketing Research*, 34 (3), 347–56.

Alley, R. S. (1989). 'Television', in *Handbook of American Popular Culture* (2nd edn). Westport, CT: Greenwood Press, p. 1368.

Antonides, G. and van Raaij, W. F. (1998). *Consumer Behaviour: A European Perspective*. Chichester: John Wiley & Sons.

Bagozzi, R. (1975). 'Marketing as exchange', *Journal of Marketing*, 39, 32–9.

Bandura, A. (1986). *Social Foundations of Thought and Action: A Social Cognitive View*. New Jersey: Prentice Hall.

Baron, R. A. (1989). *Psychology: The Essential Science*. Boston: Allyn & Bacon.

Belk, R. W. (1988). 'Possessions and the extended self', *Journal of Consumer Research*, 15, September, 287–300.

Bell, M. J. (1982). 'The study of popular culture', in M. T. Inge (ed.), *Concise Histories of American Popular Culture*. Westport, CT: Greenwood Press, p.443.

Bennett, P. D. (1988). *Dictionary of Marketing Terms*. Chicago: American Marketing Association.

Bettman, J. R. (1973). 'Perceived risk and its components: A model and empirical test', *Journal of Marketing Research*, May, 184–90.

Bettman, J. R. (1979). 'Memory factors in consumer choice: A review', *Journal of Marketing*, 43, Spring, 37–53.

Boorman, N. (2007). *Bonfire of the Brands*. London: Canongate

Brassington, F. and Pettitt, S. (2000). *Principles of Marketing* (2nd edn). London: Financial Times Prentice Hall.

Cattell, R. B. (1965). *The Scientific Analysis of Personality*. Baltimore: Penguin.

Celsi, R. L. and Olson, J. C. (1988). 'The role of involvement in attention and comprehension processes', *Journal of Consumer Research*, 15, 210–24.

Childers, T. and Houston, M. (1984). 'Conditions for a picture-superiority effect on consumer memory', *Journal of Consumer Research*, 11, September, 643–54.

Cobb, C. J. and Hoyer, W. D. (1986). 'The influence of advertising at moment of brand choice', *Journal of Advertising*, December, 5–27.

Coleman, R. P. (1983). 'The continuing significance of social class to marketing', *Journal of Consumer Research*, 10, pp. 265–80.

Collins, G. (1984). 'New studies on girl toys and boy toys', *New York Times*, 13 February, p. D1.

CSO (Central Statistics Office) (2006). *Women and Men in Ireland*. Dublin: Stationery Office.

Daly, G. (2005). 'Boom without end?', *Sunday Business Post* 'Agenda' supplement, 17 April, pp. A1–A2.

Doole, I., Lancaster., P. and Lowe, R. (eds) (2005). *Understanding and Managing Customers*. London: Prentice Hall.

Drucker, P. (1986). 'The marketing concept, what it is and what it is not', *Journal of Marketing*, pp 81–7.

FÁS (2006). *The Irish Labout Market Review 2006: A FÁS Review of Irish Labour Market Trends and Policies*. Dublin: FÁS.

Fazio, R. H., Herr, P. M. and Powell, M. C. (1992). 'On the development and strength of category–brand associations in memory: The case of mystery ads', *Journal of Consumer Psychology*, 1 (1), pp. 1–13.

Fontenella, S. M. and Zinkhan, G. M. (1992). 'Gender differences in the perception of leisure: a conceptual model', in L. McAlister and M. L. Rothschild (eds), *Advances in Consumer Research*, Vol. 20, pp. 534–40. Utah: Association for Consumer Research.

Fournier, S. (1998). 'Consumers and their brands: developing relationship theory in consumer research', *Journal of Consumer Research*, 24, March, 343–73.

Freud, S. (1959). *Collected Papers*. New York: Basic Books.

Gardner, M. P. (1985). 'Mood states and consumer behavior: A critical review', *Journal of Consumer Research*, 12 December, 281–300.

Geertz, C. (1973). *The Interpretation of Cultures*. New York: Basic Books.

Guilford, J. P. (1959). *Personality*. New York: McGraw-Hill.

Haugtvedt, C., Petty, R. E., Cacioppo, J. T. and Steidley, T. (1988). 'Personality and ad effectiveness: Exploring the utility of need for cognition', in M. J. Houston (ed.), *Advances in Consumer Research*, pp. 209–12. Utah: Association for Consumer Research.

Hawkins, D., Best, R. and Coney, K. (1995). *Consumer Behavior: Implications for Marketing Strategy*. Plano, TX: Business Publications.

Hays, C. L. (2000). 'A role model's clothes: Barbie goes professional', *New York Times* (online), 1 April.

Heckler, S. E. and Childers, T. L. (1992). 'The role of expectancy and relevancy in memory for verbal and visual information: What is incongruency?', *Journal of Consumer Research*, 18 (March), 475–92.

Hilgard, E., Atkinson, R. and Atkinson, R. (1975). *Introduction to Psychology* (6th edn). New York: Harcourt Brace Jovanovich.

Hirschman E. and Holbrook, M. (1982). 'Hedonic consumption: Emerging concepts, methods, and propositions', *Journal of Marketing*, 46, 92–101.

Hoch, S. J. and Deighton, J. (1989). 'Managing what consumers learn from experience', *Journal of Marketing*, 53 (April), 1–20.

Hogan, S. and Deegan, G. (2007). 'Being an Irish celebrity can be dangerous, warns bishop', *Irish Independent*, 7 November, p.11.

Horney, K. B. (1945). *Our Inner Conflicts*. New York: Norton.

Hornik, J. (1992). 'Tactile stimulation and consumer response', *Journal of Consumer Research*, December, 449–58.

Horton, R. L. (1979). 'Some relationships between personality and consumer decision-making', *Journal of Marketing Research*, May, 244–5.

Hoyer, W. D. and MacInnis, D. J. (2004). *Consumer Behavior* (3rd edn). New York: Houghton Mifflin.

Hutt, M. D. and Speh, T. W. (1992). *Business Marketing Management*. Fort Worth, TX: Dryden Press.

Jacoby, J. (1976). 'Consumer psychology: An octennium', in P. Mussen and M. Rosenzweig (eds), *Annual Review of Psychology*, 331–58.

Jain, K. and Srinivasan, N. (1990). 'An empirical assessment of multiple operationalizations of involvement', *Advances in Consumer Research*, 17, 594–602.

Jung, C. G. (1964). *Man and his Symbols*. New York: Doubleday.

Kahneman, D. (1973). *Attention and Effort*. New Jersey: Prentice Hall.

Kassarjian, H. H. (1971). 'Personality and consumer behavior: A review', *Journal of Marketing Research*, November, 409–18.

Kassarjian, H. H. and Sheffet, M. J. (1975). 'Personality and consumer behaviour: One more time', *American Marketing Association Combined Proceedings*, Series, no. 37, 197–201.

Keller, K. L. (1987). 'Memory factors in advertising', *Journal of Consumer Research*, December, 316–33.

Kennedy, E. (2007). 'Multiplexes dominate in €17.8m box office battle', *Sunday Business Post*, 5 August, p. M7.

Kotler, P. and Armstrong, G. (2007). *Principles of Marketing*. 12th ed. New Jersey: Prentice Hall.

Kotler, P., Armstrong, G., Saunders, J., and Wong, V. (1999). *Principles of Marketing*. London: Prentice Hall.

Lastovicka, J. L. and Joachimsthaler, E. A. (1988). 'Improving the detection of personality–behavior relationships in consumer research', *Journal of Consumer Research*, March, 583–7.

Law, S., Hawkins, S. A. and Craik, F. I. (1998). 'Repetition-induced belief in the elderly: Rehabilitating age-related memory deficits', *Journal of Consumer Research*, September, 91–107.

Lee, H., Harrell, G., and Droge, C. (2000). 'Product experiences and hierarchy of advertising effects', *AMA Winter Educator's Conference*, Chicago: American Marketing Association, pp. 41–2.

McCaughren, S. (2007). 'Show us the money: Top Irish sports stars to make €7 million', *Sunday Business Post*, 19 August, p. 3.

McClelland, D. C. (1955). *Studies in Motivation*. New York: Appleton-Century-Crofts.

Mackintosh, N. J. (1983). *Conditioning and Associative Learning*. New York: Oxford University Press.

McQuillan, D. (2007). 'True Peter', *Irish Times Magazine*, 13 October, p. 12.

McShane, I. (2007). 'Financial independence is goal most valued by Irish women', *Irish Times*, 27 September, p. 6.

McWilliams, D. (2005). *The Pope's Children: Ireland's New Elite*. Dublin: Gill and Macmillan.

Mallen, B. (1977). *Principles of Marketing Channel Management*. Toronto: Lexington Books.

Millman, R. E. (1986). 'The influence of background music on the behaviour of restaurant patrons', *Journal of Consumer Research*, September, 286–9.

Moore, T. E. (1982). 'Subliminal advertising: what you see is what you get', *Journal of Marketing*, 46, 38-47.

Mowen, J. C. (1995). *Consumer Behavior* (4th edn). New Jersey: Prentice Hall.

Mowen, J. C. and Minor, M. (1997). *Consumer Behavior* (5th edn). New Jersey: Prentice Hall.

Noonan, L. (2007). 'The special knack of marketing to migrants', *Irish Independent*, 27 September, p.8.

O'Brien, C. (2007). 'Women feel work outside home lifts standing', *Irish Times*, 27 September, p.7.

O'Connell, S. (2007). 'Firms tap into online advertising', *Irish Times*, 4 October, p.19.

O'Mahony, C. (2007). 'Paddy Power's rugby gambit targets the pink euro', *Sunday Business Post*, 25 November, p. 24.

O'Reilly, A. 2007. 'Great Irish brands', *Irish Independent* special supplement, 17 November, p. 3.

Paul, P. (2001). 'Childless by choice', *American Demographics*, November, 45–50.

Pham, M. and Johar, G. V. (1997). 'Contingent processes of source identification', *Journal of Consumer Research*, December, 249–65.

Plummer, J. T. (1974). 'The concept and application of lifestyle segmentation', *Journal of Marketing*, 38 (January), pp. 33-7.

Rassuli, K. M. and Hollander, S. C. (1986). 'Desire — induced, innate, instable?', *Journal of Macromarketing*, 6 (2), 4–24.

Rescorla, R. A. (1988). 'Pavlovian conditioning: It's not what you think it is', *American Psychologist*, 43, 151–60.

Richins, M. L. (1983). 'An analysis of consumer interaction styles in the marketplace', *Journal of Consumer Research*, June, 73–82.

Roedder John, D. (1999). 'Consumer socialization of children: A retrospective look at twenty-five years of research', *Journal of Consumer Research*, 26, 183–213.

Rogers, E. M. (1983). *Diffusion of Innovations* (3rd edn). New York: Free Press.

Rook, D. (1987). 'The buying impulse', *Journal of Consumer Research*, vol. 14, 189–99.

Rosenberg, M. (1979). *Conceiving the Self*. New York: Basic Books.

Schiffman, L. G. and Kanuk, L. L. (2007). *Consumer Behavior* (9th edn). New Jersey: Pearson Prentice Hall.

Schriver, S. (1997). 'Customer loyalty: going, going ...', *American Demographics*, September, 20–3.

Sheehan, A. (2007). '300,000 Irish children have weight problems', *Irish Independent*, 9 November, p. 3.

Simon, H. A. (1965). *Administrative Behavior* (2nd edn). New York: Free Press.

Sirgy, M. J. (1982). 'Self-concept in consumer behavior: A critical review', *Journal of Consumer Research*, 9 December, 287–300.

Skinner, B. F. (1974). *About Behaviorism*. New York: Knopf.

Smith, R. B. and Sherman, E. (1993). 'Effects of store image and mood on consumer behaviour: A theoretical and empirical analysis', in L. McAlister and M. Rothschild (eds), *Advances in Consumer Research*. Provo, UT: Association for Consumer Research.

Solomon, M. R. (2002). *Consumer Behavior*. Upper Saddle River, NJ: Prentice Hall.

Tanner, J. F., Hunt, J. B. and Eppright, D. R. (1991). 'The protection motivation model: a normative model of fear appeals', *Journal of Marketing*, July, 329–36.

Taylor, S. (1994). 'Waiting for service: The relationship between delays and evaluations of service', *Journal of Marketing*, 58, 56–69.

Thompson, L. and Walker, A. (1989). 'Gender in families: Women and men in marriage, work, and parenthood', *Journal of Marriage and the Family*, November, 845–71.

Tian, K. T., Bearden, W. O. and Hunter, G. L. (2001). 'Consumers' need for uniqueness: Scale development and validation', *Journal of Consumer Research*, 28, June, 50–66.

Ward, S. (1974). 'Consumer socialization', *Journal of Consumer Research*, September, 1–16.

Westbrook, R. A. and Oliver, R. L. (1991). 'The dimensionality of consumption emotion patterns and consumer satisfaction', *Journal of Consumer Research*, 18 June, 84–91.

Index